Personhood, Self-Consciousness, and the First-Person Perspective

Markus Herrmann (Ed.)

Personhood, Self-Consciousness, and the First-Person Perspective

BRILL | MENTIS

This publication was **funded by the Deutsche Forschungsgemeinschaft (DFG) – project number HE 7080/3-1.**
Affiliation: Section Translational Medical Ethics, University Hospital Heidelberg
Department of Medical Oncology
National Center for Tumor Diseases (NCT), NCT Heidelberg

Bibliographic information published by the Deutsche Nationalbibliothek

The Deutsche Nationalbibliothek lists this publication in the Deutsche Nationalbibliografie; detailed bibliographic data available online: http://dnb.d-nb.de

www.mentis.de

Cover design: Anna Braungart, Tübingen
Production: Brill Deutschland GmbH, Paderborn

ISBN 978-3-95743-290-2 (paperback)
ISBN 978-3-96975-290-6 (e-book)

Contents

Preface VII

Introduction IX
Markus Herrmann

I
Pre-Reflective and Reflective Self-Consciousness

1. Relationalism about the Subjective Character of Experience 3
Maik Niemeck

2. Varieties of Reflective Self-Consciousness in the Multidimensional Self 25
Heidi Haanila

3. Bodily Self-awareness 55
Irene Breuer

II
Personhood and Persistence

4. What are We? – Spatial Consciousness, Demonstrative Reference, and the First-Person Perspective 77
Markus Herrmann

5. Spatial Cognition and Bodily Objective Presence 95
Tony Cheng

6. The Metaphysics of the Continuity of Consciousness 107
Amit Anurag

III
Personal Identity and Normativity

7. A Narrative Pattern-Theory of the Self 131
Muriel Leuenberger

8. Humans and Persons: A Compatibilist Account 149
Jörg Noller

List of Contributors 169

Preface

This book originates from a workshop of the same name at Heidelberg University in August 2022. This workshop was part of the research project *The Indetermined Ego* (*Das unbestimmte Ich*), which, like this publication, was only possible thanks to the generous support of the German Research Foundation (DFG).

The workshop was held as a hybrid event and included talks by scholars from Europe to Asia to Australia:

- Amit Anurag from the FLAME University, Pune, India
- Irene Breuer from the University of Wuppertal, Germany
- Tony Cheng from the National Chengchi University, China
- Heidi Haanila from the University of Helsinki, Finland
- Pablo Fernandez from Trinity College, Dublin
- Markus Herrmann from Heidelberg University, Germany
- Muriel Leuenberger from the University of Oxford, United Kingdom
- Maik Niemek from the University of Marburg, Germany
- Jörg Noller from the University of Konstanz, Germany
- Clas Weber from the University of Western Australia, Australia

In this book, the revised results of this workshop are made available to the academic community in printed form for the first time. Excluded are the two papers by Pablo Fernandez on *Being here: Cognitive maps and the self-locating nature of perceptual experience* and Clas Weber on *First-Person Imagination and Illusions about the Self*, as they are already available.

Markus Herrmann
Heidelberg, February 2023

Introduction

Markus Herrmann

In the context of the famous *cogito* argument, Descartes already connects the philosophical themes of self-consciousness, first-person reference, and personal identity. For, the *cogito* represents a form of self-knowledge and thus self-consciousness and Descartes chooses first-person vocabulary to express this self-consciousness (*Discours* 4.2).

Such a *connection* between self-knowledge and self-consciousness may not be particularly surprising (even if it is disputed whether self-*knowledge* is the same as self-*consciousness* – i.e., whether the connection between self-knowledge and self-consciousness is that of *identity*).

Less obvious, however, is the connection between self-consciousness and personal identity. But since Descartes, in the context of the cogito argument, concludes precisely that we are not bodies (not a *res extensa*) but a *res cogitans*, he thus entered the field of personal identity, even before John Locke gave the topic its modern contour: namely, as a discussion of the transtemporal identity of persons (*Essay* 2.27). Here, the focus shifts from the question of *what* we are to the question of the identity conditions for a person at an earlier point in time and a person at a later point in time. It is precisely this broad spectrum of philosophical issues, ranging from self-consciousness to trans-temporal personal identity, that this book aims to address – and to go even beyond by investigating related ethical concerns.

*

In part 1 of this book, we take up Sartre's prominent distinction between reflective and pre-reflective self-consciousness. This influential distinction is easily illustrated by everyday cases: For example, it is a case of reflective self-consciousness, when I come out of a dressing room in a department store and announce disappointedly in front of a mirror, "These pants don't fit me." This is a rich statement that incorporates a great deal of experience and self-understanding. I have to understand *myself* as someone I see. I need to have specific notions about what it means that a pair of trousers fits someone, and that this is something that does not apply to *me* in this case, and so on. On the other hand, the case seems to be quite different when I look over a parapet and quickly pull my upper body back because the sight makes me dizzy. In such a case, I am afraid, and this fear is about *me* (because otherwise there would be no reason to withdraw *my* upper body). Thus, this is a case of self-consciousness (though this thesis is not without controversy; cf. Millikan 1990 and 1998). But even if it is self-consciousness, I do not seem to think about *who* the situation is dangerous for and *who* needs to withdraw his upper body. Nor do I see one person in danger (namely *me*). Rather, I see the danger of the depth and that causes my fear.

Thus, we have paradigmatic cases of reflective and pre-reflective self-consciousness. However, such illustrative case studies are philosophically not fully satisfying. The intriguing question is what exactly constitutes the difference between these forms of self-consciousness. A number of differences might come to mind: Reflective self-consciousness is dependent on that I become the intentional object of my mental states – or perhaps more demanding: and that in doing so I conceive of *myself* as a persisting entity in space and time. Even stronger would be the condition that reflective self-consciousness is only possible on the basis of a society in which I locate myself. But perhaps reflective self-consciousness also needs linguistic means – possibly the vocabulary of the first-person.

Pre-reflective self-consciousness, on the other hand, would be free of some – or even all – of these requirements. But this provokes the question what exactly pre-reflective self-consciousness is. How can it be distinguished from quite ordinary object consciousness? How am I conscious of myself when I am pre-reflectively self-conscious?

- This question is addressed in the first article of this volume, *Relationalism about the Subjective Character of Experience*, by Maik Niemeck. This article argues for the thesis that the *mine-ness* of conscious mental states consists in a relation. At first sight, this may seem to be a well-known position, namely that a mental state becomes a *conscious* mental state by becoming the intentional object of another mental state. Such a higher-order mental state would thus make the original mental state conscious – and therefore cast doubt on the distinction between pre-reflective and reflective consciousness. The relationalism that Maik Niemeck proposes, on the other hand, aims at an analysis that is independent of such higher-level mental states.
- In *Bodily Self-awareness* Irene Breuer examines the link between pre-reflective self-consciousness and embodiment. She argues for non-predicative self-knowledge that is rooted in bodily drives and the kinaesthetic freedom of the body. Her conclusion is that the basic form of self-awareness is the awareness of being alive.

– *Varieties of Reflective Self-consciousness in the Multidimensional Self* concludes part 1 of this book. Here, Heidi Haanila turns to reflective self-consciousness and tries to show that this phenomenon has been presented so far in a truncated way. Her aim is to develop a systematisation of reflective self-consciousness along three distinctions and to illuminate it precisely in its peripheral areas in order to draw conclusions for our mental well-being.

*

In part 2 of the book, we turn to the question of the transtemporal identity of persons. Even though Locke first raised this topic to prominence, as shown above, the Cartesian position already has far-reaching implications for this question. For, already Descartes asks the question what we are – and answers it by claiming that we are a *res cogitans*, a thinking substance. Of particular importance is what we are *not* according to him: a *res extensa*, i.e. an extended substance. Thus, Descartes links the question of transtemporal identity of persons to the question of *spatiality* even before its prominent exposition in Locke's writings. We exist beyond space as Cartesian egos. We *have* bodies, but we *are not* bodies. Thus, the criteria of personal identity would not be those of spatially extended entities. This provokes the question of what criteria of persistence a Cartesian ego could have?

In contrast, spatiality, self-consciousness, and personal identity become thematically interwoven in the second part of this book:

– In *What are we? – Spatial Consciousness, Demonstrative Reference, and the First-person Perspective* Markus Herrmann tries to develop a new position of personal identity based on our self-reference in space. This position states that we are (and do not only have) spatial consciousness that a priori locates itself and that, contrary to Descartes, this spatial consciousness that is located a priori is not only located in space but must also be extended. The foundation of this position is formed by considerations about phenomena of self-reference in symmetry scenarios.
– Tony Cheng, in *Spatial Cognition and Bodily Objective Presence*, pursues the thesis that we must conceive of ourselves as a spatial object among other spatial objects. He addresses three objections to this thesis. First, he counters the charge that a conception of ourselves as objects cannot do justice to our conception of ourselves as subjects. Then he addresses the problem of the missing self. Finally, he deals with Bálint's syndrome. Central to his considerations is Merleau-Ponty's notion of 'Subject-Object'.

- In *The Metaphysics of the Continuity of Consciousness*, Amit Anurag asks what kind of entity consciousness is. He is not concerned with the concrete kind, but asks the question about the genus. His reflections lead to the conclusion that consciousness cannot be a material object, but has a more complex temporal structure: Consciousness must be understood as an enduring process.

*

In Part 3 of this book, we turn to the normative side of personal identity. There is a reason that more attention is paid to personal identity than, for example, to the identity of stones. This reason is not only that *we* are not stones but persons, but also that the notion of a person has strong normative implications. Concepts such as *guilt, responsibility, possession*, and even *consistency* are normative and intertwined with the notion of personhood. Only on the base of transtemporal identity can I be blamed for my actions of yesterday. Only on the base of personal identity can I promise or claim something to someone. If I have screamingly inconsistent convictions, i.e. if I do not fulfil the normative conditions of rationality, this can lead to the point that I am no longer considered sane and that I am even deprived of my person status to a certain extent.

But, normative issues are not only those that answer to specific conceptions of personhood. It is not just the case that theoretical philosophy produces solutions to questions of personal identity, and we need to simply apply those fixed outcomes to normative questions.

Rather, in contrast, the theoretical discussion is already imbued with normative considerations. Questions about what one's future should look like play a significant role in the theoretical discussion of conceptions of personal identity. Already Bernard Williams (1970), and quite prominently Derek Parfit (1984), place such considerations at the centre of their reflections.

Therefore, the third part of this book deals with the normative side of personal identity:

- In *A Narrative Pattern-Theory of the Self* Muriel Leuenberger examines the different dimensions of what we call 'the self' and raises the question how they are united? Her answer is that one of the dimensions (namely the narrative self) has a special role. It unites all the other dimensions of the self and thus enables the unity of a self that is subject to temporal changes. Central to her line of reasoning is the fact that ethical considerations come into play in order to support the emphasized role of the narrative self.

– Jörg Noller raises in *Humans and Persons: A Compatibilist Account* the question of the connection between the living body and our identity. He proposes a compatibilist approach where he distinguishes between the species form and the life form. In doing so, he attempts to answer the question of personal identity not only metaphysically, but also in relation to normativity.

References

Descartes, René 1992, *Meditationes de prima philosophia*, trans. and ed. Lüder Gäbe, 3. ed. (Hamburg: Felix Meiner Verlag)

— 1997, *Discours de la méthode*, trans. and ed. Lüder Gäbe, 2. ed. (Hamburg: Felix Meiner Verlag)

Locke, John 1975, *An essay concerning human understanding*, ed. Peter H. Nidditch. (Oxford: Clarendon Press)

Millikan, Ruth Garrett 1990, 'The Myth of the Essential Indexical', in: *Nous* 24.5

— 1998, 'A common structure for concepts of individuals, stuffs, and real kinds: More Mama, more milk, and more mouse', in: *Behavioral and Brain Sciences* 21

Parfit, Derek 1984, *Reasons and Persons* (Oxford: Clarendon Press)

Williams, Bernard 1970, 'The Self and the Future', in *Philosophical Review* 79.2

I

Pre-Reflective and Reflective Self-Consciousness

Relationalism about the Subjective Character of Experience

Maik Niemeck

Abstract

It is widely believed that the phenomenal character of conscious mental states is composed of two different components: its qualitative character and its subjective character, with the latter also being referred to as 'mineness', 'for-me-ness' or 'me-ishness'. While many researchers agree that the subjective character is an essential part of conscious life, there is great disagreement about what the metaphysical nature of this component of experience has to be like. One answer to this question, originally presented in Smith (1986), conceptualizes the subjective character as being part of the modality of experience rather than as a constituent of its representational content. I call the branch of theories developed along these lines 'the self-mode approach to the subjective character of experience'. This self-mode approach to the metaphysics underlying the subjective character appears to be promising, yet it can still be developed in a number of different ways – some of which are fraught with problems, while others less so. Here I will introduce three different approaches to the idea that the subjective character is grounded in the modality of experience. I name these distinct accounts 'evaluatism' (Musholt 2015; Pereira 2018; Recanati 2007, 2012), 'adverbialism' (Thomasson 2000), and 'relationalism'. I am going to argue for relationalism, and explore how this position relates to a general representational theory of consciousness and different views about the metaphysics of the subjects of experiences, i.e. the entities in relation to which experiences are instantiated. Relationalism consists of the very simple idea that the subjective character is grounded in a sui generis mental relation that holds between a conscious mental state and the subject of experience having this state. In contrast to most of the existing accounts of subjective character, relationalism aims to account for the subjective character not by introducing something additional to our ontology of the mind and consciousness (such as a self-representational content or a higher-order state), but by adopting a different view on the grounding or basing relation holding between the representational structure of a conscious mental state and its phenomenal character.

 | DOI:10.30965/9783969752906_002

1. Introduction

It is widely believed that the phenomenal character of conscious mental states is composed of two different components: its qualitative character and its subjective character, with the latter also being referred to as 'mineness', 'for-me-ness' or 'me-ishness' (among others, Block 1995; Frank 2011; Gallagher & Zahavi 2008; Kriegel 2003, 2006, 2009; Kriegel & Horgan 2007; Levine 2001; Williford 2006b, 2014; Zahavi & Kriegel 2015; Zahavi 1999, 2004). The qualitative character of experience is usually understood as the specific feel that makes a conscious state the conscious state that it is – e.g. the felt redness, the sweet taste or the bothersome noise, whereas the subjective character is most commonly characterized as a conscious awareness that oneself is currently having a specific conscious state. According to this idea, every conscious mental state involves some undemanding (e.g. non-conceptual, non-attentive, non-observational, etc.) form of self-consciousness. To give an impression of how philosophers characterize the subjective character, here are two quotations from two of the best-known proponents of this idea.

> Arguably, for every possible experience we have, each of us can say: whatever it is like for me to have the experience, it is for me that it is like that to have it. What-it-is-like-ness is properly speaking what-it-is-like-for-me-ness. In our view, this for-me-ness is a universal feature of experience. (Zahavi & Kriegel 2015, p. 36)

> When I have a conscious experience of the blue sky, there is something it is like for me to have the experience. In particular, there is a bluish way it is like for me to have it. This 'bluish way it is like for me' constitutes the phenomenal character of my experience. Phenomenal character is the property that makes a phenomenally conscious state (i) the phenomenally conscious state it is and (ii) a phenomenally conscious state at all. The bluish way it is like for me has two distinguishable components: (i) the bluish component and (ii) the for-me component. (Kriegel 2009, p. 2)

While many researchers agree that the subjective character is an essential part of conscious life, there is great disagreement about what the metaphysical nature of this component of experience has to be like. One answer to this question, originally presented in Smith (1986), conceptualizes the subjective character as being part of the *modality* of experience and as a *manner* in which experience occurs rather than as a constituent of its representational content. I call the branch of theories developed along these lines the *self-mode approach to the subjective character of experience* (henceforth also 'self-mode approach').

This *self-mode approach* to the metaphysics underlying the subjective character appears to be promising, yet it can still be developed in a number of different ways – some of which are fraught with problems, while others less so. Here I will briefly propose a version of the self-mode approach which I call *relationalism* (see Niemeck 2022, chapter 6 for an earlier but more elaborate version of this view) and explore how this position relates to a general representational theory of consciousness and different views about the metaphysics of the subjects of experiences, i.e. the things having experiences or the entities in relation to which experiences are instantiated. Relationalism consists of the very simple idea that the subjective character is grounded in a *sui generis* mental relation that holds between a conscious mental state and the subject of experience having this state. In contrast to most (or even all) of the existing accounts of subjective character[1], relationalism aims to account for the subjective character not by introducing something additional to our ontology of the mind and consciousness (like a self-representational content or a higher-order state), but by adopting a different view on the grounding or basing relation holding between the representational structure of a conscious mental state and its phenomenal character, i.e. the way it feels to the subject of experience to be in that conscious state (Nagel 1974). I will explain in more detail what that means in what follows, but let me first say a few things about the issues I am not able to address (in great detail).

Whether this subjective character exists (e.g. Giustina 2022; Schear 2009), and if so, whether it is a ubiquitous feature of experience or something that is rarely phenomenally present (e.g. Lang 2021), are still highly debated questions that I cannot discuss here. Hence, I will not provide a justification for the existence or the ubiquity of subjective character, but simply presuppose that it really is a universal feature of conscious states. It is also beyond the scope of this chapter to provide the most accurate phenomenological description of what it is like to be in a state with subjective character (see Guillot 2017 for some useful distinctions in this regard). Moreover, some philosophers (e.g. Sebastián 2019) seem to assume that the subjective character involves some form of *de se* awareness. I agree and think that this is also one of the reasons why philosophers use indexical expressions (such as 'me-ishness', 'for-me-ness' or 'mineness') to denote the phenomenon. Yet, the metaphysics of *de se* representations is extremely complex (see García-Carpintero 2015 for an excellent overview) and requires many theoretical commitments. For this reason, I cannot go into detail on these complex issues and will merely hint at some of my views. Another major question is how we are supposed to understand the relation between the representational structure of conscious states and their phenomenal character. Is it, for instance, an identity, grounding, or supervenience

1 An exception might be O'Conaill (2019).

relation (or, perhaps, an entirely different relation)? Does the phenomenal character ground the representational structure or is it the other way around? These are important questions I will not answer. And finally, I will not be concerned with the transtemporal dimension of the subjective character, that is, I speak only about what is required for a state to have a subjective character at one specific moment, and not about what additional conditions must be met in order for an occurrence of subjective character to be extended over time. What, then, remains to be answered? One of the most fundamental questions regarding the subjective character: To which ontological category do the entities that constitute (or base, ground, etc.) the subjective character belong? The subsequent sections aim to provide a rough sketch of my answer to this question.

2. The Self-Mode Approach to the Subjective Character

To this end, I will first, in section 2.1, expose the central intuitions behind the self-mode approach originally proposed by Smith (1986, 2016) and briefly compare the position with so-called *self-representationalism* (Kriegel 2003, 2006, 2009; Williford 2006a, 2006b) and the concept of *pre-reflective self-consciousness* (Frank 2011; Zahavi 1999, 2004). I will also outline some of the shortcomings that have been associated with the last two accounts. Then, in section 2.2, I will introduce three different approaches to the idea that the subjective character is grounded in the modality of experience and demonstrate that some of them do no better than self-representationalism or a theory of pre-reflective self-consciousness. I call these distinct accounts *evaluatism* (Musholt 2015, 2019; Pereira 2018; Recanati 2007, 2009), *adverbialism* (Thomasson 2000), and *relationalism* (my view). Finally, in section 3, I will explain how relationalism can avoid these issues, how it can be embedded in a general impure representational theory of the mind (Chalmers 2010; Crane 2009, 2013), and how it relates to the metaphysics of the self. Regarding the last question, I will demonstrate that relationalism is not necessarily committed to the existence of a self or subject of experience and that this position is compatible with different reductionist and eliminativist views on such matters. This is because mental relations can be related to other mental relations and do not require an object as one of their relata.

2.1 *Self-Representationalism and the Concept of Pre-Reflective Self-Consciousness*

Self-representationalism (e.g. Kriegel 2003, 2009; Williford 2006a, 2006b) is an attempt to combine the idea of a subjective character with a well-established cluster of general theories of consciousness, the so-called *Higher-Order Representational Theories of Consciousness* (hereinafter also 'HOR-theories') (e.g. Armstrong 1968; Rosenthal 1986, 1997, 2005). HOR-theories maintain that conscious mental states are conscious in virtue of being represented by numerically distinct mental states that have specific features (such as guaranteeing some sort of immediate awareness or being first-personal) allowing them to fulfill this function. However, while these meta-representations might be conscious, they are usually unconscious until they are adequately represented by further (third-order and so on) meta-representations as well. Self-representationalists agree with HOR-theorists that conscious mental states are conscious in virtue of being represented, yet disagree with them that these meta-representations are 1) unconscious and 2) numerically distinct states. They assume that every conscious state is conscious because it contains a conscious intentional content that represents the state itself (possibly to the subject being in that state). So, this self-representational content itself is also conscious in virtue of being a property of a conscious state and not merely some unconscious meta-representation (e.g. Kriegel 2009, pp. 126–128). Thus, self-representationalism understands the subjective character of a conscious mental state as being grounded in some sort of conscious representational content that represents the state it is part of.

Although I find this account of subjective character very intuitive and quite appealing, there are some stubborn problems that might suggest the need to look for something else. The most prominent family of issues appeals to the idea that self-representationalism involves some kind of regress or circular explanation. One might, for instance, claim that self-representational contents (like all representational contents) cannot be conscious merely in virtue of being properties of conscious mental states and that self-representational contents have to be consciously represented as well for them to be conscious. Self-representationalism would then predict that conscious creatures with limited cognitive capacities must be able to entertain infinitely many self-representational contents. Furthermore, most people believe that the subjective character involves something similar to the awareness involved in first-person thinking. As previously noted, the subjective character is most commonly characterized as an awareness that oneself is currently undergoing a specific experience. That is why many people also use such terms as 'for-me-ness' to denote it. So, the assumption here is that the subjective character is not just a consciousness of something that happens to be oneself, but somehow includes an additional awareness of the identity relation holding between oneself and the object of which one is conscious. Yet, the crucial question is this: how can a self-representation ensure this additional *de se* or first-person awareness? It seems that in order to be able to recognize a representation as a representation of myself, I already need to have some prior awareness of myself given through further self-representations which enables me to do this.

Because of these and related issues, quite a few philosophers – many of them working in the continental tradition (such as Henrich 1967; Frank 2011 or Zahavi 1999, 2004) – argue that we have to take a radically different approach to the subjective character and should distinguish representational from non-representational forms of self-consciousness. Most of them appeal to the concept of pre-reflective self-consciousness. Pre-reflective self-consciousness is usually described in negative terms which makes it notoriously hard to understand what people actually mean when they use this notion. Dan Zahavi is the major figure – borrowing from Sartre – who introduced this notion into the recent anglophone philosophy of mind. This is how Zahavi defines pre-reflective self-consciousness in his seminal book of 1999:

> It is necessary to differentiate *pre-reflective self-awareness*, which is an immediate, implicit, *irrelational, non-objectifying*, non-conceptual, and non-propositional self-acquaintance, *from reflexive self-awareness*, which is an explicit, *relational*, mediated, conceptual, and *objectifying* thematization of consciousness. (Zahavi 1999, p. 33, my emphasis)

I assume that this quotation quite accurately captures the quintessence of this view. Supposedly, pre-reflective self-consciousness is not only non-representational, but it is also completely *non-relational*. For this reason, some philosophers also describe subjective character as some sort of non-objectifying awareness.[2] I am not entirely sure what it means to be conscious of a mental entity in a non-objectifying way, but it seems that they want to say that there are things which are not the intentional objects of conscious states and yet still manage to change how these experiences feel. And this is the sense in which one can be conscious of these mental entities without having any objectifying awareness of them. So, I take to be the core of this approach the

2 See, for example, how Gallagher and Zahavi characterize pre-reflective self-consciousness in their Stanford Encyclopedia article on 'Phenomenological Approaches to Self-Consciousness': 'In pre-reflective self-awareness, experience is given, not as an object, but precisely as subjective experience. For phenomenologists, intentional experience is lived through (erlebt), but does not appear in an objectified manner. Experience is conscious of itself without being the intentional object of consciousness [...] To have a self-experience does not entail the apprehension of a special self-object; it does not entail the existence of a special experience of a self alongside other experiences but different from them. To be aware of oneself is not to capture a pure self that exists separately from the stream of experience, rather it is to be conscious of one's experience in its implicit first-person mode of givenness.' (Gallagher & Zahavi 2019, section 1).

claim that some instances of self-consciousness (such as the subjective character) have to be understood as non-relational properties rather than as relations one entertains to oneself, such as specific propositional attitudes.

One obvious problem with this proposal is that the subjective character is usually characterized as being about me and my conscious mental states. But it seems simply impossible for something to be about something else unless it is relational. A mental state has to be related in some way to something else (or itself) to be about it.[3] Moreover, if we assume that the subjective character is structureless, then it is hard to see how one could embed this concept in further empirical or even philosophical research. One might even hold that this is exactly the conclusion we should draw and that there are close parallels to other supposedly unanalyzable phenomena, such as qualia. However, this is not a very desirable outcome of any theory, and I am highly skeptical that the current state of the debate would justify such a conclusion.

2.2 *Adverbialism, Evaluatism, and Relationalism*

The self-mode approach to the subjective character can be understood as a blend of the ideas introduced above. On the one hand, it is supposed to be more precise than the concept of pre-reflective self-consciousness and intended to offer an analyzable structure, yet, on the other hand, it also seeks to avoid problems that beset self-representationalism. Adherents of this type of theory maintain that the subjective character might be best conceptualized as a specific *intentional mode* in which representational contents are accessed. Advocates of this view – such as Musholt (2015, 2019), Niemeck (2020, 2022), Pereira (2018), Recanati (2007, 2009), Thomasson (2000) or Smith (1986, 2016) – tend to agree with adherents of a pre-reflective approach that the subjective character of experience is *non-representational* and draw the conclusion that it is rather a peculiar *manner* or *way* of grasping a representational content which contributes this *for-me aspect* to the phenomenal character. According to this account, conscious states do not represent themselves or their subject, but instead are *self-consciously* experienced. In this regard, it is not the representational content that contains a subjective component; rather, it is part of the *relations* we entertain towards the usual non-self-directed contents we

3 This is how Uriah Kriegel formulates this point: 'The very suggestion that subjective character is simple and unstructured is quite straightforwardly implausible. It is natural to hold that, in virtue of a conscious experience's subjective character, the subject is aware of her experience. It would be quite odd indeed to maintain that an experience is for the subject even though the subject is completely unaware of it. Since this awareness is awareness-of, it involves an of-ness relation to the experience.' (Kriegel 2009, pp. 102–104, emphasis as in the original)

grasp when having conscious states. Here is how David Woodruff Smith first characterized this idea in 1986:

> In the case of my seeing a frog, the mode of presentation in the experience is that of 'this frog', or 'this small green frog on this lily pad', whereas *the modality of presentation is that of vision, i.e. 'see' (as opposed to audition or desire, i.e. 'hear' or 'want')*. However, *this traditional distinction must be broadened.* Not only must we recognize indexical modes of presentation, e.g. 'this frog' (not all modes of presentation are descriptive, as e.g. 'the frog on the lily pad in the pond at Smith's house'). But *we must widen the modality of presentation to include not only 'see' but also 'I [see]' and indeed 'in this very experience [I see]'. The reflexive character is thus part of the modality, and not the mode, of presentation in the experience.* In the modal structure 'in this very experience', *the experience is not, strictly speaking, presented; indeed, the experience itself is not in any way presented in the experience – what is presented is 'this frog'.* (Smith 1986, p. 150, my emphasis)

Since there might be good general reasons to suppose that there are *attitudinal* parts (such as seeing, believing or desiring) shaping the phenomenal character of conscious states, we may also think that the subjective character just is such an entity. We do not easily encounter a subject in experience, just as we do not straightforwardly experience a seeing as such. Yet, we presumably think that both entities are essential features of experience. So, why not assume that both things are instances of the same type of being? In this regard, we may follow Smith's advice and expand the range of things which can be part of the modality of experience. In putting this for-me aspect in the modality of experience, one can, on the one hand, account for the *Humean* (1739) intuition that there really is *no self* appearing in (the representational content of) experience, but, on the other, also agree that a *self still is part of* (the modality of) experience and structures it in peculiar ways. The view denies that there is some experiential self-object and yet nevertheless affirms that experience has a subjective component.

There are a couple of different possibilities in terms of situating the subjective character within the framework of the self-mode approach. I think that all of them are quite attractive and at least deserve further examination. However, there is one approach that I favor. So, let me introduce three distinct views – adverbialism, evaluatism, and relationalism – to understand this self-mode idea and explain why I prefer one over the other.

Adverbialism: One way to accommodate the for-me aspect of experience within the self-mode approach could be to understand it as a *non-relational property* of other intentional modes. Just as *blurriness, intensity* or *distortedness* are possible properties of some of our perceptual relations, so we might say that intentional modes can have this *for-me* property. Strictly speaking, the for-me aspect of experience would then be something like a *second-order mode*, which is to say that it is a *way* or *manner* in which an *intentional mode* is experienced, rather than a way or manner in which a *representational content* is given to the experiencing subject. So, the central idea is that the subjective character is grounded in non-relational properties of mental relations a subject already entertains towards representational contents. This view probably comes closest to what could be called an *adverbial theory* or (*pure*) *one-level account* of consciousness and its subjective character. Let's call this approach to the self-mode *adverbialism about the subjective character* (henceforth also 'adverbialism').[4]

The general virtue of such an approach is that we can re-conceptualize those parts of experience, which prima facie seem to be intentional objects but which we have trouble situating in our ontology, as *properties* of the intentional states themselves. For instance, if we want to get rid of such apparent intentional objects as *selves, dragons* or *blue sense data*, we might say that when we have, for instance, visual experiences that seem to be directed at these kinds of entities, it is not the case that we are actually in virtue of a visual relation related to selves, dragons or blue sense data; rather, we see *self-consciously, dragon-wise* or *blue-ly*. According to such a view, concepts like *dragon, blueness* or *self* are not empty, but refer to *non-relational properties* of the mental states, that apparently stand in relations to the entities these concepts allegedly denote. Our intentional states, then, are not *genuine relations* to any ontologically independent (and perhaps questionable) entities. And for this reason, we can allow that there really are no such *objects* as dragons, selves or blue sense data even if we can have experiences which seem to involve them. As I have said, an analogous strategy would then be to understand the subjective character as based on a non-relational property of other intentional modes – such as seeing, thinking or wishing. Just as we might not entertain real representational relations to dragons, we might not usually stand in any representational relations to ourselves, but rather *subjectively, self-consciously* or *for-me-ly* think, wish or see something else.

---

4 Amie Thomasson proposes to understand Brentano's conception of the subjective character (in his terminology inner perception) in this way: 'Brentano's way of trying to preserve the idea that only one act is involved was to characterise the awareness involved in consciousness as a dependent aspect of the original act. That makes it, ontologically, something like a property of the first act, rather than an independent act of its own. If we take the notion of a mental act seriously, a way that act is might be expressed adverbially, and indeed this is a natural – perhaps the most natural – use of the word "conscious": We see, hear, think, etc. consciously' (Thomasson 2000, p. 203, my emphasis).

This approach is certainly worth considering and has not received sufficient attention. However, it might be dismissed for similar reasons as the concept of pre-reflective self-consciousness. One potential worry is that if we understand the subjective character as grounded in an *intrinsic, non-relational property*, we might also have to conclude that it lies beyond the scope of further theorizing and that we have reached an end-point of investigation.[5] So the issue is that if this for-me component itself does not have a structure that could be analyzed, the last explanatory step we can possibly take is to point to this feature. Moreover, this for-me component is supposed to make us *aware of* our mental states and therefore involves at least some form of *directedness*. But can non-relational properties exhibit intentionality? Usually we think of contents, mental states or subjects as the kinds of things that can be intentionally directed at something, but instantiations of non-relational properties are not on our list.

Evaluatism: Another branch of theories assumes that the subject functions as an unarticulated constituent of conscious states and in virtue of these evaluative relations contributes to their phenomenal character. Quite a few philosophers have stressed the idea that mental states exhibit a peculiar kind of intentionality which is not adequately explained merely in terms of their representational content (Kenny 1963; Mulligan 2007; Perry 1986, 1998; Recanati 2007; Teroni 2007). According to this view, even though conscious states are normally not *representationally* about intentional modes or their subjects, they may still entertain distinct *intentional relations* to them. This is indicated by explicating the correctness, satisfaction or adequacy conditions of different types of mental states. In accordance with this idea, even though conscious states are usually not representationally about any subjects, they may still *concern* them in some way. In this vein, a subject as such is, in most situations, not represented in conscious states, but the representational contents are still somehow directed at the subjects they belong to. Recanati (2007, 2009) and more recently Musholt (2015, 2019) – drawing on Perry's work on unarticulated constituents (Perry 1986, 1998) – maintain that this might be the right way to preserve the very common intuition that an experience somehow is about its subject without committing themselves to any implausible phenomenological views. This is how Recanati characterizes this idea: 'Thus the

5 For similar reasons, Rosenthal (1997, pp. 729, 737) maintains that the phenomenal character has to be understood in relational terms. If qualia (i.e. the components that comprise the phenomenal character) were intrinsic properties of experiences, then they might resist further explanation.

subject who sees is not herself an aspect of what is seen, but an aspect of the situation with respect to which what is seen is to be evaluated' (Recanati 2007, p. 216). Here is an example where experiential states seem to entertain this evaluative relation to their subjects. The emotion of fear for instance might represent only a particular object as dangerous but the conditions of adequacy of fear states concern the subject, since that particular object might only be dangerous for some subjects but not for others. When I fear and therefore represent a non-poisonous spider as dangerous, the attitude towards that spider is most certainly not adequate since the spider is not dangerous for me. But if a bug fears that spider in a similar type of representational state to mine, then that particular emotion is quite accurate. (Let's suppose for the sake of argument that a bug can do so.) Even if the bug and I both entertain the same type of mental state with a similar non-self-involving representational content, these states have different conditions of adequacy relative to the subject who employs them. Whereas it is quite often the case that each component of a fact which makes a certain representation adequate or veridical also corresponds to a certain constituent of the representation, this example might be taken to show that it is not always the case. In this respect, mental states can be directed at particular things, such as the subject entertaining them, without being about them representationally. Hence, we might be able to understand the subjective character of experience as based on an intentional but still non-representational relation. I call this position *evaluatism about the subjective character of experience* (henceforth also merely 'evaluatism').

One issue of this approach is based on the question of whether there are any mental states that exhibit object-directed intentionality – such as perceptions – or no intentionality at all – such as moods. The existence of these mental states would imply that evaluatism is strictly limited to a particular class of states, namely those having conditions of satisfaction or the like. In this case, the self-mode approach would not be able to take into account the assumption that the subjective character is ubiquitous and essential to all conscious states. Another related problem is that evaluatism could be considered a hidden form of self-representationalism. After all, representations are the things that are the primary (and perhaps only) bearer of semantic and evaluative properties and even though the subject is in a certain way not represented in conscious states, it is nevertheless supposed to play a central evaluative function, according to this approach. We could therefore argue that while evaluatism emphasizes crucial differences between different types of contents of conscious states (such as representational content and circumstances of evaluation), it nonetheless maintains that the subjective character is based on a representational content, albeit a very different one than most self-representationalists have considered. One might then be inclined to think that evaluatism suffers from the same problems as self-representationalism.

Relationalism: Thus, adverbialism and evaluatism seem to do no better in capturing the nature of subjective character (or at least what we take it to be) than the concept of pre-reflective self-consciousness or self-representationalism. Yet, there is a more promising variation of this self-mode idea which I call *relationalism about the subjective character of experience* (henceforth also 'relationalism'). Relationalism understands the subjective character as being grounded in a *sui generis* intentional mode that holds between us and our mental states. Intentional modes are commonly viewed as *mental relations* to representational contents. When we want to take the notion of a *self-mode* seriously, we should assume that experiences have a subjective character in virtue of specific *mental relations* and not because of non-relational properties of other mental relations or additional evaluative relations, as proposed by adverbialism or evaluatism. Hence, whereas self-representationalism and evaluatism claim that the phenomenal character of conscious states has this felt for-me aspect because they have certain *self-representational contents*, and adverbialism (and perhaps some adherents of the concept of pre-reflective self-consciousness) maintains that this is because our intentional modes have specific *non-relational properties*, the central thesis of the account proposed here is that the phenomenal character contains a subjective character in virtue of peculiar *mental relations* that a subject entertains towards his mental states and their representational contents. Thus, rather than claiming that subjective character requires the presence of additional contents, evaluative relations or specific non-relational properties of intentional modes, the main thesis of my approach is that the subjective character is based on *mental relations* whose existence most philosophers would accept anyway.

Many (if not most) philosophers would agree that all experiences are *for a subject* or that an experience is, in a certain sense, *owned by* a subject. Conscious states and their representational contents are not existence-independent events that can be found independently of someone to whom they belong or without anyone who is experientially directed at them. In other words, they only exist if there is someone *for whom* they appear to exist. This seems to be a brute metaphysical fact, i.e. a fact that is grounded in the nature of the things of which it is composed. In this regard, conscious states stand in *for-ness relations* or *ownership relations* to specific subjects (or to whatever we possibly want to reduce them to). We could also say that conscious states are always instantiated *in relation* to a subject. I think this claim is fairly uncontroversial from an ontological point of view and does not burden the account with any excessive demands. Of course, we need to accept that there are *mental relations* and, moreover, that there are mentalese *for-ness relations* or something similar, but this is not a hard pill to swallow compared to the cognitive demands that other accounts, such as self-representationalism, might place on the concept of *subjective character*.[6]

3. The Potential of Relationalism

To the best of my knowledge, no one in this debate has clearly advocated taking this theoretical path to the subjective character. This is unfortunate, since this relational view has a good deal of potential in trying to solve the problems encountered by the other accounts of subjective character, as I will explain in the section to follow.

Regress Problem: The regress problem of self-representational theories emerges because they assume that all conscious states have self-representational contents which are conscious as well. And they need to explain how it is possible that these contents are conscious too. If representing something is the only way to become conscious of something, then self-representations also have to be represented to be conscious and the theory ends up in the regress. Now, if we think that the subjective character is grounded in an intentional mode – understood as a relation and not as an adverbial modification of such – rather than a representational content, we will not run into these problems. Intentional modes are the kinds of things that relate us to contents or states but not the things that represent something like contents do. And that is why they do not provoke a regress of representations (be they contents or states). However, we might still wonder whether this for-me relation or self-mode also has to somehow relate to itself to become conscious and thus part of the phenomenal character of a mental state. Yet, the crucial advantage of my proposal is that all those questions will not even occur since there is no relation to a relation or representation of a representation involved. There is only one ontologically innocent for-ness relation that does not have to relate to itself to be conscious. Thus, the approach I suggest entails two central claims: First, the subjective character is not grounded in some sort of higher-order mental state, relation or content, but a simple relation that holds between a subject and representational contents this subject is conscious of. Second, mental relations can be conscious without being represented. So, the crucial question, then, is

6 This heavily depends on how one conceptualizes the self-representational contents. But one might wonder if a content can genuinely represent myself or my mental states without involving a concept of myself or my mental states.

what would justify the assumption that mental relations can have an impact on the phenomenal character of conscious states without being represented.

There are independent reasons as to why we should want to accept that claim. A general representational theory of the mind and consciousness which argues that mental relations play a significant role in determining the phenomenal character of conscious states is known as 'impure intentionalism' (Chalmers 2010; Crane 2009, 2013).[7] But there are many debates in which philosophers have argued that mental relations are crucial in providing the right phenomenology and metaphysics of different mental states. For instance, Matthew Soteriou (2013, pp. 111ff.) has recently emphasized that there are phenomenological differences between sense modalities that are not exhaustively described with reference to their contents. According to him, intentional modes also structure perceptual experience in peculiar ways. Other philosophers have proposed that emotions might be best theorized as attitudes rather than as specific types of contents (Deonna & Teroni 2012, 2015; Teroni 2007, 2016; Ben Ze'ev 2001, 2010). Deonna & Teroni (2015) articulate a quite elaborated attitudinal theory of emotions and argue that an account which understands them as contents fails to capture what differentiates distinct types of emotions from each other and from non-emotional states. To give another example, Marta Jorba (2016) claims that we can construe a version of Pitt's (2004) famous epistemic argument for a cognitive phenomenology which focuses on the attitudes rather than contents of cognitive states. I cannot discuss any of the arguments for these positions here, but it should be clear that there might be very good reasons to accept that mental relations play an important role in shaping how conscious states feel.

Intentionality and Structure: We have seen that one central issue of the concept of pre-reflective self-consciousness and adverbialism is that they understand the subjective character as a phenomenon which lacks intentionality and a structure that could be further analyzed. However, if we instead adopt the view I have proposed, we will not run into this problem, as relations have components (e.g. the relata) and further non-relational properties which allow us to give a more elaborated metaphysical analysis. We surely have to accept (internal or external, symmetric or non-symmetric, etc.) relations in our

7 Crane writes: 'The alternative way of developing the view that all mental states are intentional is what I call (following Chalmers 2004) impure intentionalism. This says that *the phenomenal character of an experience is determined by its entire intentional nature; in particular, by its mode and its content*. The phenomenal character of an experience therefore supervenes on its intentional nature. There cannot be two experiences which are identical in their intentional nature but differ in their phenomenal character' (Crane 2009, p. 481, my emphasis).

ontology and that they can have properties, but beyond this, not much more is required that would be controversial. Let me give a demonstration of how this relational account could proceed.

At first, we might want to give a description of very basic properties of this *for-ness relation*. Occurrences of that type of relation are certainly *non-symmetric* – representational contents of mental states are for a subject but the subject is not necessarily for these states or contents, *unigrade binary* – they merely hold between two things, and probably *external* – they do not hold with necessity between a specific subject and its respective mental states and their holding is probably not dependent on the intrinsic nature of these two entities.[8] Then we can build on these quite general formal characterizations and look for more interesting metaphysical and phenomenological features. We might find similar properties as the *blurriness* of visual relations, the *distortedness* of auditory relations or the *intensity* of emotional relations. But all this does not matter so much at this stage. The important point I want to stress here is that it is *not* the case that we cannot give an in-depth analysis of mental relations, and, as such, this approach to the self-mode is not prone to the issues which beset the concept of pre-reflective self-consciousness and adverbialism. In addition, we have options for incorporating the ideas of *directedness* into relationalism to counter the challenge posed by Kriegel (2009, pp. 102–104). Binary non-symmetric relations are considered to have a direction.[9] These relations bestow order upon their relata. When Petra loves Paul, her love may not be returned. This specific occurrence of love, therefore, goes from Petra to Paul but not vice versa. Such cases of love – which are occurrences of binary non-symmetric relations – are entertained by a subject and *directed* at something else. Hence, if we understand intentionality merely as some sort of

8 These characterizations merely serve to demonstrate that relationalism allows further investigation. Perhaps it will turn out that for-ness relations are not *binary* because the subject is nothing over and above a couple of other mental states or, in the end, they might be *internal* relations as there is something in the nature of conscious states which necessarily connects them to some specific subject. I would be fine with such results. But these are details we can worry about after we have a general rationale for this approach and a rough picture of how it could work.

9 For instance, Fraser MacBride writes: '*A non-symmetrical relation R has a direction whereby it travels from one thing to another. What distinguishes aRb from bRa is that R runs from a to b in the former case and b to a in the latter.* So differential application is possible because non-symmetric relations have direction, i.e., because non-symmetric relations run one way, rather than another, amongst the things they relate' (MacBride 2016, section 4, my emphasis).

directedness, then for-ness relations certainly exhibit intentionality, as do all binary non-symmetric relations presumably.[10]

First-Person Awareness: As stated earlier, many seem to assume that the subjective character is not just a consciousness of oneself, but a consciousness of oneself *as oneself*. When we experience a pain, we do not merely experience a property that happens to be ours, but the pain is also experienced as a state of ours. There is one insight on which most people in the debate about the nature of first-person thought have come to agree: namely that our standard picture of representational states will not work for these kinds of mental states. This is what prompted philosophers to come up with such concepts as *belief states* (Perry 1979) or *property self-ascriptions* (Lewis 1979). Those concepts have been introduced to offer *revisionary* theories of representational states, since our standard concept of representational content seems incapable of properly capturing certain features of first-person thought, such as violating the principles of *shareability* or *absoluteness* underlying other kinds of thoughts.[11] Whereas the belief state approach does so by introducing additional features next to representational contents, the self-ascription account is set up to avoid altogether the notion of representational content and instead introduces *properties* as the new intentional objects of cognitive states. So, if the concept of *representational content* is already unable to account for the peculiarities of first-person thought itself, why should we suppose that the mental entities (such as the subjective character), which have been introduced to explain how more sophisticated forms of self-consciousness (such as first-person thought) are possible, are just some other kinds of representational contents? Considering the current state of discussion, it seems more natural to suppose that we need something other than simply more self-representational contents to explain the possibility of first-person awareness. Relationalism

10 Tim Crane recommends avoiding the notion of *aboutness* when defining intentionality: 'Hence, we *should not become too attached to the words "about" and "aboutness" in describing intentionality*. If we do, then we might find it hard even to understand the view that conscious states are intentional. For example, intentionalists say that a headache is an intentional state, but the question 'What is your headache about?' makes little sense. Here we can avoid this superficial problem by thinking of intentional states in a more general, abstract, and semi-technical way to begin with: *intentional states are "directed upon" objects, and "objects", by definition, are what intentional states are directed on*. Sometimes intentionality is described even more abstractly as "self-transcendence": the idea being that intentional states are concerned with what transcends the state itself' (Crane 2009, p. 476, my emphasis).

11 A content is shareable if it is in the same way accessible by different thinkers, and it is absolute if it has a truth value that depends solely on the world and not on the subject accessing it (once the content is fixed). See also García-Carpintero (2017, p. 256) and Ninan (2016, pp. 100ff.) on this point.

appears to accommodate this way of seeing things. This will, of course, not suffice to prove that positing something as *sui generis* mental relations is *the best way* to explain the possibility of first-person awareness, but it speaks in favor of such an approach compared to other attempts. In respect thereof, we can at the very least say that the self-mode theory is closer to the truth than other accounts, such as self-representationalism, which try to address this topic in a more traditional framework that has been considered to fail.

Metaphysics of Selves: Finally, let me say a few things about how relationalism might be conceptually connected to different metaphysical views about the subjects of experiences, or 'selves' for short. My focus will be on *reductionist* (e.g. Hume 1739; Strawson 2011) and *eliminativist* (e.g. Metzinger 2003, 2011; for Buddhist views see Priest 2018 or Siderits 2011) positions, as one might be inclined to think that these views pose specific challenges to relationalism.[12] Theories that conceptualize selves as *substances* (e.g. Lowe 1996) seem to fit well with relationalism, since it is easy to see that mental states and their representational contents can *be for* or *owned* by such entities. Selves would, then, seem to be very ordinary relata of these relations. But while it seems plausbile, for instance, that we can have representations of things that do not exist and mental states as such, it might be considered counterintuitive that we can be non-representationally related to non-existent beings and that the *sui generis* relations, which relationalism posits, can be instantiated without any substance-like subject standing in them. However, let me very briefly demonstrate that relationalism is not necessarily committed to the existence of selves, understood in this way, and that it could be compatible with different reductionist and eliminativist views. This is partially because relations can be related to other relations and do not require any sort of substance as one of their relata. It seems unproblematic to suppose, for instance, that it is *more common* that *bigger-than-relations* are instantiated than *famous-than-relations*. According to such a position, selves could be reduced to mental relations and thus the subjective character to specific mental relations that hold between other mental relations. Relationalism is in this respect compatible with some sort of ontic structural realism (Ladyman & Ross 2007) about the mind and can allow 'relations all the way down', but it is in no way committed to such a position. Similarly, relationalism would work well with views that understand the subjects of experiences as bundles of mental states instead of substances or relations. It also seems unproblematic to accept that mental states can *be for* other mental states. I can think about my desires I had as a

12 Eliminativists, as I understand them, hold that selves simply do not exist, and reductionists claim that selves exist but are nothing other than the experiences (or their properties etc.) themselves.

child. My past desires would then *be for my* current thoughts. Perhaps the main consequence would be that the for-ness relations, posited by relationalism, are not binary. Nonetheless, they can still be considered non-symmetric and therefore to exhibit some sort of directedness (my past desires *are for* my current thoughts but not vice versa). A genuine eliminativism about selves appears to be more problematic for relationalism, since it raises the question of whether the subjective character could be based on a relation without relata. However, there are also (plausible) answers to this question that relationalism has to offer. For instance, one could claim that there are things that do not exist in the actual world and yet they still manage to stand in certain mental relations. After all, I can think of Pegasus and round squares, even though my thinking might not imply that Pegasus or round squares actually exist. Hence, relationalists about the subjective character (who are also eliminativists about selves) might want to accept that mental for-ness relations are not *existence-entailing relations* (just like *being thought of* by someone is not). Although these relations can actually occur, their relata need not. It is important to note that this is not to say that relationalism about the subjective character has to be committed to eliminativism about selves, or any of these views. But I take it to be a theoretical advantage of relationalism that it can be consistently combined with different positions about the nature of selves.

4. Conclusion

The simple idea that the subjective character is grounded in (or based on, etc.) a mental relation may seem too obvious to be considered an interesting philosophical claim. However, this chapter has aimed to prove that this is not the case. It becomes more than clear that relationalism is a viable theory when considering the current theoretical alternatives which try to account for the phenomenon by introducing additional entities to our ontology underlying consciousness (such as self-representational contents or special non-relational properties of intentional modes). In contrast, relationalism seeks to avoid superfluous ontological commitments and provides answers to heavily debated issues by relying on fairly uncontroversial metaphysical claims (such as that conscious experiences are always *for* someone/something or *had* by someone/something). In this respect, relationalism is not only parsimonious, but is also able to avoid the problems that seem to beset other theories and provides novel conceptual resources to account for features philosophers have ascribed to the subjective character.

References

Armstrong, David. 1968. *A Materialist Theory of the Mind.* London: Routledge.

Ben Ze'ev, Aaron. 2001. *The Subtlety of Emotions.* Cambridge, MA: MIT Press.

Ben Ze'ev, Aaron. 2010. "That Thing Called Emotion: On the Nature of Emotional Experiences". In: *Oxford Handbook of Philosophy of Emotion.* Peter Goldie (ed.). Oxford: Oxford University Press, 41–61.

Block, Ned. 1995. "On a Confusion about a Function of Consciousness". *Behavioral and Brain Sciences* 18 (2): 227–247.

Chalmers, David (ed.). 2010. "The Representational Character of Experience". In: *The Character of Consciousness.* Oxford: Oxford University Press, 339–380.

Crane, Tim. 2009. "Intentionalism". In: *The Oxford Handbook of Philosophy of Mind.* Ansgar Beckermann et al. (eds.). Oxford: Oxford University Press, 474–491.

Crane, Tim. 2013. "Unconscious Belief and Conscious Thought". In: *Phenomenal Intentionality.* Uriah Kriegel (ed.). New York: Oxford University Press, 156–173.

Deonna, Julien & Teroni, Fabrice. 2012. *The Emotions: A Philosophical Introduction.* London: Routledge.

Deonna, Julien & Teroni, Fabrice. 2015. "Emotions as Attitudes". *Dialectica* 69 (3): 293–311.

Frank, Manfred. 2011. *Ansichten der Subjektivität.* Berlin: Suhrkamp.

Gallagher, Shaun & Zahavi, Dan. 2008. *The Phenomenological Mind.* New York: Routledge.

Gallagher, Shaun & Zahavi, Dan. 2019. "Phenomenological Approaches to Self-Consciousness". In: *The Stanford Encyclopedia of Philosophy* (Summer 2019 Edition). Edward N. Zalta (ed.). URL = https://plato.stanford.edu/archives/sum2019/entries/self-consciousness-phenomenological/.

García-Carpintero, Manuel. 2015. "De Se Thought". In: *Oxford Handbooks Online.* URL = http://www.oxfordhandbooks.com/view/10.1093/oxfordhb/9780199935314.001.0001/oxfordhb-9780199935314-e-61?rskey=16DYmt&result=1.

García-Carpintero, Manuel. 2017. "The Philosophical Significance of the De Se". *Inquiry* 60 (3): 253–276.

Giustina, Anna. 2022. "A Defense of Inner Awareness: The Memory Argument Revisited". *Review of Philosophy and Psychology* 13 (2): 341–363.

Guillot, Marie. 2017. "I Me Mine: on a Confusion Concerning the Subjective Character of Experience". *Review of Philosophy and Psychology* 8: 23–53.

Henrich, Dieter. 1967. *Fichtes ursprüngliche Einsicht.* Frankfurt: Klostermann.

Hume, David. 1896 (reprint from 1739). *Treatise of Human Nature.* L. A. Selby-Bigge (ed.). Oxford: Clarendon Press.

Jorba, Marta. 2016. "Attitudinal Cognitive Phenomenology and the Horizon of Possibilities". In: *The Phenomenology of Thinking: Philosophical Investigations into the Character of Cognitive Experiences*. Thiemo Breyer & Christopher Gutland (eds.). New York: Routledge, 77–96.

Kenny, Anthony. 1963. *Action, Emotion and Will.* London: Routledge.

Kriegel, Uriah. 2003. "Consciousness, Higher-order Content, and the Individuation of Vehicles". *Synthese* 134: 477–504.

Kriegel, Uriah. 2006. "The Same-Order Monitoring Theory of Consciousness". In: *Self-Representational Approaches to Consciousness*. Uriah Kriegel & Kenneth Williford (eds.). Cambridge, MA: MIT Press, 143–170.

Kriegel, Uriah & Horgan, Terry. 2007. "Phenomenal Epistemology: What is Consciousness that we may know it so well?" *Philosophical Issues* 17 (1): 123–144.

Kriegel, Uriah. 2009. *Subjective Consciousness: A Self-Representational Theory*. Oxford: Oxford University Press.

Ladyman, James & Ross, Don. 2007. *Everything Must Go: Metaphysics Naturalized*, Oxford: Oxford University Press.

Lang, Stefan. 2021. "A Methodological Objection to a Phenomenological Justification of the Ubiquity of Inner Awareness". *ProtoSociology* 38: 59–73.

Levine, Joseph. 2001. *Purple Haze: The Puzzle of Consciousness*. New York: Oxford University Press.

Lewis, David. 1979. "Attitudes De Dicto and De Se". *The Philosophical Review* 88 (4): 513–543.

Lowe, Edward Jonathan. 1996. *Subjects of Experience*. Cambridge: Cambridge University Press.

MacBride, Fraser. 2016. "Relations". In: *The Stanford Encyclopedia of Philosophy* (Winter 2016 Edition). Edward N. Zalta (ed.). URL = https://plato.stanford.edu/archives/win2016/entries/relations/.

Metzinger, Thomas. 2003. *Being No One: The Self-Model Theory of Subjectivity*. Cambridge MA: MIT Press.

Metzinger, Thomas. 2011. "The No-Self Alternative". In: *Oxford Handbook of the Self*. Shaun Gallagher (ed.). Oxford: Oxford University Press, 279–296.

Mulligan, Kevin. 2007. "Intentionality, Knowledge and Formal Objects". *Disputatio* II (23): 205–228.

Musholt, Kristina. 2015. *Thinking About Oneself: From Nonconceptual Content to the Concept of a Self*. Cambridge, MA: MIT Press.

Musholt, Kristina. 2019. "From Non-Self-Representationalism to the Social Structure of Pre-Reflective Self-Consciousness". In: *Senses of Self: Approaches to Pre-Reflective Self-Awareness*. Marc Borner, Manfred Frank & Kenneth Williford (eds.). *ProtoSociology* 36: 243–263.

Nagel, Thomas. 1974. "What is it like to be a bat?" *The Philosophical Review* 83 (4): 435–450.

Niemeck, Maik. 2020. "Current Accounts of Subjective Character and Brentano's Concept of Secondary Consciousness". In: *Franz Brentano's Philosophy after Hundred Years: From History of Philosophy to Reism*. Denis Fisette, Guillaume Fréchette & Hynek Janoušek (eds.). New York: Springer, 55–71.

Niemeck, Maik. 2022. *First-Person Thought: Action, Identification and Experience*. Leiden/Paderborn: Brill | mentis.

Ninan, Dilip. 2016. "What is the Problem of De Se Attitudes?" In: *About Oneself: De Se Attitudes and Communication*. Manuel García-Carpintero & Stephan Torre (eds.). Oxford: Oxford University Press, 86–120.

O'Conaill, Donnchadh. 2019. "Subjectivity and Mineness". *Erkenntnis* 84 (2): 325–341.

Recanati, François. 2007. *Perspectival Thought: A Plea for Moderate Relativism*. Oxford: Oxford University Press.

Recanati, François. 2009. "De Re and De Se". *Dialectica* 63 (3): 249–269.

Rosenthal, David. 1986. "Two Concepts of Consciousness". *Philosophical Studies* 49 (3): 329–359.

Rosenthal, David. 1997. "A Theory of Consciousness". In: *The Nature of Consciousness – Philosophical Debates*. Ned Block et al. (eds.). Cambridge, MA: MIT Press, 729–753.

Rosenthal, David. 2005. *Consciousness and Mind*. Oxford: Oxford University Press.

Pereira, Roberto Horácio de Sá. 2018. "A New Deflationary Account of the 'Primitive Sense of Selfhood'". *Grazer Philosophische Studien* 95 (3): 309–328.

Perry, John. 1979. "The Problem of the Essential Indexical". *Noûs* 13 (1): 3–21.

Perry, John. 1986. "Thought without representation". *Proceedings of the Aristotelian Society* 60: 137–166.

Perry, John. 1998. "Indexicals, Contexts and Unarticulated Constituents". In: *Proceedings of the 1995 CSLI-Amsterdam Logic, Language and Computation Conference*. Atocha Aliseda-Llera, Rob J. Van Glabbeek & Dag Westerståhl (eds.). Stanford: CSLI Publications, 1–16.

Pitt, David. 2004. "The Phenomenology of Cognition or What is it Like to Think that P?" *Philosophy and Phenomenological Research* 69 (1): 1–36.

Priest, Graham. 2018. *The Fifth Corner of Four: An Essay on Buddhist Metaphysics and the Catuskoti*. Oxford: Oxford University Press.

Schear, Joseph. 2009. "Experience and Self-Consciousness". *Philosophical Studies* 144 (1): 95–105.

Sebastián, Miguel Ángel. 2019. "Subjective Character, the Ego and De Se Representation". *ProtoSociology* 36: 316–339.

Siderits, Mark. 2011. "Buddhist Non-Self: The No-Owner's Manual". In: *The Oxford Handbook of the Self*. Shaun Gallagher (ed.). Oxford: Oxford University Press, 297–315.

Smith, David Woodruff. 1986. "The Structure of (Self-)Consciousness". *Topoi* 5 (2): 149–156.

Smith, David Woodruff. 2016. "The Several Factors of (Self-)Consciousness". *Rivista Internazionale di Filosofia e Psicologia* 7 (3): 291–302.

Soteriou, Matthew. 2013. *The Mind's Construction: The Ontology of Mind and Mental Action*. Oxford: Oxford University Press.

Strawson, Galen. 2011. "The Minimal Subject". In: *Oxford Handbook of the Self.* Shaun Gallagher (ed.). Oxford: Oxford University Press, 253–278.

Teroni, Fabrice. 2007. "Emotions and Formal Objects". *Dialectica* 61 (3): 395–415.

Teroni, Fabrice. 2016. *"Emotions, Me, Myself and I"*. In: *International Journal of Philosophical Studies* 24 (4): 433–451.

Thomasson, Amie. 2000. "After Brentano: A One-Level Theory of Consciousness". *European Journal of Philosophy* 8 (2): 190–210.

Williford, Kenneth. 2006a. "Zahavi versus Brentano: A rejoinder". *Psyche* 12 (2): 1–8.

Williford, Kenneth. 2006b. "The Self-Representational Structure of Consciousness". In: *Self-Representational Approaches to Consciousness*. Uriah Kriegel & Kenneth Williford (eds.). Cambridge, MA: MIT Press. 111–143.

Williford, Kenneth. 2014. "Representationalisms, Subjective Character, and Self-Acquaintance". In: *Open MIND*. Thomas Metzinger & Jennifer Windt (eds.). URL = http://open-mind.net/papers/representationalisms-subjective-character-and selfacquaintance.

Zahavi, Dan. 1999. *Self-awareness and Alterity: A Phenomenological Investigation*. Evanston, IL: Northwestern University Press.

Zahavi, Dan (ed.). 2004. "Back to Brentano?" *Journal of Consciousness Studies* 11 (10–11): 66–88.

Zahavi, Dan & Kriegel, Uriah. 2015. "For-me-ness: What it is and what it is not." In: *Philosophy of Mind and Phenomenology: Conceptual and Empirical Approaches*. Daniel Dahlstrom et al. (eds.). London/New York: Routledge, 36–53.

Varieties of Reflective Self-Consciousness in the Multidimensional Self

Heidi Haanila

Abstract

The capacity to reflect on oneself is of utmost importance to human personhood. To elaborate on the manifold forms of reflective self-consciousness, this article endorses a multidimensional conception of self, according to which self-reflection essentially involves an experiential dimension. While classical analyses of reflective self-consciousness have highlighted unique epistemic and motivational features of self-conscious thoughts, I propose that the mere remarking of self-conscious thinking is insufficient for a complete analysis of reflective self-consciousness and more fine-grained conceptual tools are required. I complement the classical analyses by exploring three conceptual distinctions within different modes of self-reflection: one can reflect on oneself deliberately or theoretically, voluntarily or involuntarily, and with or without identification. In order to illustrate the significance of these conceptual distinctions, I consider changes in self-reflection in two altered states of consciousness, namely pathological depersonalization and meditation, which can also be studied to elucidate typical self-reflection. Utilizing this investigation of the variation in self-reflection, I demonstrate that reflective self-consciousness is important for mental well-being.

Self-reflection is vital to human personhood, as it provides rich opportunities to make and modify judgments about oneself and to direct one's actions.[1] In this article, I elaborate concepts that are needed to understand the manifold forms of reflective self-consciousness. First, I show that self-reflection involves an experiential dimension, and I examine classical analyses of reflective self-consciousness, which have highlighted unique epistemic and motivational features of self-conscious thoughts (§1). Second, I propose that in order to analyze reflective self-consciousness as a whole, the remarking of self-conscious thinking must be extended by introducing more elaborate conceptual tools

1 Many of the ideas elaborated in this article are discussed in greater detail in the author's dissertation (Haanila 2022).

 | DOI:10.30965/9783969752906_003

(§2). Third, I complement the classical framework by presenting three conceptual distinctions within different modes of self-reflection: one can reflect on oneself deliberately or theoretically, voluntarily or involuntarily, and with or without identification. The significance of these conceptual distinctions is illustrated by considering changes in self-reflection in two altered states of consciousness: pathological depersonalization and meditation (§3). The study of altered self-consciousness also elucidates typical functions of self-reflection. Finally, I emphasize that reflective self-consciousness is important for mental well-being (§4). The proposed conceptual picture of the varieties in self-reflection can be applied in further studies to build a complete theory of self-consciousness (§5).

1. Theoretical Basis for the Study of RSC

1.1 *Concepts of Self-Consciousness*

Although the notion of self is notoriously ambiguous, the first step in an analysis of self is to recognize its different dimensions. In this article, I focus only on *self-consciousness*, that is, to experience oneself.[2] Self-consciousness provides a suitable starting point for the study of self because it is a prominent feature of selfhood, and reflective self-consciousness in particular has been described as a crucial human capacity. In addition, studies have argued that metaphysical inquiries concerning the nature of self are subordinate to inquiries of self-consciousness (Strawson 2000). Strawson (2000) points out that the investigation of self-experience in self-consciousness is decisive, as it provides knowledge that defines the self, and this knowledge is needed in order to answer metaphysical questions concerning the nature of self. However, self-consciousness also comes in many varieties. The most general distinction can be drawn between two different forms of self-consciousness: minimal and reflective.[3]

---

2 Here, I do not address metaphysical questions concerning self (for metaphysical perspectives in this volume, see, e.g., Anurag, Niemeck, Noller). For an overview of the concepts of self, see, e.g., Gallagher (2011) or Siderits et al. (2010), the latter also involves conceptions of self in eastern philosophies.

3 This frequent distinction is conceptualized in different forms in separate theories, for instance, as 'nonconceptual and conceptual self-consciousness' (Bermúdez 2001), 'implicit and explicit self-awareness' (Grünbaum and Zahavi 2013), 'intransitive and transitive self-consciousness' (Kriegel 2004), 'minimal and narrative self' (Gallagher 2000), and 'pre-reflective and reflective self-consciousness' (Zahavi 2005). In this article, the terms 'minimal' and 'reflective self-consciousness' are used as general concepts that can be applied across different theories.

The *minimal self-consciousness* (MSC) refers to the most fundamental form of selfhood. This elementary or 'thin' form of self-consciousness forms the basis for the cognitively more complex dimensions of self (e.g., Bermúdez 2001; Grünbaum and Zahavi 2013; Kriegel 2003, 2004; Zahavi 2005, 2014; in this volume, see, Breuer; Niemeck). MSC identifies self as the *subject* or *subjectivity* of experience, which is a constitutive feature of consciousness. This subtle awareness of oneself is present in all conscious mental states, including those that are not directed toward oneself. For example, while one is focused on perceiving the environment, one is aware of oneself as the owner or *subject* of the experience. In other words, MSC does not refer to self as a content or object of consciousness, that is, a *what* of experience. Instead, MSC concerns the *how* of experience: the experiences I am living through are *first-personal*. I am immediately familiar with my own experiences, but I do not have this same connection to the experiences of others; my experiences are given differently to me than to anybody else. The embodied and affective features of pre-reflective MSC are frequently highlighted: even when one's body or affects are not the focus, one's experiences are lived through the body and affectivity functions as a tacit background of experience.

The concept of MSC needs to be complemented with the 'thicker' notion of the *reflective self-consciousness* (RSC), which is higher in the cognitive hierarchy (e.g., Bermúdez 2001; Gallagher and Zahavi 2007; Kriegel 2004; Zahavi 2005, 2014). RSC aligns with the use of 'self-consciousness' in everyday language, as it refers to the capacity to identify oneself as the *object* of one's reasoning and to think of oneself *as* oneself.[4] RSC is essentially linked to our linguistic capacities and reasoning skills, that is, one's ability to form concepts, beliefs, and inferences about oneself. Importantly, one can use RSC to evaluate and direct one's action: self-reflection is necessary for moral self-responsibility and self-critical deliberation.

---

4 This article focuses on linguistic human RSC. However, several other species have the (simply defined) capacity to take oneself as the object of cognition and to recognize oneself as oneself. In developmental psychology and comparative psychology, the capacity of (reflective) self-consciousness has often been operationalized by the highly influential paradigm of the mirror self-recognition task (see, e.g., Gallup, 1970 1982; Rochat and Zahavi 2011). Infants 'pass' the mirror test at the age of 18 months on average. In addition, several non-human species also pass the test, including chimpanzees, orangutans, bottlenose dolphins, and Asian elephants. However, the mirror tests have been criticized, as it is difficult to precisely define the relationship between self-consciousness and mirror self-recognition (see, e.g., Broesch et al. 2011; Zahavi 2014). Nonetheless, human RSC exceeds mere mirror tests and is unique among species because of our complex cognition and linguistic skills.

Furthermore, RSC has been connected with memory and the capacity to formulate self-narratives and a long-term personal identity in a Lockean sense (e.g., Baker 2012; Gallagher and Zahavi 2007; Gallagher 2000; Kriegel 2004; Schechtman 2011). These connections highlight the wider time-perspective of RSC, which extends from past to future; in contrast, MSC relates to an immediate experience. Overall, RSC has a distinct role within cognition and facilitates certain ways of thinking and acting that are characteristically human: the capacity to acknowledge one's own thoughts and to reflect upon them on a significant scale enables one's engagement in many intellectual activities and helps to direct one's life.

The distinctive role of self-reflection has led some theorists to define 'self-consciousness' solely in terms of RSC. In other words, certain theories do not consider MSC self-consciousness and only use the notion of 'self-consciousness' at a cognitively higher level of self-reflection (see, e.g., Baker 2012; MacIntyre 1981; Musholt 2013; Revonsuo 2006; Taylor 1989). This article, however, endorses a multidimensional approach to self that identifies MSC and RSC as complementary (see, e.g., Gallagher 2013; Zahavi 2014). This multidimensional concept highlights the idea that self-consciousness involves several features of self. The involvement of MSC in RSC reveals the amalgamation of different forms of selfhood: when self is the object of (reflective) self-consciousness, self is simultaneously the (minimally self-conscious) subject of consciousness. The whole picture of self-consciousness involves aspects of both minimal and reflective self-consciousness and recognizes the dynamics between them (Haanila 2022). This multidimensional conception of self-consciousness can be illustrated using the recently developed pattern theory of self (Gallagher 2013; Gallagher and Daly 2018; see also, Newen 2018).[5] According to the pattern theory, an individual self includes a complex pattern of characteristic features or certain aspects of self; various interpretations of self can be seen as commensurable, and thus the theory provides a useful framework for discussions on what constitutes a self (Gallagher 2013). This article investigates the dimensions of reflective self-consciousness on a wide scale with an aim to provide a general picture of the diverse forms of self-reflection and their connections to mental well-being. This investigation employs a multidisciplinary methodological approach, which combines conceptions of self in analytic and

5 While this article does not explore pattern theory in more detail, the analyses provided here could be considered an elaboration of the reflective aspects of self in particular. At a minimum, MSC involves embodied, experiential, and affective features of self, whereas RSC involves at least psychological-cognitive, reflective, and narrative aspects. For a more complete examination of pattern theory and especially the narrative aspects of self, see Leuenberger (in this volume).

phenomenological philosophical traditions with the study of self in empirical sciences.

1.2 *Classical Analyses of Reflective Self-Consciousness: The Uniqueness of Self-Conscious Thoughts*

Reflective self-consciousness is essentially connected to language;[6] therefore, examining the unique features of first-personal language use is a prominent route in the study of self-reflection. The classical analyses of RSC in analytic philosophy have highlighted the peculiarities of *self-conscious thoughts*, that is, thoughts referring to oneself using the first-person concept 'I' (e.g., Castañeda 1967; Perry 1979; Shoemaker 1968; Wittgenstein 1958; see also Grünbaum and Zahavi 2013). Analytic philosophers have found that self-conscious thoughts involve specific semantic, epistemic, and motivational peculiarities, which reveal how self-consciousness is different to a consciousness of things other than oneself. However, these peculiarities only hold when one refers to oneself in the first person. Thus, the most common distinction within RSC is drawn between first- and third-personal thinking about oneself. This distinction is briefly reviewed below to outline the contrasting characteristics between first-personal RSC and third-personal RSC.[7]

A fundamental feature of all self-conscious thoughts is *immunity to failure of reference:* these thoughts are guaranteed to succeed in referring to the subject of the thinking. For example, when I think of myself with an 'I'-concept, I know that I am referring to myself and there is no possibility of reference failure ('as Descartes's "cogito argument" brings out', Shoemaker 1968, p. 557). It is impossible to think an I-thought and not refer to oneself. This is also connected to

6 Thus, reflective self-consciousness is also called a 'conceptual self-consciousness', e.g., by Bermúdez 2001, 2007.

7 The aim here is to provide only a brief introduction to the discussion of 'I'. Wittgenstein's (1958, p. 66–7) distinction between two different uses of the word 'I' is frequently mentioned as an initiator of the discussion in analytic philosophy: the use of 'I' as object (e.g., 'My arm is moving') and the use of 'I' as subject (e.g., 'I think it will rain'). Shoemaker's (1968) interest in this distinction led to the development of his now famous idea that a particular class of statements in which 'I' is used as the subject is immune to the error through misidentification relative to the first-person pronoun. According to Shoemaker (1968), this is the use of 'I' that philosophers have found puzzling, and it reveals the uniqueness of self-consciousness. Castañeda (1966, 1967) reported a closely related observation when studying third-person sentences such as 'The editor believes that he* is F'. However, James (1890) had already provided a parallel distinction between 'I' and 'me' ('I' reflecting the self as a subject of experience and 'me' the self as an object of experience) and the distinction can also be found in Kant's philosophy (see, e.g., Brook 2001). For more detailed discussions on these topics, see, e.g., Brook & DeVidi 2001; Gertler 2010; Smith 2020; in this volume, see, Herrmann.

reference without identification: as one refers to oneself by an 'I'-concept, one is aware of oneself as the subject of thinking without knowing any identifying properties of the subject. Furthermore, the knowledge that one is referring to oneself makes whatever one is ascribing to oneself stand out as something significant to one's practical reasoning (Grünbaum and Zahavi 2013; Perry 1979; Shoemaker 1968). That is to say, self-conscious thinking entails specific epistemic and motivational features, which are elaborated below.

First, a first-person reference to oneself reveals an *epistemic* uniqueness: by thinking an 'I'-thought one necessarily *knows* and *understands* that one is thinking about oneself (Castañeda 1967; Grünbaum and Zahavi 2013; Perry 1977; Shoemaker 1968). This knowledge is based on immediate familiarity with one's own experience and does not include any identificatory step. Identification involves the possibility of misidentification, but this is not the case for self-conscious thinking: my self is accessible to me in a way in which it is not to others. In contrast, when one refers to oneself in the third-person mode – that is, by a definite description, a name, or a perceptual demonstrative – there are more identificatory steps, and the danger of making a mistake is always present. For example, one can make a mistake by actually referring to someone else or not realizing that one is referring to oneself.

The possible errors of third-person self-reference can be seen, for instance, in Perry's (1977) thought experiment of Rudolf Lingens, an amnesiac who wanders in the Stanford Library. While in the library, Lingens happens to read a biography about himself, but he does not realize that he is in fact the main character. A very detailed description or even his name does not provide self-knowledge to amnesiac Lingens: he does not understand that he is referring to himself when he thinks about Lingens' life. On the other hand, a third-person self-reference can fail to refer to oneself. For instance, if Lingens observed only young people in the library, he might refer to himself with the definite description of 'the oldest person in this library'. However, if there are older individuals browsing through the books when Lingens is present, the description does not actually hold true for Lingens.

Second, first-person self-reference includes specific motivational features that are significant in relation to the subject's emotional feelings, practical reasoning, and action (Baker 2012; Castañeda 1966, 1967; Grünbaum and Zahavi 2013; Perry 1977, 1979; Shoemaker 1968). That is to say, first-personal thoughts enable and motivate action, while non-first-personal thoughts are not linked to action in the same direct way.

A famous example is Perry's (1979) story about his own shopping experience during which he noticed a trail of sugar on the floor of the supermarket. Perry thought that someone had been sloppy, and he sought out the shopper with the torn sack in order to tell him that he was making a mess. After a while, Perry realized that he himself was actually the shopper with the torn sack, and this realization made him change his action: he stopped his search and rearranged the torn sack in his cart. Kaplan's (1989, p. 533) example also clearly illustrates the connection between self-conscious thinking and motivation for action. In this example, I see in a window the reflection of a woman whose pants appear to be on fire. If I believe 'Her pants are on fire', pure self-interest does not necessarily motivate me to do anything about it. However, if I believe 'My pants are on fire', pure self-interest is very likely to motivate me, and I will behave differently.

2. Elaborated Analysis of Reflective Self-Consciousness

Although self-conscious thoughts have distinctive epistemic and motivational features, I propose that the mere remarking of self-conscious thinking does not provide a sufficient analysis of the varieties of RSC. Self-reflection is used in numerous different experiences, and we need fine-grained conceptual tools to advance the understanding of the subtleties of these experiences. In this section, I examine self-conscious thoughts with three additional distinctions that can classify and systematize the conception of RSC manifestations. Rather than being in competition with each other, these distinctions are complementary: they provide answers to different questions and thus can be used in parallel. The first distinction is drawn between the deliberative and theoretical stances, that is, stances or attitudes with which one can exercise RSC. The second distinction between voluntary and involuntary RSC refers to the start of the process of reflection, when self is taken as the object of consciousness. The third distinction concerns the degree of identification with self-related content: the analysis of RSC is extended to also cover cases in which one does not identify with oneself and withdraws from self-referential thinking.

2.1 *Theoretical and Deliberative Stances*

In his analysis of self-reflection, Richard Moran (2001) distinguishes between deliberative and theoretical stances that one can take toward oneself. By defining these stances, we can illustrate the complexity of RSC and deepen the classical analysis of self-conscious thought. Moran argues that even if one is immediately aware of one's mental state and has self-conscious thoughts, it is possible that one may still only have an outsider's perspective on one's mental state. In order to recognize this kind of case, we require a more complete picture of first-person awareness.[8] Moran (2001) proposes that we need to acknowledge the difference between two different manners through which one can inspect oneself. In both cases, self is taken to be the object of consciousness and the pronoun 'I' is used, but the self is approached with different *stances*. The *deliberative stance* is associated with practical reasoning and is essential for understanding first-person self-awareness and action. In contrast, the *theoretical stance* is rather descriptive and involves more explanatory examinations of one's mind. Each stance is needed in its own domain; one stance does not eliminate the other, and RSC is characterized by their interplay. We can however gain a more accurate picture of a particular self-reflection by acknowledging the differences between the stances and clarifying the question, 'With which stance does one employ RSC?'

According to Moran (2001), questions from the theoretical stance concerning oneself can come in the form of 'What do I believe?' or 'What is it that I feel?' Answers to these kinds of theoretical inquiries provide true descriptions of one's mental state, as they result in a discovery of a fact of which one was ignorant (Moran 2001, p. 58–63). However, answers to theoretical questions about oneself merely provide attributional self-knowledge, a knowledge that concerns one's state of mind but is mediated by an identifying description – which prompts a reference to oneself in a third-personal form. Moran (2001, p. 128–9) also describes the theoretical stance as a rationalizing interpreter's stance by which one seeks to explain one's actions and attitudes. From this viewpoint, one's beliefs function as psychological data that explain one's behavior purely in terms of its role as a psychological state, giving a fairly good indication of one's beliefs. Capacity for this stance is important because it assists, for instance, in the normative evaluation of one's actions – in the same way that the actions of others are normatively evaluated. However, Moran highlights that the theoretical stance is not sufficient for capturing the special characteristics of self-consciousness.

The deliberative stance, on the other hand, is a position fundamentally different from that of another person: it is essential to human nature and plays a crucial role in making us who we are (Moran 2001). Deliberative questions of oneself are presented in the form of 'What am I to believe?' or 'What shall I intend?' This kind of deliberative inquiry requires one to determine what is

8 It can be noted that Moran generally argues for 'a tradition of thought, roughly Kantian, but with sources both in Locke and in early Stoicism, which aligns, or even identifies, reflective self-consciousness with rational freedom' (Moran 2001, p. 139). However, Moran's wider context is not within the scope of this article; instead, the distinction between deliberative and theoretical stances is primarily considered an elaboration of different forms of self-reflection.

true, and thus it plays a constitutive role in psychological facts. Deliberative questions are answered by a decision or commitment of some sort, whereas theoretical questions can simply be answered by a response to ignorance of some antecedent fact about oneself. Since the result of deliberative inquiry is the formation of an endorsement of an attitude, one's reflections on one's own state have a self-transforming aspect: one plays a role in formulating how one thinks and feels.

Moran emphasizes the idea that deliberative reflection is connected to practical reflection; this reflective process 'does not conclude with a normative judgment *about* what would be best to do, but with the formation of an actual intention *to do* something' (Moran 2001, p. 59). Moran also describes the deliberative stance as a stance of the reasoning agent who does not treat her beliefs as opaque psychological facts. For the agent herself, her beliefs are not psychological data that could justify, even in principle, her 'behavior purely in its role as a psychological state' (Moran 2001, p. 128–129). The agent stands in a first-personal relation to herself, which is not the same type of relation the agent has with other things. As Moran (2001, p. 113) describes, 'I do not "move my body" as I might move a piece of equipment, nor do I relate to my attitudes as mental furniture to be arranged.' Instead of merely arranging one's mental states, deliberative endorsement involves an element of shaping one's mental states. For instance, when one sees one's anger as childish or one's feelings of guilt as false, the 'seeing' is not purely descriptive but a deliberative reflection about how to feel. Moreover, when one answers the question 'Is this what I really want?' by considering what is worth wanting, one thereby clarifies the structure of one's desires. Moran (2001, p. 142–5) describes this form of self-reflection using a metaphor of distancing (following Korsgaard 1996), that is, 'stepping back' from one's current mental activities. According to Moran, the metaphor presents a very rich image of our self-reflection: 'stepping back' involves observation as well as identification, differentiation, and acknowledgment of one's mental states. This deliberative confrontation is an unavoidable human characteristic, as one needs to take a stance on what to believe and how to act.

Although the deliberative stance has specific first-person features, Moran (2001) emphasizes that self-consciousness requires both stances. Each stance has prestige in its own domain: instead of being inconsistent, the stances are complementary.[9] Moran (2001, p. 161–2) demonstrates the complementary roles of the stances by considering Sartre's (1956) example of the akratic gambler

9 However, there are also situations which involve a conflict between the two styles of thinking – for example, between one's reflection *about* a desire and one's reflection that has a *conclusion* that is a desire.

who resolves to stop gambling. The case illustrates how each stance presents its own demands as unavoidable and requires an answer in its specific terms. Since the gambler is a deliberative agent who is committed to her decision to stop gambling, the empirical evidence from her history does not determine what she will do. On the other hand, in the theoretical stance, her decision is a psychological fact that is examined in relation to her empirical history. Since (due to her akrasia) the gambler has failed to adhere to her antecedent decisions to stop, the theoretical point of view presents her current decision as ungrounded and inconstant in regard to determining her actual decisions and actions. The benefit of the theoretical stance is that it advices the gambler to be empirically realistic about herself and to not engage in pretense or wishful thinking. However, the theoretical stance cannot tell her when such 'realism' is simply an appearance that has resulted from avoiding the practical question before her. The benefit of the deliberative stance is that it advices the gambler that she is not bound by her history and needs to face the question of what she *is to do*, otherwise she is exhibiting a form of evasion. However, the deliberative point of view does not reveal when her assumption of agency is artificial, since there are empirical conditions undermining her normal strength to form an intention that will lead to constructive action. Thus, each stance offers a useful viewpoint without denying the truth of the other stance. While the theoretical viewpoint is crucial in acknowledging the relevance of facts in one's history, the deliberative viewpoint is essential for denying the completeness and decisiveness of these facts and providing the insight that one is not bound by one's history. As the stances have complementary roles, Moran (2001) argues that the capacity to shift between them is a vital component of psychological well-being (this idea is extended in §4).

2.2 *Voluntary and Involuntary Reflective Self-Consciousness*

In order to grasp the subtleties of self-conscious thinking, it is useful to draw a further distinction between voluntary and involuntary reflective self-consciousness. While the content of consciousness can be consistent (one's self), the distinction concerns a difference in the initiation of the process of self-consciousness. Seigel (2005) uses the terms 'reflexivity' and 'reflectivity' to describe this type of distinction while Colombetti and Ratcliffe (2012) employ the terms 'involuntary and voluntary noematic feelings' (for a parallel distinction between voluntary and involuntary neural activation, see also, Gerrans 2015). *Involuntary self-reflection* (i.e., reflexivity) refers to reflection that has a passive character: it is 'an automatic, reflex-like exaggerated self-intimation of a first-order experience' (Colombetti and Ratcliffe 2012, p. 146). In contrast, *voluntary self-reflection* (i.e., reflectivity) refers to the more active reflection (deliberate distancing) to self; in this case, the attention to self establishes a new relationship between consciousness and its contents. This distinction can be detected in manifestations of RSC by asking 'is the reflective self-consciousness voluntarily or involuntarily initiated?' Although the distinction refers to the start of self-conscious thinking, it can also be related to experiential differences in employing RSC (elaborated in §3.1).

Up to this point, the cases described in this article have illustrated voluntary uses of RSC in which one chooses to contemplate one's mental states and actions. It is this voluntary character that makes RSC so significant: one not only reacts to stimuli, but one also has the capacity to decide how to respond and act in various situations. Indeed, voluntariness has been identified as a feature that distinguishes RSC from MSC (Kriegel 2003).

However, RSC can also occur involuntarily, that is, without active commencement by the subject. One can be concentrating on a task that is not focused on oneself when a sudden occurrence shifts the attention to oneself involuntarily. For example, when I decide to swim to a rocky shore, my attention is focused solely on the environment: the location of the rocks, the rising of the waves, and the beauty of the seascape. However, a sudden pain in my foot causes me to immediately turn my attention to myself as I realize that I have been wounded by a sharp rock. I now focus on how badly I have hurt myself, and I also change my action: I change my course and head to the nearest shore in order to inspect the wound. The wounded foot may also trigger chains of self-reflection: I remember swimming on many shores like this, what didn't I notice this time? How will I manage to get back to town? What will my friends think of me now since I have always boasted about my skillful swimming? Ultimately, however, this involuntarily initiated sudden self-reflection and quick shift of attention demonstrates the usefulness of RSC. RSC provides a means to quickly utilize new relevant information, reorientate oneself, and then adjust one's actions accordingly. Once one attends to the urgent need for self-consciousness, one can shift attention back to the tasks one considers most relevant.

In addition, forms of 'periodic' involuntary RSC seem to be present at least in episodes of mind-wandering, moments in which thoughts occur spontaneously while one is not actively focused on anything in particular (e.g., Christoff et al. 2016; Christoff & Fox 2018). It has been observed that during mind-wandering, many thoughts tend to concern one's self. Although excessive mind-wandering can be undesirable[10], transient mind-wandering can be considered functional 'resting' between intense task-oriented cognitions. Mind-wandering

10 See, e.g., Killingsworth and Gilbert's (2010) famous paper 'A Wandering Mind Is an Unhappy Mind'. However, a detailed examination of mind-wandering is outside the scope of this article.

is also related, for instance, to creative thinking, which is regarded as a useful mental process (e.g., Christoff et al. 2016).

In this article, I also want to highlight that *frequent* involuntary RSC is characteristic of several mental disorders. That is to say, excessive involuntary self-reflection is related to psychological distress. For instance, excessive negative rumination is a feature of depression: individuals with depression can continuously reflect on themselves and their condition. Another example is depersonalization disorder, which is characterized by a tendency to observe one's feelings of self-alienation in a hyper-reflective manner (this case is elaborated in §3.1).

2.3 *Self-Reflection with and without Identification*

In addition to different stances and means of initiation, reflective self-consciousness can be exercised in different modes. Two opposing modes of self-reflection involve thinking of oneself with and without identification. The distinction between these two modes reveals a variant of RSC in which one thinks of oneself without the intention of identification and consciously refrains from self-identification (e.g., Fasching 2008). The recognition of this distinction provides an answer to the question, 'Does RSC involve identification with the self as the content?' This case in part resembles the distinctions between first-person and third-person thinking about oneself or the deliberative and theoretical stances toward oneself, but it can also be considered a separate further elaborate example of RSC. In fact, both the theoretical and deliberative stances seem to involve identification: these stances are used in self-conscious thinking, which is often identificatory. The deliberative stance in particular entails a strong sense of the first-person and an identification that is related to commitment and practical reasoning. Although the theoretical stance has a more descriptive character, it does involve a level of identification and can result in the discovery of identification.

Moreover, many discussions of RSC in analytic philosophy have placed self-identification in an advanced and aspired position (e.g., Frankfurt 1988; Moran 2001). In these discussions, identification in action has been contrasted with somewhat deficient action that is ambivalent or halfhearted. In other words, 'identification' and being active have frequently been commended in the studies of RSC; in contrast, a lack of identification has been associated with mental distress.

I wish now to highlight that RSC forms also involve the capacity to observe one's mental states directed toward oneself without the intention to identify with oneself; in this state, one consciously refrains from identification. This mode of reflection is not intended to stand in opposition to 'wholeheartedness' in traditional discussions, but it can be used to explore further variations of RSC. Instead of being deficient or inferior to identification, this *capacity* for the non-identification mode of self-consciousness should be recognized as significant and functional since excessive self-reflecting can lead to distress that is a risk for mental well-being, particularly if it becomes chronic. The non-identificatory mode directed toward oneself can be purposely exercised, at least in (some) meditative practices. This is evident in Fasching's (2008, p. 478) characterization in which the 'essence of the meditative process … is … a de-identification from what we normally ascribe to ourselves'. However, it is notable that RSC is employed in the exercise of the non-identificatory mode: self-reflection is used to withdraw from identification with the self-related contents of consciousness and to maintain a neutral stance when observing the flow of mental states (elaborated in §3.2).

3. Altered Self-Consciousness as a Methodological Tool to Elucidate Varieties of Self-Reflection

In order to illustrate the significance of the proposed three conceptual distinctions within self-reflection, I consider the manifestation of reflective self-consciousness in two example cases. Both of these cases, meditation and pathological depersonalization, concern profound changes in self-reflection in altered states of consciousness. Studies of altered states of consciousness have been utilized in recent empirically informed philosophy of mind and self (e.g., Gallagher 2013; Mandik 2007; Metzinger 2004; Thompson 2014; Windt 2015). In a multidisciplinary analysis of self, an *altered state of consciousness* (ASC) functions as a contrast condition that can elicit the features of typical self-consciousness. That is to say, ASCs can be used as a methodological tool to clarify the dimensions of self-consciousness. An ASC has been defined as 'a temporary change in the overall pattern of subjective experience' (Farthing 1992, p. 205).[11] The variations between altered and typical experiences assist in revealing the tacit aspects of self that generally receive little attention: only when these aspects alter or are absent do we see their initial role in self-experience.

11 For definitions of an ASC, see e.g., Revonsuo et al. (2009). Analyses of ASCs in the study of self have involved a range of forms: (i) induced illusions (Blanke and Metzinger 2009), (ii) dreaming (Haanila 2021; Thompson 2014; Windt 2015), (iii) experiences under psychedelic drugs (Letheby and Gerrans 2017), (iv) meditative practices (Fasching 2008; Metzinger 2020), and (v) pathological conditions such as depersonalization disorder (Ciaunica et al. 2021). The last two forms of ASC mentioned in this list are briefy discussed in this article. In this volume, see also, Cheng, Fernandez.

3.1 *Depersonalization*

Depersonalization refers to feelings of estrangement or alienation from one's self, one's body, and/or one's surroundings (Ciaunica et al. 2021; Medford et al. 2016; Sass et al. 2013; Sierra 2009; Sierra and David 2011). Characteristic symptoms of depersonalization include 'emotional numbing, loss of sense of agency, inability to focus, feelings of the unreality of the external world, altered experience of the body, time, and space, and heightened self-observation' (Sass et al. 2013, p. 433; Simeon and Abugel 2006). The feelings of unreality regarding the external world are referred to as 'derealization'. The depersonalized experience has been described, for example, in the following patient reports:

> When part of my body hurts, I feel so detached from the pain that it feels as if it were somebody else's pain. (Sierra and Berrios 2000, p. 163)

> Essentially it felt like there was a divorce or fracture between the world and me so that although my body was still in the world, my mind was only an observer. (Ciaunica et al. 2021, p. 6)

The reports of depersonalization indicate significant alterations in self-consciousness. Transient episodes of depersonalization are rather common in the general adult population, with an estimated lifetime prevalence of 26–74% (Hunter et al. 2004; Michal 2009). However, in some cases, the experiences of depersonalization generate a chronic condition that is diagnosed as Depersonalization/Derealization Disorder (DPD), with an estimated prevalence of 1–2% in the adult population (Tibubos et al. 2018).[12] Transient experiences of depersonalization have been considered an adaptive response when dealing with a traumatic situation, whereas chronic depersonalization involves persistent increased anxiety and stress (e.g., Hunter et al. 2003). In this article, the focus is on pathological depersonalization in DPD, which involves prolonged feelings of alienation from self.

In order to briefly describe the altered dynamics of self-consciousness in depersonalization, I refer to a self-disturbance model of psychopathology, which represents phenomenologically oriented psychiatry. The model was originally developed by Sass and colleagues in a study of schizophrenia (e.g., Sass and Parnas 2003, 2007) and was later applied to depersonalization (Sass et al. 2013). According to the self-disturbance model, an alteration of self-consciousness in depersonalization has two main aspects: hyper-reflectivity and diminished

12 In addition to DPD, experiences of depersonalization are present in other mental disorders, including schizophrenia, depression, and post-traumatic stress disorder.

self-affection.[13] While these aspects may initially appear mutually contradictory, they are in fact complementary. *Diminished self-affection* refers to an attenuation of self-presence – that is, depersonalization. According to Sass and colleagues (2013, p. 431), diminished self-affection is 'a reduction in the very sense of existing as an aware subject or agent of action, i.e., to a diminished sense of existing as a first-person perspective on the world'. Typically, tacit self-affection is an essential feature of MSC, which also involves embodied aspects of self and the sense of agency. *Hyper-reflectivity*, in turn, refers to an exaggerated and non-volitional self-consciousness. This 'focal, objectifying or alienating attention' is directed to features and processes of self that are considered part of oneself in a typical experience. These tacit processes normally remain in the background of awareness and involve tacit self-affection, but in hyper-reflectivity, the processes are experienced with an object-like quality. Although hyper-reflective patients continually reflect on their experiences, the reflection lacks typical first-personal familiarity and instead the individuals regard themselves as unfamiliar objects. That is to say, the hyper-reflective self-monitoring does not restore the lost tacit self-awareness and in fact can exacerbate the problem by deepening the experienced alienation.

When hyper-reflectivity is coupled with diminished self-affection, these two processes form a 'vicious circle' that dominates an individual's experience. Although 'depersonalization is, by definition, a way of feeling the self to be unreal (diminished self-affection), yet it apparently involves or engenders experiences involving intense self-consciousness' (hyper-reflectivity) (Sass et al. 2013, p. 437–8). In other words, the distortions of MSC include the feelings of unrealness and estrangement from one's self; these feelings lead to heavy

---

13 While this article does not consider the model in further detail, it should be noted that when defining the original model, Sass and colleagues used the concept of 'hyperreflexivity'. In this article, I instead use the concept of 'hyper-reflectivity' for brevity and to explicitly conceptualize RSC. By applying a simple definition of RSC, hyper-reflectivity can be regarded as a manifestation of RSC; moreover, it is considered a dysfunction of RSC in this article. However, in the original model of self-disturbance, Sass and Parnas state that although hyperreflexivity includes hyperreflectivity (that is, 'an exaggerated intellectual or reflective process'), it is not an intellectual, volitional, or 'reflective' kind of self-consciousness at its core (see, e.g., Nelson et al. 2009; Sass and Parnas 2003, 2007). The original descriptions specify the varying manifestations of hyperreflexivity. In operative or basal hyperreflexivity, the normal experience is interrupted by an automatic popping-up or popping-out of phenomenal processes, which form a tacit pre-reflective background of awareness in everyday experiences. In consequential hyperreflexivity, these primary disturbances lead to further attention and a process of self-scrutiny and self-objectification. Finally, an individual can voluntarily engage in reflective self-monitoring in compensatory hyperreflexivity in order to compensate for the anomalous feelings of diminished self-affections and self-objectification.

self-reflection, which in turn results in a heightened attention toward one's self and one's feelings of estrangement. The vicious circle between diminished self-affection and hyper-reflectivity dominates the experience and thus displaces the routine flexible connections between MSC and RSC (see also, Ciaunica et al. 2021; Haanila 2022).

This analysis of disturbances of self-consciousness in depersonalization can elucidate the factors that are typically involved in self-reflection. As described above, depersonalized RSC operates in a special hyper-reflective mode that is an exaggerated, non-volitional, and objectifying self-attention. This characterization proposes that the use of RSC in depersonalization is essentially involuntary, which in turn highlights the significance of the distinction between voluntary and involuntary self-reflection; although continuous involuntary RSC is rare, it is recognized in the pathological condition and thus important to understand.

Furthermore, in terms of the distinction between the theoretical and the deliberative stances, objectifying hyper-reflectivity seems to involve a prolonged and continual theoretical stance toward oneself: oneself is approached only in a descriptive manner and in the same way that outer objects are observed. Despite aspiring to take a deliberative stance, the patients with depersonalization appear unable to fully attain this stance. Without the deliberative stance one cannot shape one's mental states and enact one's self-reflection in a typical manner. Although the patients express a desire to restore feelings of familiarity and the first-personal relation to themselves, their feelings of estrangement prevail. That is to say, the patients cannot shift between theoretical and deliberative stances and remain captured in a theoretical attitude toward themselves. Furthermore, in terms of the identification and non-identification modes in RSC, depersonalization seems to involve involuntary non-identification: patients have not chosen to be in this condition, and the lack of identification is experienced as disruptive. In addition, depersonalization involves disruptions in their self-narrative: the patients describe a disconnection from their personal stories, memories, and future plans (e.g., Ciaunica et al. 2021).[14] This loss of narrative flow can be associated with dysfunctions in RSC since the narrativity of self is employed by RSC.

When reviewing self-consciousness as a whole, depersonalization could be characterized as a pathological imbalance or a disintegration in the dynamics of self-consciousness: both MSC and RSC lack their typical features and

14 Alterations in self-narratives and involuntary RSC are also observed in other mental disorders, including depression and schizophrenia (see, e.g., Gallagher and Daly 2013, Sass et al. 2013).

instead a third-personal self-experience dominates. RSC is permeated with hyperreflectivity, which involves a lack of the deliberative stance, a continual theoretical stance, and a non-identification with oneself – all of which are involuntary. Hyper-reflective RSC does not involve the feeling of being an agent of an operative deliberative stance; although self-reflection aims to restore typical first-personal familiarity, hyper-reflective RSC ensures that the self remains distant and object-like in an experience.

3.2 *Meditation*

Extensive changes in self-consciousness are also present in another altered state of consciousness, meditation. In meditation, one aims to detach from the normal operations of the mind in order to reach a mental state in which one does not identify with the contents of RSC. This self-detachment is often considered pleasant, and meditation is practiced because it can promote many positive effects, such as stress reduction and improvements in cognitive performance and mental well-being (e.g., Dambrun 2016; Fox et al. 2016; Gu et al. 2015; Tang et al. 2015).[15] Considering these positive associations, it is interesting that meditation appears to share at least some features with depersonalization: both have been described as involving de-identification with one's self. Thus, a closer analysis of meditation is needed to further elucidate the subtleties of self-consciousness.

Meditation has been defined 'as a form of mental training that aims to improve an individual's core psychological capacities, such as attentional and emotional self-regulation' (Tang et al. 2015, p. 213).[16] Meditation is highly relevant to the study of self because meditation-induced alterations of mind concern the different manifestations of self-consciousness, and meditative training can yield insights about one's self. Indeed, many philosophical traditions that address meditation consider that our ordinary sense of self causes psychological distress and that meditative practice is beneficial because it reorganizes self-consciousness – although the character of self has been defined in

15 However, it would be misleading to conclude that meditation necessarily leads to mental well-being (see, e.g., Lindahl & Britton 2019). As a self-exploratory practice, meditation can raise challenging aspects of self-experience, such as hidden feelings of distress or traumatic memories. For brevity, only the positive experiences of meditation and their connection to mental well-being are considered in this article.

16 That is to say, meditation is typically defined as a technique to train one's mind or attention. By developing this techique, one can bring about or arrive at an ASC, which is also frequently the aim of meditative practice (e.g., Tang et al. 2015). However, the distinction between meditation as mental training or an ASC is not elaborated here; instead, the focus is primarily on the features of meditative ASC.

different ways in different traditions.[17] The details of the different meditation schools cannot be described here; instead, the main ideas of meditation are discussed in order to illuminate the varieties of RSC.

Wolfgang Fasching (2008) provides a useful characterization of meditation that covers various meditative styles and is directly linked to concepts of self-consciousness. Fasching (2008, p. 464) draws a distinction between two meanings of 'self-consciousness':

1) the self-identification with certain configurations of what one experiences, and
2) the self-presence of experiencing itself.

According to Fasching, meditation aims at a temporary inhibition of the former in order to uncover the more fundamental latter, which constitutes the very being as subjectivity. In other words, Fasching describes meditation as de-identification that involves a withdrawal from the 'emotional investment' used to appraise things according to their value in relation to oneself. In terms of the concepts used in this article, a meditator refrains from evaluative RSC involving self-identification and instead focuses on self-presence in immediate MSC. By cultivating present-centered awareness, meditation assists in disengaging from narrative forms of self-identification (e.g., Thompson 2014; Tang et al. 2015).

In order to briefly elaborate on the alterations of self-consciousness in a meditative state, I focus here on characterizing mindfulness meditation. Mindfulness meditation has been defined as nonjudgmental attention directed toward experiences in the present moment (e.g., Hölzel et al. 2011; Kabat-Zinn 1994; Tang et al. 2015).[18] In mindfulness, one choicelessly and non-reactively observes the flow of one's mental contents. According to Fasching (2008), the

17 For instance, Buddhist philosophy, which is the foundation for modern mindfulness meditation, aims at disidentification from the everyday self; this letting go can lead to the freedom to experience life in more genuine ways (see, e.g., Hölzel et al. 2011; Tang et al. 2015; Vago and Silbersweig 2012). For an introduction to the conceptions of self in different meditative traditions, see, e.g., Siderits et al. 2010. For studies of meditation in recent philosophy of mind and mind sciences, see, e.g., Flanagan 2011; Metzinger 2020; Thompson 2014; Wallace 2007.

18 Mindfulness has been the most popular and studied method of meditation in western countries (see, e.g., Gu et al. 2015; Tang et al. 2015). However, it should be noted that in addition to mindfullness, there are other forms of meditation: for example, meditation techniques that aim explicitly at a state of 'pure consciousness' or 'pure subjectivity', which is a state of simply being wide-awake without the contents of consciousness or even spatiotemporal self-location (Albahari 2006; Fasching 2008; Metzinger 2020).

decisive point of mindfulness does not concern the observed content but the attitude of observing itself: one does not react to the mental contents that arise in the mind; instead, one experiences oneself non-observationally, not as an object but in the act of observing. This process of observation involves three interacting components: 1) enhanced attention control, 2) improved emotion regulation, and 3) altered self-awareness, which includes diminished self-referential processing and enhanced body awareness (Tang et al. 2015, p. 214; Hölzel et al. 2011). Constituted by these components, a meditative process involves interactions between minimal and reflective self-consciousness. RSC is associated with attention control, regulation of mental states, and the continuation of the objective mode in diminished self-referential thinking. At the same time, MSC is involved in enhanced present moment (bodily) self-consciousness and a withdrawal from emotional load.

The study of meditation offers an interesting viewpoint to examine self-reflection since reflective self-consciousness is actively modified in meditative practices. As presented above, a mindfulness meditator regards her mental states with an open, neutral, and de-identifying manner. Thus, meditation provides an exemplar of exercising a non-identification mode of self-reflection: it reveals a variant use of RSC that can extend the picture of RSC examined in traditional analytic philosophy. Furthermore, meditation involves an interplay between the theoretical and deliberative stances. The meditative endeavor to apply an objective approach to oneself can be viewed as an exercise of the theoretical stance toward oneself in which self is considered a neutral object of description. The neutral observation of one's mental states can be beneficial in reducing excessive narrativity and self-referential thinking. On the other hand, it seems that the deliberative stance toward oneself is also needed to enter and sustain a meditative state. This stance can be seen in one's efforts to maintain the withdrawal from affectivity and uphold the non-identification with the self-related contents of consciousness. In addition, meditation might be regarded as a deliberative shaping of one's mental states, for example, when distancing oneself from one's impulses and realizing that one is not dominated by these impulses. Since meditation involves a combination of theoretical and deliberative reflective elements, it can be considered a training ground for their interplay and flexible alternation.

Utilizing the conceptual distinctions proposed in this article, I also want to specify that meditation is initiated voluntarily: a conscious effort of RSC is required to enter a meditative state. Meditative RSC deviates from everyday self-reflection and requires regulation in order to maintain the meditative state (and avoid mind-wandering). This voluntariness also distinguishes the meditative detachment from self from the disruptive de-identification that is experienced in depersonalization disorder. The latter is an involuntarily initiated altered state of consciousness, whereas meditation is a voluntary endeavor toward de-identification.

Collectively, the features of meditation transform the dynamics of self-consciousness. Meditation can be described as a shift from a self-related 'narrative' focus to one that is more 'experiential'. The reflective self-identification with the (narrative and emotional) contents of consciousness is inhibited in favor of exploring the self-presence of experiencing. This process involves active modification of RSC or more specifically, a flexible and nonjudgmental use that enables a voluntary non-identification mode. The interplay between the theoretical and deliberative stances is needed in order to maintain a neutral state toward oneself. Overall, meditative practices appear to bring balance or integration to self-consciousness by strengthening the connectivity and the flexible modulation of the different features of self-consciousness.

4. Reflective Self-Consciousness and Mental Well-Being

As the analyses above indicate, I want to highlight that RSC is significant for mental well-being. This article observed an initial connection between the manner of self-reflection and mental well-being in the classical analyses, which emphasize the practical and motivational dimensions of RSC that are directly related to action (§1.2). The practical side of self-reflection facilitates aspirations toward deeds that advance one's well-being and alter harmful intentions or narratives. The connection to well-being is clarified when the picture of self-reflection is deepened by extending the recognition of the varieties of RSC (§2); moreover, the association with well-being is evident in the discussion of the altered states of consciousness (§3). Identifying the connection between the manner of self-reflection and well-being is significant: the endeavor to understand self is important not only for meaningful conceptual analyses, but also for opportunities to increase mental well-being.

Moran (2001) explicitly points out the connection between self-consciousness and well-being in distinguishing the theoretical and deliberative stances. Moran acknowledges that the capacity for first-person awareness has particular relevance for the psychological well-being of a person, and he proposes that this idea has operated as a background assumption in contemporary philosophy of mind, although it has not been investigated on its own (Moran 2001, p. 136). Moran argues that the psychological health of a person is dependent on the exercise of a deliberative stance and the ability to flexibly alternate between the theoretical and deliberative stances. The deliberative stance is important, as it assists in the formation of one's mental states and one's intentions to act. However, even if deliberative thinking is significant in terms of action and determining oneself, it is equally important that one is able to examine oneself descriptively in the theoretical stance, as this capacity enables the adoption of an objective point of view. It is vital that one can shift between these stances because each stance is needed in different cognitive tasks. Indeed, some mental disorders are characterized by a chronic lack of the deliberative stance and an inflexibility to move between the stances. The analysis of depersonalization indicated that involuntary hyper-reflectivity involves a prolonged and continual theoretical stance toward oneself, a stance in which one approaches oneself in an objectifying manner. Without the deliberative stance and the ability to shift between the stances, one cannot shape one's mental states in a typical manner and a critical viewpoint of oneself is lost.

In terms of the distinction between voluntary and involuntary RSC, the analysis attested that voluntary RSC is connected to psychological well-being. It is also noteworthy that transient involuntary RSC is a useful variant because it can assist in orienting oneself to a situation, thus drawing out the flexibility and functionality of self-consciousness. Likewise, transient involuntary RSC occurring in mind-wandering episodes can be functional, as it assists in 'refreshing' the mind between different cognitive tasks and has connections, for instance, to creative thinking. However, continuous involuntary RSC can generate psychological distress, which is evident in depersonalization disorder. Depersonalization involves non-volitional hyper-reflectivity in which the self is continuously taken as the object of consciousness; however, the reflection lacks feelings of being an active self as well as the ability to transform one's mental states in a typical manner to restore a sense of familiarity. The involuntary exercise of RSC without the desirable effects appears to be a significant cause of anxiety and distress in depersonalization.

Furthermore, the distinction between the identification and non-identification modes of RSC elaborated the picture of the spectrum of self-reflection, and the analysis indicated that the appropriate application of both modes is beneficial to mental well-being. The self-identification in self-conscious thinking and acting has been highlighted as important to mental well-being in many theories of RSC: it is well argued that an involuntary lack of identification is related to reduced mental well-being and could be described in terms of a theoretical stance toward oneself or a 'half-hearted' or unwilling action. However, in addition to acknowledging the benefits of the identificatory mode, it is important to recognize the non-identification mode of RSC, as exercising this mode can also improve well-being by relieving, for example, the psychological distress that results from excessive self-referential thinking. This benefit is evident in the positive effects of meditation: meditation explicitly involves de-identification from everyday self-conscious thinking, and the focus on the nature of experiencing can provide insights into the nature of self.

5. Opportunities for Further Studies

The analyses in this article have highlighted how different dimensions of self-consciousness function collectively. Reflective self-consciousness involves a multiplicity of varieties, and not all of them can be considered here. However, the elaborations of the different forms of self-reflection detailed in this article provide multiple opportunities for further studies.

In order to formulate a more extensive theory of self-consciousness, a relevant future research topic is the study of how the different modes of RSC relate to other aspects of self. For instance, it would be interesting to elaborate on the relation between RSC and the narrative aspects of self. Narrative reflection has a significant role in our everyday life and is important for understanding oneself as a person who has a past and a future. However, a rich self-narrative is not necessarily evoked by the simple definition of RSC presented in this article: one can reflect on oneself (as oneself) and deliberate one's actions without an extensive narrative of oneself. Nevertheless, as mentioned in the case of depersonalization, distortions of (reflective) self-consciousness are related to disruptions in a self-narrative. In addition, narrativity featured in the case of meditation, which can be considered as a withdrawal from an excessive self-narrative. The specification of RSC and the narrative aspects of self could involve, for instance, differences in self-narratives that are related to the dominant use of either the theoretical or the deliberative stance.

Furthermore, it would be useful to explore the relation between RSC and the aspects of self that are present in MSC. In this article, affective and embodied aspects of MSC were mentioned in the discussion of the altered states of consciousness. In depersonalization, the disruptive diminution of these aspects inflicts hyper-reflectivity and is related to the reduction of the deliberative stance toward oneself. On the other hand, the examination of meditation indicated that RSC can be employed in an endeavor to withdraw from affective aspects and enhance the experience of the embodied self. However, there are likely to be many varieties of bodily self-consciousness that could be elaborated. In addition, studies of self-reflection could include, for instance, the intersubjective and extended/situational aspects of self that concern one's relation to other people and the environment and culture. These aspects involve pre-reflective elements of MSC, but at the same time, they are important in self-reflection: one identifies oneself as a member of various social groups and in relation to the environment.

The analyses in this article also encourage a continued multidisciplinary study of (reflective) self-consciousness. Precise concepts of self can assist, for example, in more detailed comparisons between different altered states of consciousness. These comparisons enable a more thorough understanding of individual altered states of consciousness and also of the structure and features of everyday self-consciousness. Furthermore, these studies can potentially contribute to the development of diagnostic tools and treatment programs for mental disorders as well as to positive psychology. The conceptual distinctions shaped in philosophy of mind can also be relevant to neuro-cognitive empirical research. Although self-consciousness cannot be reduced to neural processes (according to the multidimensional approach to self that is endorsed in this article, see, e.g., Gallagher 2013; Zahavi 2014), these processes underlie self-conscious mental states and constitute their non-conscious mechanisms. In other words, differences in self-conscious states are related to variations in neural processing. This observation implies that precise concepts are needed to understand the diverse range of neural processing related to self. The neural processes of MSC and RSC can be differentiated (e.g., Christoff et al. 2011; Legrand and Ruby 2009), and it would be interesting to apply, for instance, the distinction between the theoretical and deliberative stances toward oneself to neural studies.

6. Summary

Reflective self-consciousness is a key feature in human personhood. However, reflective self-consciousness comes in many varieties. The aim of this article was to elucidate the varied aspects in self-reflection and their connections to mental well-being. The first step in understanding RSC was to place it within the wider theory of selfhood by endorsing a multidimensional conception of self-consciousness in which MSC functions as a basis for RSC. The analysis of the different forms of self-reflection began with a reference to classical studies in analytic philosophy, which have established that self-conscious thoughts have unique epistemic and motivational features. I proposed that in addition to noting the difference between first- and third-personal self-reference, more elaborate conceptual tools are needed to understand the full scope of RSC. I presented three complementary conceptual distinctions that can be identified within the variations of self-reflection. The first distinction, which relates to the theoretical and deliberative stances, concerns the attitude or position in the examination of oneself. In the theoretical stance, the self is observed as an object of description and explanation. In the deliberative stance, however, the self is considered an agent of practical reasoning that can make decisions and transform its attitudes. Instead of addressing the content or stance of self-reflection, the second distinction involves the initiation of the self-reflection and is apparent in the differences between voluntary and involuntary RSC. The third distinction, which concerns the identification and non-identification modes, relates to the manner in which self is approached as a content of reflection and also acknowledges the use of RSC that refrains from self-identification. The relevance of these conceptual distinctions was demonstrated by examining the alteration of self-consciousness in meditation and pathological depersonalization. Overall, the analyses in this article clearly indicate that RSC is important for mental well-being. In particular, well-being is promoted by the capacity to assume the deliberative stance and the ability to flexibly shift between the different forms of self-reflection. Involuntary, reduced, and inflexible RSC can be seen in depersonalization, whereas meditation involves a sophisticated exercise of RSC and a flexible interplay between its different forms. The depth of the connections between self-reflection and mental well-being also encourages further multidisciplinary studies. The proposed elaborations of self-reflection can be used to build a complete theory of self-consciousness and be complemented with other aspects of self in future studies.[19]

References

Albahari, Miri 2006. *Analytical Buddhism: The Two-Tiered Illusion of Self.* London: Palgrave Macmillan UK.

Baker, Lynne Rudder 2012. 'From Consciousness to Self-Consciousness', in *Grazer Philosophische Studien* 84(1).

Bermúdez, José Luis 2001. 'Nonconceptual Self-Consciousness and Cognitive Science', in *Synthese* 129(1).

——— 2007. 'Self-Consciousness', in *The Blackwell Companion to Consciousness*, eds. S. Schneider & M. Velmans. Blackwell Publishing.

19 I am grateful to the participants of the Heidelberg Workshop on Personhood, Self-Consciousness, and the First-Person Perspective for their comments and discussions during the development of this article. This research was funded by Academy of Finland (project number 342166).

Blanke, Olaf, and Thomas Metzinger 2009. 'Full-Body Illusions and Minimal Phenomenal Selfhood', in *Trends in Cognitive Sciences* 13(1).

Broesch, Tanya et al. 2011. 'Cultural Variations in Children's Mirror Self-Recognition', in *Journal of Cross-Cultural Psychology* 42(6).

Brook, Andrew 2001. 'Kant, Self-Awareness and Self-Reference', in *Self-Reference and Self-Awareness*, eds. A. Brook & R. C. DeVidi. Amsterdam: John Benjamins.

Brook, Andrew, and DeVidi, Richard C. eds. 2001. *Self-Reference and Self-Awareness.* Amsterdam: John Benjamins.

Castañeda, Hector-Neri 1966. '"He': A Study in the Logic of Self-Consciousness', in *Ratio* 8.

——— 1967. 'On the Logic of Self-Knowledge', in *Noûs* 1(1).

Christoff, Kalina et al. 2016. 'Mind-Wandering as Spontaneous Thought: A Dynamic Framework', in *Nature Reviews Neuroscience* 17(11).

Christoff, Kalina, Diego Cosmelli, Dorothée Legrand, and Evan Thompson 2011. 'Specifying the Self for Cognitive Neuroscience', in *Trends in Cognitive Sciences* 15(3).

Christoff, Kalina, and Fox, Kieran C. R. eds. 2018. *The Oxford Handbook of Spontaneous Thought.* Oxford University Press.

Ciaunica, Anna, Jane Charlton, and Harry Farmer 2021. 'When the Window Cracks: Transparency and the Fractured Self in Depersonalisation', in *Phenomenology and the Cognitive Sciences* 20(1).

Colombetti, Giovanna, and Matthew Ratcliffe 2012. 'Bodily Feeling in Depersonalization: A Phenomenological Account', in *Emotion Review* 4(2).

Dambrun, Michaël 2016. 'When the Dissolution of Perceived Body Boundaries Elicits Happiness: The Effect of Selflessness Induced by a Body Scan Meditation', in *Consciousness and Cognition* 46.

Farthing, G. W. 1992. *The Psychology of Consciousness.* Englewood Cliffs, NJ: Prentice-Hall.

Fasching, Wolfgang 2008. 'Consciousness, Self-Consciousness, and Meditation', in *Phenomenology and the Cognitive Sciences* 7(4).

Flanagan, Owen 2011. *The Bodhisattva's Brain : Buddhism Naturalized.* MIT Press.

Fox, Kieran C. R., Yoona Kang, Michael Lifshitz, and Kalina Christoff 2016. 'Increasing Cognitive-Emotional Flexibility with Meditation and Hypnosis: The Cognitive Neuroscience of de-Automatization', in *Hypnosis and Meditation: Towards an Integrative Science of Conscious Planes*, eds. A. Raz and M. Lifshitz. Oxford University Press.

Frankfurt, Harry G. 1988. *The Importance of What We Care About.* Cambridge: Cambridge University Press.

Gallagher, Shaun 2000. 'Philosophical Conceptions of the Self: Implications for Cognitive Science', in *Trends in Cognitive Sciences* 4(1).

——— ed. 2011. *The Oxford Handbook of the Self.* Oxford: Oxford University Press.

——— 2013. 'A Pattern Theory of Self', in *Frontiers in human neuroscience* 7(August), 443.

Gallagher, Shaun, and Anya Daly 2018. 'Dynamical Relations in the Self-Pattern', in *Frontiers in Psychology* 9(May), 664.

Gallagher, Shaun, and Dan Zahavi 2007. *The Phenomenological Mind*. London: Routledge.

Gallup, Gordon G. 1970. 'Chimpanzees: Self-Recognition', in *Science* 167(3914).

Gallup, Gordon G. 1982. 'Self-Awareness and the Emergence of Mind in Primates', in *American Journal of Primatology* 2(3).

Gertler, Brie 2010. *Self-Knowledge*. London: Routledge.

Gerrans, Philip. (2015). 'All the Self We Need', in *Open MIND*, 15.

Grünbaum, Thor, and Dan Zahavi 2013. 'Varieties of Self-Awareness', in *The Oxford Handbook of Philosophy and Psychiatry*, eds. K. W. M. Fulford et al. Oxford University Press.

Gu, Jenny, Clara Strauss, Rod Bond, and Kate Cavanagh 2015. 'How Do Mindfulness-Based Cognitive Therapy and Mindfulness-Based Stress Reduction Improve Mental Health and Wellbeing? A Systematic Review and Meta-Analysis of Mediation Studies', in *Clinical Psychology Review* 37.

Haanila, Heidi 2021. 'The Dream Self and the Waking Self', in *Reasons and Responsibilities: Proceedings of the Philosophical Society of Finland Colloquium 2020*, eds. I. Koskinen & T. Toppinen (*Acta Philosophica Fennica; Vol. 97*).

——— 2022. *Neurophilosophy of Self-Consciousness: Clarifications for the Connection between Minimal and Reflective Form*. Turku: Univerity of Turku.

Hölzel, Britta K. et al. 2011. 'How Does Mindfulness Meditation Work? Proposing Mechanisms of Action from a Conceptual and Neural Perspective', in *Perspectives on Psychological Science* 6(6).

Hunter, E. C. M. et al. 2003. 'Depersonalisation Disorder: A Cognitive-Behavioural Conceptualisation', in *Behaviour Research and Therapy* 41(12).

Hunter, E. C. M., M. Sierra, and A. S. David. 2004. 'The Epidemiology of Depersonalisation and Derealisation – A Systematic Review', in *Social Psychiatry and Psychiatric Epidemiology* 39(1).

James, William 1890. *The Principles of Psychology, Vol I*. New York: Henry Holt and Co.

Kabat-Zinn, Jon 1994. *Wherever You Go, There You Are: Mindfulness Meditation in Everyday Life*. Hyperion.

Kaplan, David 1989. 'Demonstratives: An Essay on the Semantics, Logic, Metaphysics and Epistemology of Demonstratives and Other Indexicals', in *Themes From Kaplan*, eds. J. Almog, J. Perry, and H. Wettstein. Oxford University Press.

Killingsworth, M. A., and D. T. Gilbert 2010. 'A Wandering Mind Is an Unhappy Mind', in *Science* 330(6006).

Korsgaard, Christine M. 1996. *The Sources of Normativity*. Cambridge University Press.

Kriegel, Uriah 2003. 'Consciousness as Intransitive Self-Consciousness: Two Views and an Argument', in *Canadian Journal of Philosophy* 33(1).

——— 2004. 'Consciousness and Self-Consciousness', in *Monist* 87(2).

Legrand, Dorothée, and Perrine Ruby 2009. 'What Is Self-Specific? Theoretical Investigation and Critical Review of Neuroimaging Results', in *Psychological review* 116(1).

Letheby, Chris, and Philip Gerrans 2017. 'Self Unbound: Ego Dissolution in Psychedelic Experience', in *Neuroscience of Consciousness* 2017(1).

Lindahl, Jared R, and Willoughby B. Britton 2019. 'Buddhist Meditation and Changes in the Sense of Self', in *Journal of Consciousness Studies* 26(7–8).

MacIntyre, Alasdair C. 1981. *After Virtue: A Study in Moral Theory*. Notre Dame, Ind: University of Notre Dame Press.

Mandik, Pete 2007. 'The Neurophilosophy of Consciousness' in *The Blackwell Companion to Consciousness*, eds. S. Schneider and M. Velmans. Blackwell Publishing.

Medford, Nick et al. 2016. 'Emotional Experience and Awareness of Self: Functional MRI Studies of Depersonalization Disorder'. *Frontiers in Psychology* 7.

Metzinger, Thomas 2004. 'Why Are Identity Disorders Interesting for Philosophers?' in *Philosophy and Psychiatry*, eds. T. Schramme and J. Thome. De Gruyter.

——— 2020. 'Minimal Phenomenal Experience Meditation, Tonic Alertness, and the Phenomenology of 'Pure' Consciousness', in *Philosophy and the Mind Sciences* 1(2020).

Michal, Matthias et al. 2009. 'Prevalence, Correlates, and Predictors of Depersonalization Experiences in the German General Population', in *Journal of Nervous & Mental Disease* 197(7).

Moran, Richard 2001. *Authority and Estrangement: An Essay on Self-Knowledge*. Princeton NJ: Princeton University Press.

Musholt, Kristina 2013. 'A Philosophical Perspective on the Relation between Cortical Midline Structures and the Self', in *Frontiers in Human Neuroscience* 7(SEP), 536.

Nelson, B et al. 2009. 'A Disturbed Sense of Self in the Psychosis Prodrome: Linking Phenomenology and Neurobiology', in *Neuroscience and biobehavioral reviews* 33(6).

Newen, Albert 2018. 'The Embodied Self, the Pattern Theory of Self, and the Predictive Mind', in *Frontiers in Psychology* 9(NOV), 2270.

Perry, John 1977. 'Frege on Demonstratives', in *The Philosophical Review* 86(4).

——— 1979. 'The Problem of the Essential Indexical', in *Noûs* 13(1).

Revonsuo, Antti 2006. *Inner Presence: Consciousness as a Biological Phenomenon*. Cambridge, Massachusetts: MIT Press.

Revonsuo, Antti, Sakari Kallio, and Pilleriin Sikka 2009. 'What Is an Altered State of Consciousness?' in *Philosophical Psychology* 22(2).

Rochat, Philippe, and Dan Zahavi 2011. 'The Uncanny Mirror: A Re-Framing of Mirror Self-Experience', in *Consciousness and Cognition* 20(2).

Sartre, Jean-Paul. 1956. *Being and Nothingness. An Essay on Phenomenological Ontology* (*1943. L'Être et le Néant*), trans. Hazel Barnes. New York: Philosophical Library.

Sass, Louis A., and Josef Parnas 2003. 'Schizophrenia, Consciousness, and the Self', in *Schizophrenia Bulletin* 29(3).

——— 2007. 'Explaining Schizophrenia: The Relevance of Phenomenology', in *Reconceiving Schizophrenia*, eds. M. C. Chung, K. W. M. Fulford, and G. Graham. Oxford University Press.

Sass, Louis A., Elizabeth Pienkos, Barnaby Nelson, and Nick Medford 2013. 'Anomalous Self-Experience in Depersonalization and Schizophrenia: A Comparative Investigation', in *Consciousness and cognition* 22(2).

Seigel, Jerrold 2005. *The Idea of the Self.* Cambridge University Press.

Shoemaker, Sydney 1968. 'Self-Reference and Self-Awareness', in *The Journal of Philosophy* 65(19).

Siderits, Mark, Evan Thompson, and Dan Zahavi eds. 2010. *Self, No Self?: Perspectives from Analytical, Phenomenological, and Indian Traditions.* Oxford: Oxford University Press.

Sierra, Mauricio. 2009. *Depersonalization: A New Look at a Neglected Syndrome.* Cambridge: Cambridge University Press.

Sierra, Mauricio, and German E. Berrios 2000. 'The Cambridge Depersonalisation Scale: A New Instrument for the Measurement of Depersonalisation', in *Psychiatry Research* 93(2).

Sierra, Mauricio, and Anthony S. David. 2011. 'Depersonalization: A Selective Impairment of Self-Awareness', in *Consciousness and Cognition* 20(1).

Simeon, Daphne, and Jeffrey Abugel 2006. *Feeling Unreal: Depersonalization Disorder and the Loss of the Self.* New York: Oxford University Press.

Smith, Joel 2020. 'Self-Consciousness', in *Stanford Encyclopedia of Philosophy*, <https://plato.stanford.edu/archives/sum2020/entries/self-consciousness/>.

Strawson, Galen 2000. 'The Phenomenology and Ontology of the Self', in *Exploring the Self*, ed. D. Zahavi. John Benjamins.

Tang, Yi-Yuan, Britta K. Hölzel, and Michael I. Posner. 2015. 'The Neuroscience of Mindfulness Meditation', in *Nature Reviews Neuroscience* 16(4).

Taylor, Charles 1989. *Sources of the Self.* Cambridge, Mass: Harvard University Press.

Thompson, Evan 2014. *Waking, Dreaming, Being.* Columbia University Press.

Tibubos, Ana N. et al. 2018. 'Emotion Regulation Strategies Moderate the Relationship of Fatigue with Depersonalization and Derealization Symptoms', in *Journal of Affective Disorders* 227.

Vago, David R., and David A. Silbersweig 2012. 'Self-Awareness, Self-Regulation, and Self-Transcendence (S-ART): A Framework for Understanding the Neurobiological Mechanisms of Mindfulness', in *Frontiers in Human Neuroscience* 6, 296.

Wallace, Alan 2007. *Contemplative Science: Where Buddhism and Neuroscience Converge*. New York: Columbia University Press.

Windt, Jennifer M. 2015. *Dreaming: A Conceptual Framework for Philosophy of Mind and Empirical Research*. MIT Press.

Wittgenstein, Ludwig 1958. *The Blue and Brown Books*. Oxford: Blackwell.

Zahavi, Dan 2005. *Subjectivity and Selfhood*. The MIT Press.

——— 2014. *Self and Other: Exploring Subjectivity, Empathy, and Shame*. Oxford University Press.

Bodily Self-Awareness

Irene Breuer

Abstract

This article enquires into the relation between pre-reflective awareness and the lived body and, in particular, into the notion of self-affection. It claims only the 'innermost' lived-experiences such as the affective awareness of my own body-self are immediately given as acts of an originally, pre-reflective proto-consciousness. What affective consciousness experiences is its own acts understood as the actualization of its capacity of sensing. Bodily self-awareness is thus the consciousness of my continuing self-affection. It will further claim that the unity of body and consciousness in its totality is made possible by the force of bodily drives onto consciousness, which, on the grounds of an awareness of both the reflexive process of touch and of the kinaesthetic freedom of the body, grants the subject a non-predicative self-knowledge or *experiential knowledge*. It further distinguishes between different modalities of self-affection, since not all experiences are self-aware in the same sense. It also enquires into their order of foundation, to arrive to a primal form of self-awareness, that of the awakening of consciousness to life. Here we grasp consciousness and self-consciousness in *statu nascendi*: to exist is to discover oneself as being existent. Hence, the primary form of self-awareness consists in the sudden *realization of being alive*.

1. Introduction

Much has been written about the relation between experience, self-awareness, and selfhood. What is urgently needed is a clarification not only of our most basic and fundamental acts, by which we, as embodied beings, open up first to ourselves, and then to the world, but even most importantly, how our consciousness awakens to life. In order to shed light on these issues, I will begin by inquiring into the relation between pre-reflective awareness and the lived body and in particular, into the notion of self-affection. I will suggest that only the 'innermost' lived-experiences such as the affective awareness of my own body-self are immediately given as acts of an originally, pre-reflective proto-consciousness: What affective consciousness experiences is its own acts understood as the actualization of a capacity. Acts are the continuous *activity* by which consciousness not only manifests itself as being embodied, that is, as an achieved state or *entelechia*, but by which it is conscious of a

© BRILL MENTIS, 2023 | DOI:10.30965/9783969752906_004

continuous activity or *energeia*, that of sensing. Bodily self-awareness is thus the consciousness of my continuing self-affection. I will further claim that the unity of body and consciousness in its totality is made possible by the force of bodily drives onto consciousness, which, on the grounds of an awareness of both the reflexive process of touch and of the kinesthetic freedom of the body, grants the subject a non-predicative self-knowledge or *experiential knowledge*. We must, however, distinguish between different kinds of bodily experience and accordingly, between *different modalities of self-awareness*, since not all experiences are self-aware in the same sense. We will also enquire into their order of foundation, in order to arrive to a primal form of self-awareness, that of the awakening of consciousness to life.

In order to disclose this thesis, this article will first introduce the concepts of living body, the concomitant kinesthetic sensations, and tactile sensings. It is the task of the bodily intentionality to interrelate them and thus to allow for the unity of the lived body's experiential field. The second part engages in the core of the proposal by developing the notion of a bodily self-affection and experiential self-knowledge, which is here conceived of as the actualization of our innermost capacity of sensing. It sustains that the bodily, unthematized proto-consciousness provides a *minimal form of self-awareness* arising from self-affection/sensing. Thus, feelings and sensations allow us to recognize and experience ourselves as experiencing lived bodies. While intentional kinesthetic sensations objectify the own body and allow for a pre-reflective objectifying self-awareness corresponding to the consciousness of kinesthetic movements, intentional sensations as lived experiences provide a *pre-reflective self-awareness* corresponding to the consciousness of the act of sensing oneself in the sense of having *Empfindnisse*. However, lived experiences are of two kinds: Insofar as sensations as extended or localized allow for the constitution of a *living body*, these *sensations are intentional and objectifying* and ground *a pre-reflective affective self-awareness*, while *sensations as impressions* or *carnal sensations* stemming from the self-affection of the own *flesh* are non-intentional ones and ground *a pre-reflective, impressional and carnal self-awareness*. Self-sensuous sensing seems thus to be the most fundamental level of a lived experience.

The third part enquires into impressional consciousness, its time-constituting activity, and the constitution of a *temporal bodily and spiritual self-awareness*, that is, an objectifying intentionality of an impressional, temporal consciousness that constitutes my present and my retentional self, grounding thus an impressional, temporal self-awareness. This will enable us to distinguish between an objectifying intentionality of kinesthetic feelings and time-constituting consciousness and the non-intentional/non-objectifying impressional activity of carnal sensations. At this point we will return to the issue of proto-consciousness and claim that experiencing (*Erleben*), that is the consciousness of the activity of sensing, grounds a *pre-reflective carnal self-awareness*, that is, an *affective awareness of my own self-affection*. This sensing oneself is genetically the most original activity, since it involves the constitution of the body, which is presupposed by the constitution of the Ego. In contrast, time constituting consciousness as *Erleben* is primary from the transcendental point of view, since it involves the constitution of consciousness itself. The fourth part deals with the driving force of this process of evolving consciousness and self-awareness, which we located at the level of an originary sensuousness or proto-hyle. The last step involves the limit issue or proto-event of the awakening of the transcendental life of a being, which involves the emergence of an *impressional and minimal form of anonymous consciousness*: Here we grasp consciousness and self-consciousness in *statu nascendi*: to exist is thus to discover oneself as being existent. Hence, the primary form of self-awareness consists in the sudden and instant *realization of being alive*. Finally, the conclusion summarizes the main results of the enquiry.

2. The Lived Body, Kinesthetic Feelings and Sensings

Edmund Husserl's analysis of perception departs from the body as a '*medium of all perception,* [...] *the organ of perception*' (Husserl, Hua IV, p. 56; *Ideas* II, p. 61), which ensures the relationship between things. Its role is essentially productive or constitutive: The lived-body as 'freely moving sense-organ' has a special kind of sensations, the kinesthetic feelings, which motivate the visual adumbrations of things and of their surrounding space (cf. Breuer 2020). Kinesthetic feelings are a system of possible subjective movements that by unfolding itself within the scope of a familiar, habitual motility system enable presentation of things and space without 'coming into presence themselves' (Husserl, Hua XVI, p. 161). Each image-change is essentially related to kinesthetic change (*ibid.*, p. 350) insofar as each possible movement, whose system is governed by me in the sense of an 'I can', intentions a possible image. Only a body, which is physically extended and psychically located in a space, can bind 'sense-things and subjective occurrences in a regulated way' (Husserl, Hua IV, p. 66; *Ideas II*, p. 71). Hence, it is a 'material body, upon which are constructed new strata of being, the Bodily-psychic' (*ibid.*, p. 143/151). Husserl still conceives of the lived body not only as a stratification of material and psychic realities but views it from the perspective of an observer (*ibid.*, p. 144/152), that is, as a phenomenon among others.

This approach changes when he comes to consider the body as body, that is, how the lived body not only senses but knows itself, the body as living body. What Husserl realizes is that the lived body is a privileged body, because it can feel or sense thanks to bodily events which material bodies lack. The process of touching, that is, when my body touches exterior bodies or when two parts of the body touch one another (*ibid.*, p.147/155), arouses a specific kind of sensorial, tactile sensations, which Husserl calls 'sensings (*Empfindnisse*)'. Sensings are specific body feelings through which it senses itself; they not only allow the lived body to experience itself, or, better, live itself, but to constitute itself as a living object, a body (*ibid.*, p. 146/154). These sensings as lived- experiences (*Erlebnisse*) allow the body to feel or 'find' itself through touch, thus relating the body to itself before it opens up to the experience of the world and the perception of outer phenomena. In this '"innermost" perception' in the sense of self-affection, the body originally appears to itself (Husserl, Hua VIII, p. 188). These sensings are therefore body-immanent before they transcend this sphere towards the world. Kinesthetic sensations differ from sensings: While kinesthetic sensations are thematically *erfahren* and correlate to bodily movements that are intersubjectively perceived, the tactile sensings are unthematically lived or *erlebt* and are 'given in purely originary perception' as 'immanent data' to the subject (Husserl, Hua IV, p. 199, *Ideas II*, p. 209).

Consequently, Husserl not only unites the body to the world but to itself insofar as these sensings constitute the body into a unity. At this point we may ask how this unity is achieved. Husserl speaks of a double constitution in the tactile sphere, on the one hand the constitution of an outer object through tactual, objective sensations, and on the other hand the constitution of the lived body through the tactual, subjective sensings. Husserl emphasizes that both processes belong to a different order of analysis, but in bodily experience they are undoubtedly related to one another: It is the task of the bodily intentionality to interrelate them both and thus allow for the unity of the lived body's experiential field.

Now we may pose the question about the special kind of motivational correlation at play within the body itself. But first, let us focus on the process by which the body comes to constitute and know itself.

3. Bodily Self-Affection and Experiential Self-Knowledge

In touching myself, I become aware of the fact that it's *me* whom I am touching. Here, the process of touching is '*reflexive*' (Welton 1999, p. 45), because in touching, my body is at the same time touching *and* touched. Thus, the body becomes constituted as a unity through the ongoing process of self-touching and the retention of the touched/touching fields, being built in an ordered succession. In self-touching the body not only touches itself but senses itself; a process which Husserl views as a 'haptic intuitability (*haptische Anschaulichkeit*)' (Husserl, Hua XV, p. 299) in analogy with the optic intuitiveness. Only haptic intuitability is able to constitute my body as a unity between its interiority, that is, as an organ, and its exteriority, as a material body; in Husserl's words, 'if visual constitution would be for itself, there would be an abyss between material and lived-body' (*ibid.*, p. 8).

The second process involved in the constitution of the lived body is set forth by the kinesthetic feelings and the perceptions of movement of the hand that touches *and* moves. In Husserl's words: 'Touching my left hand, I have touch-appearances, that is to say, I do not just sense, but I perceive and have appearances of a soft, smooth hand, with such a form.' Husserl defines them respectively as 'indicational sensations of movement' and 'representational sensations of touch', as sensations remit us to movements that arouse them while tactile sensations represent the hand which appears as a thing. He goes so far as to understand this process as a '*tactual* regarding' (Husserl, Hua IV, p. 134; *Ideas II*, p. 152) since both sense organs act in concordance. Hence, each subjective 'I touch' implies a sequence of 'haptic appearances' of a thing, which as tactile sensations, are localized in the tactual organs. Husserl further remarks a 'peculiar priority' of the sense of touch, that is, of the touching of things (Husserl, Hua XXXIX, p. 398f.), as regards the optical sphere. This is because the typicality of things is originally grasped through their being touched; it requires a constitution of a higher order to build up things in their perceptual visibility through our kinesthetic experience (Husserl, Hua XV, p. 307). The sense of touch sets up an originary communion of my living-body and the world, while my tactile sensations and the corresponding sensuous feelings enable the first sensitive contact with the world, with which my body is united thanks to the constitutive force of our feelings and sensations (cf. Breuer 2015).

At this point we may ask how all these processes relate to the one and the same body. How is that unity guaranteed? As Dan Zahavi remarks, whatever experience we have, they are 'characterized by a dimension of *mineness*, or *for-me-ness*', that is, by their 'first-personal character' (Zahavi 2014, p. 19). Consequently, the body's self-affection shows a 'double' dimension of *mineness*: It is not only my experience, but the experience of my own body. Husserl seems to imply this when he sustains that I can thematize myself and thus 'actually get to know myself' (Husserl, Hua XV, p. 120), because I am passively self-aware of my own body; I can grasp it, because I am originally affected by myself (*ibid.*, p. 78): 'My body cannot act without affecting itself, itself as functioning' (Husserl, Hua Mat. VIII, p. 193). Affection is thus not extraneous to the 'pre-ontic lived experience, but one of the modus of the I' (*ibid.*, p. 189) who is 'ceaselessly (*ständig*) "conscious"' – but not 'in the ordinary sense' as 'intentional object in the sense of nature' of both its being in time and constituting itself in it (*ibid.*, p. 338, cf. pp. 365, 366). This means that I am *self-aware in the sense of my being conscious of my self-affection grounding my very self as subject in and of the world.* Hence, this self-affection grounds self-consciousness as consciousness of a lived experience (*ibid.*, pp. 202, 308) – a consciousness which Husserl calls 'proto-original life of consciousness' (*ibid.* p. 368) or even 'proto-consciousness (*Urbewusstsein*)', whose '"content" is primally conscious (*urbewusst*) in itself and necessarily' (Husserl, Hua X, p. 119; 1991, p. 123). Since the lived experience as its content cannot be objectified by any further consciousness, it can be defined in Zahavi's terms as an 'original and immediate nonobjectifying self-givenness' (Zahavi 2008, p. 70)[1], which is prior to reflection:

> Whenever I reflect, I find myself 'in relation to' something, as affected or active. That, which I am related to, is lived-experientially (*erlebnismäßig*) conscious – it is something for me as a 'lived experience (*Erlebnis*)', so that I can relate myself to it. (Husserl, Hua Mat. VIII, p. 196)

The I is able to grasp itself through reflection, but this reflective 'self-experience' uncovers a pre-reflective consciousness of not only its own body, but of a 'background of the unnoticed (*Hintergrund des Unbeachteten*)' (*ibid.*, p. 192), which is not yet 'thematically experienced' (Husserl, Hua XV, p. 493). However, Husserl stresses that one 'must not misunderstand this primal consciousness [...] to be an apprehending act' (Husserl, Hua X, p. 119; 1991, p. 123). Accordingly, Husserl distinguishes between 'intentional lived experiences' conceived of as 'consciousness of (*cogitationes*)' and 'non-intentional' lived experiences, that is, the 'sensuous' ones (Husserl, Hua XXIII, p. 330). Kinesthetic feelings and perceptions of movements are conscious acts that constitute my own body and its surrounding space and objects, such that they are characterized by a pre-reflective objectifying self-awareness, that is, I am aware of myself as the self that not only objectifies itself, but also space and objects. But it is important to notice that each and every intentional act involves not only consciousness of an object, but also consciousness of an act: 'Every lived experience (*Erlebnis*) is "sensed", is immediately perceived (internal consciousness), although naturally

1 As Zahavi explains, this is necessarily so because no unconscious content can be retained.

not posited, not meant' (Husserl, Hua XXIII, p. 307; 2005, p. 369). By stating that each act conceived of as lived experience is 'sensed', Husserl suggest that each and every conscious act is characterized by 'a tacit, immediate, pre-reflective and non-objectifying self-awareness' (Geniusas 2022, p. 79).

This means that one should not mistake the consciousness of an objective background or of an act and the consciousness understood in the sense of being sensuously experienced (*erlebt*), as Zahavi rightly remarks (Zahavi 2008, p. 70; cf. Zahavi 2003, p. 169). We may add to this distinction, that one should not mistake a pre-reflective objectifying self-awareness corresponding to the consciousness of kinesthetic movements and a *pre-reflective non-objectifying self-awareness* corresponding to the consciousness of the act of sensing oneself in the sense of having *Empfindnisse*. Moreover, and contrary to experience in general, lived-experiences are non-objectifying perceptions, they are not themselves perceived – otherwise we would face an infinite regress (Husserl, Hua XXIX, p. 252; cf. 1991, p. 123; Hua X, p. 119, Hua XXIII, p. 307; 2005, p. 369). Rather, lived experiences are immediately given as pre-reflective acts and are 'sensed (*empfunden*)'. It is neither posited nor intended, but only 'inwardly perceived (*inmanent wahrgenommen*)', while it has to be noticed that the term 'perception' appears here in quotation marks (Hua XXIII, p. 307; 2005, p. 369): What does Husserl mean with this internal perceiving?

4. Internal Perceiving and Impressional Consciousness

The perceiving of the internal is not a lived experience (*Erlebnis*), but experience (*Erleben*) as *activity* or *dynamis*. In this connection, Husserl singles out three structural moments that characterize perception as presentations (*Gegenwärtigungen*): 1) 'the inner consciousness, the *experiencing* (*das innere Bewusstsein, das* Erleben)', 2) '*lived experience* (*das* Erlebnis)', 3) the intentional *object* of the lived experience (*der intentionale* Gegenstand *des Erlebnisses*)' (Husserl, Hua XXIII, p. 326; 2005, p. 397). This means not only that each presentation entails these three moments, but also that every lived experience is the result of experiencing (*Erleben*), that is, the result of an activity or *energeia*. Husserl clearly distinguishes between *Erlebnis* and *Erleben*: 'Every experience (*Erlebnis*) […] presents itself as an experience that endures, that flows away, and that changes in such and such a way' (*ibid.*, p. 307/ 369). Some pages latter, Husserl adds: 'Impressions in the wider sense as experiences (*Erlebnisse*) in which an originary present, an originary now, becomes constituted […] (these are) impressions in the strict sense, impressional experiences (*impressionale Erlebnisse*)' (*ibid.*, p. 316/ 381). In fact, we may claim that far from opposing an objectifying[2] intentionality of kinesthetic and retentional self-consciousness to a non-intentional impressional self-consciousness stemming from carnal sensations, Husserl discovers in Rudolf Bernet's words, a preceding 'self-consciousness, which has the form of an impressional intentionality', in which the 'appearing of the life of the subject in the form of an object of reflection is preceded and made possible by an appearing of this life to itself' (Bernet 1994, p. 244), and, in our present context, of consciousness to itself.

This appearing of the consciousness to itself is the result of a reflexive act, so that it involves an impressional, objectifying intentionality. However, 'impressions in the strict sense, every phenomenon of original presentation' not only involves consciousness of the present 'now' or instant, but 'also involves components of post-presentation (*Nachgegenwärtigung*) and fore-presentations (*Vorgegenwärtigung*) [...] internal consciousness is precisely time consciousness' (*ibid.*, p. 316/381). Therefore, each impressional lived experience as temporal unity comprises not only presentations as 'original acts' (*ibid.*, p. 309/371), but also retentions and protentions as their 'modifications' (*ibid.*). To this, Husserl adds that internal consciousness presents these impressive lived experiences in 'internal perceptions (*Perzeptionen*)', that are nothing other than the 'experiencing of experiences (*das Erleben von Erlebnissen*), but not itself an experience (*Erlebnis*)', avoiding thus infinite regress (*ibid.* p. 325/395). Hence, while an impressive experience (*Erlebnis*) is a constituted temporal unity, experiencing (*Erleben*) is conceived of as the activity by which this experience (*Erlebnis*) is originally constituted. Insofar as on the one hand, this experiencing entails its own retentions and protentions (*ibid.*, p. 308/370), and on the other, as Husserl claims in his *Lectures on Internal Time-Consciousness* from 1905, the conjunction of longitudinal and transversal intentionality enables consciousness both to be conscious of the succession of phases and to intend enduring acts, time constituting consciousness becomes aware of its own performance and contents. As Husserl further claims, 'it is just non-sense to talk about an "unconscious" content [...]. Consciousness is necessarily *consciousness* in each of its phases' (Husserl, Hua X, p. 119; 1991, p. 123). This means that this 'double intentionality of the stream of consciousness' (transversal and longitudinal), (Husserl, Hua X, p. 116, cf. pp. 80–81; 1991 p. 120) enables consciousness to be self-conscious, that is, to be self-aware of its own experiencing (*Erleben*). This implies that *self-awareness* is necessarily *twofold:* While every original act involves awareness of myself as the self who experiences, every

2 Here, Bernet considers this kind of intentionality as 'non-objectifying'. Since kinaesthetic feelings constitute the own body not only as *Leib*, but as *Körper*, they have in our eyes an objectifying function.

reproduction involves awareness of myself as the self who 'has' experienced. This self-awareness is *twofold* in another sense, insofar as it concerns past and present consciousness of both my body as seat of affections and actions and my Ego as pole of these affections and seat of spiritual lived experiences (cf. Husserl, Hua XIV, p. 23; Hua I, p. 101).

5. Self-Awareness as Self-Experience or Consciousness of Self-Affection

We may return now to the afore mentioned conclusions regarding self-affection: We had claimed that self-affection grounds self-consciousness as consciousness of a lived experience (Husserl, Hua Mat. VIII, pp. 202, 308) – a consciousness which Husserl calls 'proto-original life of consciousness' (*ibid.* p. 368) or even 'proto-consciousness (*Urbewusstsein*)' (Husserl Hua X, p. 119; 1991, p. 123). We then may ask whether any lived experience (*Erlebnis*) and any experiencing (*Erleben*) may count as content of the above-mentioned primal consciousness. I would like to suggest in contrast to Zahavi's claims that self-experience is *not* 'simply a question of being pre-reflectively aware of one's own consciousness' (Zahavi 2014, p. 4), but rather a question of being aware of our most primitive actions, through which we affect ourselves: *Self-experience is thus the consciousness of my self-affection.* Only the primary lived-experiences such as the affective awareness of my own body-self are immediately given to me as acts of an originally, pre-reflective proto-consciousness: What affective consciousness experiences is its own acts understood as actualization of a potentiality, that is, as *energeia*. Acts in the sense of *Erlebnisse* are the result of continuous activity by which consciousness not only senses or manifests itself as embodied – consciousness of a *state* – but by which it is conscious of sensing or *Erleben* – consciousness of an *activity*. This sensing oneself is genetically the most original activity, since it involves the constitution of the body, which is presupposed by the constitution of the Ego. In contrast, time constituting consciousness as *Erleben* is primary from the transcendental point of view, since it involves the constitution of consciousness itself.

Let us now further inquire into the nature of sensings: Sensings are characterized by a double structure: As extended or localized in the corresponding sensing part of the body, they allow for its constitution, while as act they enable a bodily self-awareness. While in the first case, there is a bodily intentionality running between the parts sensed and the ones sensing – their mutual difference allowing for the manifestation of a body composed by heterogeneous parts – in the second, no intentionality is involved, since the self-awareness of the experience of having a body is immanent to the experience itself. While the first one involves a hetero-manifestation, the second one is simply an auto-manifestation. In this connection, Husserl evokes the possibility of 'formless stuffs', as sensuous pleasure, pain and tickle sensations, and so forth, that insofar as they belong to the sphere of 'drives' may not bear some 'animating construing' (*Ideas I*, § 85). Here, Husserl makes room for the possibility of affective sensations or impressions that only reveal the state of a consciousness in some way affected by itself, and, as we may add, a state of incarnated consciousness affected by its own *flesh*. As Husserl remarks, to delve into what is experienced is not to be mistaken with the intentional consciousness of perception which involves position-takings (Husserl, Hua XXIX, p. 252; cf. 1991, p. 123; Hua X, p. 119) or – we may add – with the intentional consciousness of a sensuous kinesthetic bodily experience. Hence, by understanding consciousness as affectively embodied we not only avoid the subject-object model, but infinite regress as well.[3] Therefore, to the above distinction we may add that lived experiences are of two kinds: While *intentional and objectifying ones ground a pre-reflective affective self-awareness, non-intentional and non-objectifying ones ground a pre-reflective carnal self-awareness.*

The kinesthetic freedom of our body provides us with another valuable clue: As a moving body and as 'a field of localization of its sensations', the body is 'an organ of the will' insofar as only bodies are immediately spontaneously ('freely') movable (Husserl, Hua IV, p. 152; *Ideas II*, p. 159). The subject has the '"faculty" (the "I can") to freely move this body', in Husserl's words (*ibid.*, p. 154/159–60). Thus, the subjective capacity of my body to move freely belongs to the horizon of my kinesthetic freedom (cf. Rang 1973, pp. 159–63).[4] Husserl adds in this context that our will is not only guided by 'rational motives', but by 'original "drives or impulses" and (is) passively submitted to them'. In reflective experience we are able to come to predicative consciousness as the unity of the modes of comportment, but already at the level of self-perception and self-experience we can enter into the patent and latent intentionalities of motivation, that is, 'I am "conscious" in pre-givenness' prior to any reflection on my modes of comportment (Husserl, Hua IV, pp. 249–50; *Ideas II*, pp. 262–4). In this connection, Husserl remarks that the conscious ordering of sensations to

3 Cf. Zahavi 2003, who conceives inner time consciousness as 'the pre-reflective self-awareness of the act'. He sustains that 'Husserl's description of the structure of inner time-consciousness [...] is exactly an analysis of the structure of the pre-reflective self-manifestation of our acts and experiences' (Zahavi 2003, p. 168).

4 Cf. Zahavi 1994 for an account of the role of transcendental subjectivity for the constitution of one's own body.

the position of the limbs opens up a horizon of possible appearances of things. Thus, the subject is conscious about its possibilities and views itself as the subject who is capable to freely command its kinaesthesias (Husserl, Hua XI, p. 14; 2001, p. 51).

Hence, we may conclude that

1. sensings as intentional bodily affections allow us to recognize and experience ourselves as experiencing lived-bodies, while as acts, they disclose an underlying bodily proto-consciousness which is pre-reflectively aware of its own performing of lived-experiences.
2. feelings and sensations allow us to know and recognize ourselves as the bodies who are able – at least insofar as kinesthetic sensations are concerned – to freely command them.
3. my being aware of my self-perception as a living body, my self-experience as a bodily self-awareness and my kinesthetic freedom is provided by a consciousness that not only 'knows' about its bodily capacities but also knows itself as the body originating them and is originally *self-aware in the mode of a self-manifestation of its acting.*

Despite not being '*erfahren*' or 'known', this 'reflective immanently directed experience' (Husserl, Hua XXV, p. 89), as Husserl calls it, provides us with a consciousness of ourselves as experiencing, that is, an *experiential knowledge* of ourselves insofar as we get to know ourselves as the ones who are actualizing our innermost capacity of experiencing. As Husserl says,

> The flow of consciousness that constitutes immanent time not only *exists* but is so remarkably and yet intelligibly fashioned that a self-appearance of the flow necessarily exists in it, and therefore the flow itself must necessarily be apprehensible in the *flowing*. (Husserl, Hua X, p. 83; 1991, p. 88, emphasis in the original).

This flow is nothing other than the field of lived experience generated by consciousness. To grasp something in the 'flowing' that is, as *energeia*, would seem to suggest that self-manifestation is concomitant with the continuous exercise of a capacity (*dynamis*) that is actualized in a *carnal and temporal auto-affection*. Hence, exercising the most fundamental capacity entails ceaselessly sensing ourselves as a living, functioning (*fungierender*) body. Thus, along with proto-consciousness, the continuous exercise of auto-affection in the sense of self-sensuous sensing seems to be the most fundamental level of a lived experience (*Erlebnis*). In conclusion, passive experience is grasped by an *affective bodily self-consciousness*, which in its turn, allows for a bodily self-knowledge, an *experiential self-knowledge* that expresses itself in bodily drives and affections.

Now, we are able to resume the question posed above about the motivational correlation at work in these lived experiences. Husserl remarks that total consciousness is bound to the body by means of its 'hyletic substrate', but, he adds that 'the *intentional lived experiences themselves are no longer directly and properly localized, they no longer form a stratum on the body*', insofar as '*(p)erception, as the touching apprehension of form, does not have its seat in the touching finger in which the touch sensation is localized*'. Therefore, for Husserl we can 'only metaphorically' say that intentionalities are 'related to the body or in the body' (Husserl, Hua IV, p. 153; *Ideas II*, p. 160). Metaphorically or not, Husserl explicitly distinguishes in *Ideas II* between the intentionality of bodily lived experiences and the intentionality of predicative consciousness. The root of the problem lies in the static stratification of the constitutional process, built up by three layers: first, the non-intentional diffuse, non localisable sensings as warmth and coldness, immanent to the body second, those bodily immanent intentional tactile sensings of my own body, which are localized on its surface and passively lived or *erlebt*, and finally, those intentional kinesthetics feelings which are aroused by a tactual vision and are actively i.e. thematically and intersubjectively experienced or *erfahren*.

6. The Originary Sensuousness of the Proto-Hyle

At this point we may ask ourselves what the driving force of this process of evolving consciousness and self-awareness is. I'd suggest that this driving force is due to Husserl's groundbreaking conception of an 'originary sensitivity (*ursprüngliche Sinnlichkeit*)' or proto-*hyle* (Husserl, Hua XXXIII, p. 275), developed in his studies on the structure of temporality as published in the *Bernauer Ms*. This originary sensuousness opens up a dynamic continuous process of evolving consciousness, which leads from the affective hyletic data to the proper intentional consciousness. This process is not driven by an active intentionality correlating conscious experience to the appearing world, but in Husserl's words by a *passive intentionality* ruled by sensuous drives or impulses. These impulses are the driving force which ensures the continuity and dynamics of the constitutional process of the body. Let us take a closer look into these notions.

Husserl claims that everything affecting us conforms to a quasi 'blind' unity of constituting characteristics or predicates having their source in feelings (Husserl, Hua XXXI, p. 7; 2001, p. 278). But the most primitive line of development is not motivated by any of these active affective performances, it rather begins at the hyletic data, which become involved with one another building up homogeneous 'affective [hyletic] units' in the 'living present' (Husserl, Hua XI, p. 162; 2001, p. 210). An hyletic blending is produced within each of the sensuous fields out of the time-continuity. This hyletic data has its origin in the proto-hyle which is not a mere content of apprehension that should be affectively 'enlivened' by an intentional apprehension, that is, something as a 'pure affective nothingness (*pures affektives Nichts*)', but a *hyle* endowed with an 'affective vitality' (Husserl, Hua XI, p. 165). This *hyle* produces an 'affective relief' composed of data with varying affective efficacy, which are 'also for the Ego insofar as they affect the Ego' (*ibid.*, p. 162). Husserl understands this originally affectivity of the *hyle*, that is, this 'sensuousness devoid of Ego (*ichlose Sensualität*)' as an 'originally vitality (*ursprüngliche Lebendigkeit*)', a 'universal drive-intentionality (*universale Triebintentionalität*)', consisting of affections on the Ego and his passive 'being attracted' to. By this Ego Husserl means a pole of stimuli, it is the one 'without name', 'not-being', only 'functioning' through touching, handling, assessing, etc. (Husserl, Hua XXXIII, p. 275). This primary sensuousness owes its vitality to the drive-intentionality or 'passive proto-intentionality' (Husserl, Hua Mat VIII, p. 335), which we may call a *bodily intentionality* insofar as it consists of sensuous stimuli and the correlative passive reaction of the Ego as irritability. At this point, Husserl immediately realizes that he has to abstract from this Ego to reach the sphere of primary sensuousness, which he finally defines as composed by passive tendencies of association and reproduction.

Thus, Husserl's conception of *hyle* takes up an Aristotelian concept and endows it with a particular vivacity. Only the affective power of the *hyle* can produce such strong and vivid drives or sensuous tendencies governed by bodily affections. In response to these affections, our body reacts with varying degrees of attraction and repulsion; it is the power of drives, which governs our bodily responses.

7. Impressional and Primary Form of Anonymous Consciousness: its Awakening to Life

But this is still not the primary level: Returning to Husserl's *Lectures on Internal Time-Consciousness*, we may suggest that grasping this flowing of time *in* the flowing involves the awakening of this consciousness to life: This is suggested by a passage of the *VI Cartesian Meditation*, where Eugen Fink analyses the appearing of the life of the subject in the form of an object of reflection that is preceded and made possible by an awakening of this life to the world. This implies that the concomitant appearing of this life to itself in the form of a carnal and temporal auto-affection is but a second step in this process. For this purpose, the VI. *Cart. Med.* uncovers an impressional and minimal form of 'anonymous' consciousness (Hua Dok II/1, p. 144), that is, a consciousness devoid of Ego, which appears to itself by the 'proto-event (*Urereignis*)' (*ibid.* p. 124) of its awakening to life. This event is brought about by the 'transcendental self-movement of constitutive life (*das Geschehen der transzendentalen Selbstbewegung des konstituierenden Lebens*)' (*ibid.*), that is, a reflexive movement of life itself, through which life transcends and thereby exceeds itself, engendering thus an existent, still impersonal, neutral, and anonymous being of which we can only say, following Emmanuel Lévinas, that 'there is' (*il y a*)' (Lévinas 1998, pp. 93–94).

What is thematically awakened is the transcendental life of a being, that in its nude exposure to the world returns to itself, that is, he passes from the 'oldest world's sleep of being-out-of-itself (*aus dem weltalten 'Schlaf' des Aussersichtseins*)' to its 'being-for-itself (*'Für-sich-Seins*)' (Hua Dok II/1, p. 125). Being awakened and beginning at the instant, he refers to himself such that, by objectifying himself (*ibid.* p. 164) he both becomes an individual I and inaugurates the present time. As Lévinas claims, 'the return of the present to itself is the affirmation of an I that has already turned to itself, that is, is doubled by a *self'* (*Le retour du present à lui-même est l'affirmation du Je déjà rivé à soi, déjà double d'un* soi)' (Lévinas 1998, pp. 135–136). While the instant marks the passage to existence, the present is the result of the return of the self to itself, such that it becomes the carrier of an existent being as an individualized Ego. In this context, it is important to notice that there is a *double movement* that affects both the self and its life: On the one hand, this self-return of the Ego implies the birth of self-consciousness, on the other, the 'self-split (*Selbstentzweiung*)' (Hua Dok II/1, p. 121) – and Husserl adds in a footnote – of the 'act of living (*Lebensakt*)' (*ibid.*, fn. p. 385) gives rise to the transcendental or reflexive Ego. Husserl leaves the question open of whether the phenomenalizing I as reflexive Ego is posited by the transcendental, individuated Ego or whether the last determination of the phenomenalizing activity should be traced back to the 'most originary depth of the absolute life (*ursprünglichere Tiefe des absoluten Lebens*)' (*ibid.*, p. 164). At this stage of the analysis, Husserl redefines the concept of the absolute in phenomenological terms, by affirming that

> the absolute is the overarching totality of the transcendental life in general, which is itself articulated in opposing terms: This splitting between the constitutive and phenomenalizing life now determines the concept of the absolute: It is the synthetic unity of antithetical moments. (*Ibid.*, p. 157)

Far from meaning the homogeneous and universal totality of beings in ontological terms, the absolute is 'the overarching unity of being in general and pre-being (of mundane and "transcendental" being), of the world and of the origin of the world' (*ibid.*). Through the phenomenological reduction we arrive thus at the 'depths of the constitutive "pre-being"' and the birth of transcendental self-consciousness. In his *Studies on the Structure of Consciousness* (Hua XLIII) recently published, Husserl defines such 'pre-being' of consciousness as a 'limit case, *zero case of life* (Grenzfall, *Nullfall des Lebens*)' and as '*zero case in the genesis* (*Nullfall in der Genesis*)' (Hua XLIII/2, 203). This state is characterized by a 'discontinuity of that which stands out (*Diskontinuität der Abhebung*)', which even if it might be the case of a discontinuity against a continuous standing out of the background, would impede synthesis and with it, any 'particular consciousness (*Sonderbewusstsein*)' (*ibid.*). We now realize why is it not possible to leap over the gap between non-being and being: The birth of consciousness is something that we can only retroactively, that is, reflectively, account for. Hence, at this level we grasp consciousness in *statu nascendi*: to exist is thus to return to oneself and discover oneself as being existent. Therefore, the *primal form* of *self-awareness consists in the sudden and instant realization of being alive.*

8. Conclusions

We can now apply these insights to the process of constitution and conclude that insofar as the function of the bodily affections guiding our drives is to localize hyletic data, tactual sensings and feelings, anchoring them to the body itself, these sensuous drives can be said to belong to a bodily proto-intentionality which allows for an intentional lived experience. We can conceive of this *bodily proto-intentionality* as a force with varying degrees of *intensity*, which correlates our drives and sensuous affections and expresses itself in sensings and kinesthetic feelings. Thus, the affective power of the *hyle* triggers the dynamic constitutional process, which runs from the drive as lived experience or *Erlebnis* to the conscious intentional experience as *Erfahrung*. This conception of a bodily intentionality allows us to understand the body as a system ruled by driving forces or motility vectors that enable the body's self-constitution as a unity by correlating our immanent feelings and sensations to parts or places of the lived body, that is, through localization. Hence, our bodily, unthematized proto-consciousness provides a minimal form of carnal self-awareness arising from our self-affection and self-sensing, which allows us to recognize ourselves as experiencing lived bodies.

In this connection, we have distinguished between on the one hand, intentional kinesthetic sensations, which insofar as they objectify the own body as *Körper*, they allow for the constitution of a *pre-reflective kinesthetic self-awareness* corresponding to the consciousness of kinesthetic movements, and on the other, intentional sensations as lived experiences, which insofar as they objectify the own body as *Leib*, they provide for a *pre-reflective affective self-awareness* corresponding to the consciousness of the act of sensing oneself in the sense of having *Empfindnisse*. While kinesthetic movements constitute my own body as a *Körper* and its surrounding world in space and time, *Empfindnisse* constitute my own body as sensed/sensing *Leib*. Here, we may recall that lived experiences are of two kinds: On the one hand, insofar as sensations as extended or localized allow for the constitution of a lived body as *Leib*, they are both *intentional and objectifying* and ground a *pre-reflective affective self-awareness*. On the other, insofar as sensations as impressions or carnal sensations stem from the own body as *flesh*, they are *non-intentional* and ground a *pre-reflective impressional self-awareness*, such that in conjunction, sensations allow for the constitution of a bodily consciousness. Self-sensuous sensing seems thus to be the most fundamental level of a lived experience.

These levels presuppose the constitution of an impressional temporal consciousness that not only constitutes time but allows for the constitution of a *temporal self-awareness* which is in a double sense *twofold*, since it constitutes me as the unity of body and ego as an embodied spiritual self, who is self-aware of both its present I that *is* presently experiencing and a retentional form of itself as the one who *has* experienced. Hence, we may distinguish between an objectifying intentionality of kinesthetic feelings and retentional impressional consciousness grounding an *impressional temporal self-awareness* and on the one hand, non-intentional, non-objectifying impressional carnal sensations that ground an *impressional carnal self-awareness*, according to which I am aware of having sensations stemming from my flesh and on the other, intentional and objectifying affective sensations that ground an *affective self-awareness* according to which I am aware of having sensations that constitute my body as *Leib*. Furthermore, we have shown that experiencing (*Erleben*), that is the consciousness of the activity of sensing, grounds a pre-reflective carnal self-awareness, that is, an *affective awareness of my own self-affection*, according to which I am aware of myself as the body who is affecting itself, that is, I am aware of myself as performing the act of affecting myself. We have further pointed out that we must consider the primary level from two points of view: While genetically, sensing oneself is the most original activity, since it involves the constitution of the body that is presupposed by the constitution of the Ego, time constituting consciousness as *Erleben* is primary from the transcendental point of view, since it involves the constitution of consciousness itself. But the most originary depth of the absolute life concerns the limit issue or proto-event of the awakening of the transcendental life of a being, which involves the emergence of an *impressional and minimal form of anonymous consciousness*. Here we grasp consciousness and self-consciousness in *statu nascendi*: the primary form of consciousness and *self-awareness* consists in the sudden and instant *realization of being alive*.

Summarizing the above, we are now able to distinguish between different forms of self-awareness, which are organized according to an order of foundation as follows:

1. a primal form of self-awareness consisting in the realization of being alive and concomitantly,
2. an impressional and minimal form of anonymous consciousness in its awakening,
3. an impressional, temporal self-awareness of my present and my retentional embodied spiritual self,
4. a pre-reflective bodily self-awareness (I am the one who is sensing – awareness of an activity), which is concomitant with an awareness of my own self-affection (I am the one who is affecting itself – awareness of an act). This bodily self-awareness has two modalities:
   4.1. a pre-reflective, impressional and carnal self-awareness stemming from non-intentional, non-objectifying carnal sensations of my own *flesh*,
   4.2. a pre-reflective affective self-awareness stemming from intentional, objectifying carnal sensations that constitute my own body as *Leib*.
5. a pre-reflective kinesthetic self-awareness corresponding to objectifying, intentional kinesthetic movements, constituting my own body as *Körper* and its surrounding world in space and time.

As already anticipated at the beginning of this paper, we are now able to conclude that the unity of body and consciousness in its totality is made possible by the constitutive force of sensitive feelings, sensations and sensings. In conclusion, passive experience is grasped by an *affective bodily self-consciousness*, which in its turn, allows for a bodily self-knowledge, an *experiential self-knowledge* that expresses itself in bodily drives and affections.

References

Bernet, Rudolf 1994, 'An intentionality without subject or object?', in *Man and World* 27, pp. 231–255

Breuer, Irene 2015, 'Die haptisch korrelative Genesis von Raum/Ort und eigener bzw. "intersubjektiver" Leiblichkeit an den Rändern der Phänomenologie Husserls. Die originäre Entstehung der Ur-präsenzen an den Grenzen der Gegebenheit', in *The Yearbook on History and Interpretation of Phenomenology 2015. New Generative Aspects in Contemporary Phenomenology*, pp. 95–115

——, 2020, *Ort, Raum, Unendlichkeit. Aristoteles und Husserl auf dem Weg zu einer lebensweltlichen Raumerfahrung* (Würzburg: Königshausen & Neumann)

Claesges, Ulrich 2001, *Edmund Husserls Theorie der Raumkonstitution* (Den Haag: Nijhoff)

Depraz, Natalie 2001, *Lucidité du corps. De l'empirisme transcendental en phénoménologie* (Dordrecht: Kluwer)

Geniusas, Saulius 2022, 'Phantasy and Self-awareness: Remarks on the Phenomenology of Mineness', in Th. Breyer, M. Cavallaro, R. Sandoval (eds.), *Phenomenology of Phantasy and Emotion* (Darmstadt: WGB), pp. 77–100

Husserl, Edmund, Abbreviations: Hua = Husserliana, Edmund Husserl Gesammelte Werke. Hua Mat = Husserliana Materialien. Hua Dok = Husserliana Dokumente

——, Hua I, 1950, *Cartesianische Meditationen und Pariser Vorträge*, ed. St. Strasser (Den Haag: Nijhoff)

——, Hua IV, 1952, *Ideen zu einer reinen Phänomenologie und phänomenologischen Philosophie. Zweites Buch. Phänomenologische Untersuchung zur Konstitution*, ed. M. Biemel (Den Haag: Nijhoff). Engl. trans.: 2000, 5th ed.. *Ideas II. Ideas pertaining to a Pure Phenomenology and to a Phenomenological Philosophy. Second Book. Studies in the Phenomenology of Constitution*, trans. R. Rojcewicz and A. Schuwer (Dordrecht: Kluwer)

——, Hua VIII, 1959, *Erste Philosophie (1923/1924). Zweiter Teil. Theorie der phänomenologischen Reduktion*, ed. R. Boehm (Den Haag: Nijhoff)

——, Hua X, 1966, *Zur Phänomenologie des Inneren Zeitbewusstseins (1893–1917)*, ed. R. Boehm (Den Haag: Nijhoff)- Engl. transl.: 1991, *On the Phenomenology of the Consciousness of Internal Time* (1893–1917), transl. J. B. Brough (Dordrecht: Kluwer)

——, Hua XI, 1969. *Analysen zur passiven Synthesis. Aus Vorlesungs- und Forschungsmanuskripten 1918–1926*, ed. M. Fleischer Den Haag: Nijhoff; and Hua XXXI, 2000, *Aktive Synthesen: Aus der Vorlesung 'Transzendentale Logik' 1920/21. Ergänzungsband zu 'Analysen zur passiven Synthesis'*, ed. R. Breeur (Dordrecht:

Kluwer). Engl. transl.: 2001, *Analyses concerning Passive and Active Synthesis. Lectures on Transcendental Logic*, transl. A. J. Steinbock (Dordrecht: Kluwer)

——, Hua XIV, 1973, *Zur Phänomenologie der Intersubjektivität. Texte aus dem Nachlass. Zweiter Teil: 1921–1928*, ed. I. Kern (Den Haag: Nijhoff)

——, Hua XV, 1973, *Zur Phänomenologie der Intersubjektivität. Texte aus dem Nachlass. Dritter Teil 1929–1935*, ed. I. Kern (Den Haag: Nijhoff)

——, Hua XVI, 1973, *Ding und Raum. Vorlesungen 1907*, ed. U. Claesges (Den Haag: Nijhoff)

——, Hua XIX/1, 1984, *Logische Untersuchungen. Zweiter Band. Erster Teil. Untersuchungen zur Phänomenologie und Theorie der Erkenntnis*, ed. U. Panzer (Den Haag: Nijhoff)

——, Hua XXIII, 1980, *Phantasie, Bildbewusstsein, Erinnerung. Zur Phänomenologie der anschaulichen Vergegenwärtigung*, ed. E. Marbach (Den Haag: Nijhoff). Engl. trans.: 2005, *Phantasy, Image Consciousness and Memory (1898–1917)*, trans. J. B. Brough (Dordrecht: Springer)

——, Hua XXV, 1987, *Aufsätze und Vorträge (1911–1921)*, ed. Th. Nenon, H. R. Sepp (Dordrecht: Nijhoff)

——, Hua XXIX, 1993, *Die Krisis der Europäischen Wissenschaften und die transzendentale Phänomenologie. Ergänzungsband. Texte aus dem Nachlass 1934–1937*, ed. R. N. Smid (Dordrecht: Kluwer)

——, Hua XXXIII, 2001, *Die Bernauer Manuskripte über das Zeitbewusstsein (1917–1937)*, ed. R. Bernet and D. Lohmar (Dordrecht: Kluwer)

——, Hua XXXIX, 2008, *Die Lebenswelt. Auslegungen der vorgegebenen Welt und ihrer Konstitution. Texte aus dem Nachlass (1916–1937)*, ed. R. Sowa (Dordrecht: Kluwer)

——, Hua XLIII/2, 2020. *Studien zur Struktur des Bewusstseins. Teilband II. Gefühl und Wert. Texte aus dem Nachlass (1896–1925)*, ed. U. Melle and Th. Vongehr (Cham: Springer)

——, Hua Mat. VIII, 2006, *Späte Texte über Zeitkonstitution (1929–1934). Die C-Manuskripte*, ed. D. Lohmar (Dordrecht: Springer)

——, Hua Dok II/I, 1988, *Eugen Fink. VI. Cartesianische Meditation. Teil 1. Die Idee einer transzendentalen Methodenlehre*, ed. H. Ebeling, J. Holl, G. van Kerckhoven (Dordrecht: Kluwer)

Lévinas, Emmanuel 1988, *De l'existance a l'existant*. Paris: Vrin

Melle, Ullrich 2012, 'Husserls deskriptive Erforschung der Gefühlserlebnisse', in R. Breeur, U, Melle (eds.), *Life, Subjectivity & Art. Essays in Honor of Rudolf Bernet* (Dordrecht: Springer), pp. 51–99

Rang, Bernhard 1973, *Kausalität und Motivation* (Den Haag: Nijhoff)

Waldenfels, Bernhard 2013, *Sinnesschwellen. Studien zur Phänomenologie des Fremden 3* (Frankfurt a.M.: Suhrkamp)

Welton, Don 1999, 'Soft, smooth hands: Husserl's phenomenology of the lived-body', in D. Welton (ed.), *The Body. Classic and contemporary Readings* (Massachusetts: Blackwell), pp. 39–56

Zahavi, Dan 1994, 'Husserl's Phenomenology of the Body', in *Études Phénoménologiques* 19, pp. 63–84

——, 2003, 'Inner Time-Consciousness and Pre-reflective Self-awareness', in D. Welton (ed.), *The New Husserl. A Critical Reader* (Bloomington: Indiana University Press), pp. 157–180

——, 2008, 2. ed., *Subjectivity and Selfhood. Investigating the First-Person Perspective* (Cambridge: MIT Press)

——, 2014, *Self and Other. Exploring Subjectivity, Empathy and Shame* (Oxford: Oxford University Press).

II

Personhood and Persistence

What are We? – Spatial Consciousness, Demonstrative Reference, and the First-Person Perspective

Markus Herrmann

Abstract

This article argues for the thesis that we are (and do not merely have) spatial consciousness. But the arguments presented also imply that we must conceive ourselves as necessarily extended. The line of reasoning starts with a thought experiment of universal symmetry as entertained by P. F. Strawson. Even though particulars in such a thought experiment are objectively indiscernible, persons can nevertheless successfully distinguish between themselves and their indiscernible counterparts via demonstrative and first-person reference. This would lead into mysticism if those ways of reference were not constitutive for the criteria of transtemporal identity. Comparing demonstrative reference with the coordinates of a Cartesian coordinate system, we can learn that demonstrative reference is dependent on spatial consciousness that a priori locates itself. This leads to the crucial point: In a Cartesian coordinate system, the axes of this system are defined as the system. Therefore, spatial consciousness locates a priori itself *as spatial consciousness*. We *are* spatial consciousness and do not merely *have* it. However, as the Cartesian coordinate system needs extended subsections for being able to provide coordinates, we need to have a definite extension for being able to demonstratively refer to particulars. Hence, we are spatial consciousness that a priori locates itself and that is necessarily spatially extended.

If I encounter a person on Monday and I encounter a person on Tuesday, I could ask whether it is one and the same person. To this question of transtemporal personal identity, there are two major approaches: the psychological and the physiological one. The former claims that psychological criteria (like memories or psychological similarity) determine whether the person on Monday and the one on Tuesday is one and the same.[1] The latter tries to determine identity by physiological criteria (like the identity of the biological organism; Snowdon 1990 and 2014, and Olson 1997).

1 John Locke is the classical proponent for this position (Locke 1975, ch. 2.27). It is also advanced by David Lewis (Lewis 2003).

 | DOI:10.30965/9783969752906_005

In this article, I want to argue for a position that that does not smoothly fit into either of these two schools of thought.[2] I want to argue that we *are* (and do not merely *have*) spatial consciousness that a priori locates itself (and that thereby a specific psychological outfit like certain memories or psychological similarity is not essential for determining our transtemporal identity). This might seem like a merely uncommon version of the psychological approach because consciousness is a psychological concept. However, the argument that I present will also imply that we are necessarily spatially located and *extended.* We *are* an extended entity (like a body) and do not merely *have* one.

I will start by developing a framework for the question of personal identity. Next, I address a thought experiment by Peter F. Strawson about the dependencies of reference, which implies that reference and personal identity are related topics. In the following two paragraphs, I will examine this relation by comparing demonstrative reference to a Cartesian coordinate system. This constitutes the main argument for the thesis that we are (*and do not merely have*) spatial consciousness. Then, I discuss an important implication of this comparison: namely, that we necessarily are located and extended. After addressing objections to the position advanced in this article, I finally address certain implications of my line of reasoning.

1. A Kantian Framework

I try to give an answer to the question of transtemporal personal identity by answering the question *what kind of entity* the indexical 'I' does refer to (does it refer to a biological organism, a set of memories or character traits etc.). That I frame the question in this way is due to a specific framework of transtemporal identity in general. I will call it further the Kantian framework of spatiotemporal identity (or short: the Kantian framework).

To understand the Kantian framework, let us first examine the identity criteria of an everyday object like a table. If I see a table at noon in the living room and I see a table an hour later in the kitchen, I can base my judgment about whether it is one and the same table on the salient properties I perceive. For example, on each occasion I might see a table of the same structure. Maybe, I can even perceive an indiscernible scratch at both points in time. By these salient properties, I judge that it is one and the same table.

2 In this article I summarize a position that I have developed in depth earlier (Herrmann 2021). This article is part of a research project that has been funded by the Deutsche Forschungsgemeinschaft (DFG; project number HE 7080/3-1).

Although such a judgment is well justified, the criteria applied (the perceived properties) cannot be constitutive for the transtemporal identity of the object in question. For, it is possible that there might be two indiscernible tables (i.e., two tables of the same structure, even with indiscernible scratches).[3] The logical possibility of multiple instances of any set of internal properties entails the danger of indeterminateness if we simply judge by these properties. Therefore, such criteria cannot be *constitutive* for the transtemporal identity of such objects like a table, but merely *indicative*.

However, we can judge identity by different criteria. Instead of simply comparing the properties we perceive at noon and an hour later, we can *keep track* of the table. If I constantly perceive it for the entire hour, I can easily judge whether the table that was at noon in the living room is one and the same table as the one that is an hour later in the kitchen. Even some changes of the salient properties during this period (like getting additional scratches) are no problem. What matters is less the properties, but the *spatiotemporal relation* between the table at noon and the table one hour later. It seems, with the proper spatiotemporal connection, we have found robust criteria for our judgment of transtemporal identity.

Is the spatiotemporal connection as described above sufficient for transtemporal identity? Unfortunately, the discussion about contingent identity (Gibbard 1975) and material constitution (Baker 1997) has provided us with cases that indicate the contrary. I want to examine a case inspired by the statue cases of this discussion (Gibbard 1975, p. 191): Let us assume we have an object A at time t1 that is cubical. When keeping track of it, we discover that its cohesive mass changes its shape so radically that we get an object that is spherical at time t2. Is the object A we perceive at t1 and the object we perceive at t2 one and the same? We have a spatiotemporal connection that is similar to the table that has been moved from the living room to the kitchen: If we keep track of the object A we can see that its cohesive mass is one and the same cohesive mass as the one we can perceive at t2. Nevertheless, if we ask whether the object A is the same as the object at the t2, the question becomes more difficult. What is A? If A is a cube and we ask the question whether it is one and the same cube, the object A and the spherical object at t2 are not one and the same object. For, the object at t2 is no cube. However, if A is simply a cohesive mass and we ask the question whether it is one and the same cohesive mass, the object A and the spherical object at t2 are one and the same object. Therefore,

3 For in depth defense of the possibility of indiscernibles (even relational indiscernibles) cf. Black 1952 and Koch 2006, §§ 43ff.

the *property* in question (being a cube or being a cohesive mass) is also decisive for determining transtemporal identity.[4]

Hence, we have two necessary ingredients for identity over time: It depends on the proper spatiotemporal connection *and* on an essential property (i.e., on *what* the entity in question *is*).

Therefore, within the framework presented above, the question about transtemporal personal identity takes the following shape: *What is the kind of entity that we are* and that we must keep track of over time? I name this a Kantian framework as it mirrors Kant's position that an object needs intuition (which is spatiotemporal in his philosophy) *and* concepts: "Gedanken ohne Inhalt sind leer, Anschauungen ohne Begriffe sind blind" ("Thoughts without content are empty, intuitions without concepts are blind", Kant, KrV, B 75).[5]

The obvious answer to the question what kind of entity we are is that we are *persons*. Hence, we simply need to keep track of persons in space over time when we try to resolve questions of personal identity. Of course, this prompts the question about the essential features of personhood? As has been mentioned above, some claim that persons are biological organisms. Hence, we would need to keep track of those. Descartes notoriously claimed that we are thinking substances. His account already raises a question about our Kantian framework: This framework presupposes that persons are spatiotemporal entities. But if we were Cartesian substances, we would not be spatial.

For now, I will ignore this problem. The following argument for my claim that we are spatial consciousness will imply (and not only presuppose) that we are indeed spatially located and extended – and therefore it will rule out Cartesianism.

2. Subjectivity and Symmetry

As I have mentioned, I try to give an answer to the question what kind of entity the indexical 'I' does refer to. And I try to give this answer by arguing that the unique characteristics of first-person reference already determines the kind of entity it refers to. This might seem strange. For, the properties that determine the referent of an expression do usually not determine its identity criteria. If I

4 This might sound like Peter Geach's conception of relative identity (Geach 1973). However, the necessity of a spatiotemporal connection is a crucial difference.

5 It is important to highlight that Kant has never explicitly developed this framework for transtemporal identity. Nevertheless, I name it 'Kantian' because it mirrors his understanding of an empirical object.

refer to a person by the expression 'the lady in the red sweater', it is hardly the case that her identity criteria are dependent on a red sweater. Otherwise, if she took it off, she would cease to exist. However, as we will see, with the indexical 'I' the situation is different. In this case, the way of reference determines the identity criteria.

First, I would like to start with an observation about reference by Peter Frederick Strawson. In his famous book 'Individuals' he considers possible worlds containing planets with nearly similar intrinsic and extrinsic structures (Strawson 1959, p. 20). Following him, we can conceive a possible world with a point symmetric structure. In this world, there is not one, but two planets called 'Earth', both of exactly the same shape, size and material configuration (cf. Koch 2016, p. 314ff.). Both planets instantiate the same objective properties. For example, they are inhabited by human civilizations which gave rise to philosophers who author an article about subjectivity and symmetry.

Because the possible world has a point symmetric structure, both planets are located in qualitatively identical solar systems, galaxies etc. In other words, each particular in this possible world has an indiscernible counterpart. I am here, and my counterpart in the other part of the universe has exactly the same objective properties – relational and monadic ones.

Strawson draws our attention to a quite disturbing fact: Although all objective properties are mirrored to the extent of total indiscernibility of all particulars, its inhabitants face no problems when they make an identifying reference to themselves (or to their environment). They can easily distinguish between themselves and their objectively indiscernible counterparts. Each one can simply say, "I am here, and he is over there." Although they do not use any objective criteria like 'the person who is 1.82m tall and has quite short hair' they do not get into identity troubles.

One might object that this is merely reference, not metaphysics. Why should the way we refer to people tell us anything about their identity criteria (cf. Geach 1973, 288)? As I have mentioned above, referring by a property (like wearing a red sweater) does not imply that the property in question is essential for the entity that has the property (the lady wearing the red sweater).

However, two premises highlight a link between our identity and the self-reference in the Strawsonian thought experiment:

(p1): The criteria of our identity are not in principle cognitively opaque to us.

(p2): The criteria of our identity are the same in all possible worlds.

Denying the first premise is outright mysticism. Because criteria that are in principle beyond our grasp result in principally indetermined personal identity – in every single case. On the other hand, declining the second premise without a further argument would be ad hoc. In addition, one could make a Kripkean case for this premise, as "person" (like "water") would be a rigid designator and therefore refer to the same property in every possible world (Kripke 1980).[6]

With these two premises and Strawson's thought experiment at hand, we can conclude that our ability to refer to ourselves is somehow linked to the issue of our identity: The only cognitive accessible criteria in the thought experiment are the indiscernible (and therefore irrelevant) objective facts on the one hand and our first-person perspective reference as last distinguishing criterion available on the other hand. For, whatever set of properties I pick to determine my identity (e.g. 'being a human being who is 1.82m tall and has quite short hair') – and even if I enrich this set of properties by relational properties (e.g. 'who is sitting on a chair of this or that specific structure in a city with these or those salient features') –, all these properties cannot sufficiently constitute my identity. There is always a counterpart who has exactly the same properties.[7]

Although I think that this argument is valid, it is far from satisfying. It raises too many questions: Apart from the fact that due to first-person reference I can distinguish between me and my counterpart, demonstrative reference makes it similarly possible for me to distinguish between any spatiotemporal object and its counterpart. Does that imply that demonstrative reference constitutes the identity of spatiotemporal objects? In addition, what exactly is the link between first-person reference and personal identity? How does the entire argument fit into the Kantian framework presented above?

3. A Priori Self-location

To answer these questions, I want to compare our practice of referring with a Cartesian coordinate system.[8] With such a system, we can use the coordinates

6 But even if one is not inclined to accept a Kripkean approach to naming, the second premise could be slightly altered (p2*: *The criteria of personal identity are the same in all possible worlds with inhabitants that are intrinsically similar to us*). As in the Strawsonian thought experiment persons can even be intrinsically identical to us, it does not matter if the argument presented here is based on p2 or p2*.

7 One might object that the counterparts can be distinguished by their identity relations (like being identical with themselves). However, Max Black has already pointed out that presupposing identity when defining identity criteria becomes circular (Black 1952, p. 11f.; similarly, Koch 2006, p. 315).

8 Already, Anton Friedrich Koch compared indexical reference to a Cartesian coordinate system (Koch 2016, p. 54).

provided by the x and y axes to refer to a point P (see figure 4.1). For example, P in the center of the circle has the coordinates (2|2).

This is similar to some cases of demonstrative reference, like when I point with my finger at a chair and use the expression 'this chair'. In the latter case, I use the characteristics of my body and its relation to the chair to refer to the entity in question. In the former case, I use characteristics of the Cartesian coordinate system and its relation to the point at the center of the circle to refer to the entity in question.

As has been argued by Hector-Neri Castañeda (2001) and John Perry (2001), demonstrative reference, even if directed at ourselves, is not self-reference as it occurs when we use the indexical 'I'. Only the latter can express self-consciousness. For, I can point at myself without recognizing that I point at myself (like in a Wittgensteinian case when I am entwined with another wrestler and I point at a body part I perceive, but I do not recognize to whom the body part belongs; cf. Wittgenstein 1980, § 170). In such a case, I do not recognize that it is myself who I am referring to. But this cannot happen if I refer to myself via the indexical 'I'. Therefore, there is a substantial difference between demonstrative reference and self-reference via first-person pronouns.

This raises the question whether there is something analogue to first-person reference in the case of the Cartesian coordinate system. Insofar as providing coordinates is similar to demonstrative reference, how can we describe reference via the indexical 'I'?[9]

Let us assume that we have a world that does contain nothing but our Cartesian coordinate system and our circle. Where is the location of the coordinate system? I could answer that its Y-axis is formed by all points that have the X-coordinate of 0, and that its X-axis is where all the points are that have 0 as their Y-coordinate. However, the obvious problem with this answer is that it already presupposes that we know the location of the coordinate system.

A second approach would be to determine its location by its relation to the circle. In that case, the location of the coordinate system could be determined as being half the circle's diameter away from the circle. However, such a description would not only be incomplete (as there is an infinite number of

9 Throughout this article, I address only obviously spatiotemporal kinds of demonstrative reference, like when pointing a finger at something and using a demonstrative. There might be other kinds of demonstrative reference (e.g., when I use the expression 'this last thought'). However, this does not invalidate the line of reasoning presented in this article, as it is only dependent on the fact that there *is* spatiotemporal demonstrative reference. It does not presuppose that *all* demonstrative reference is spatiotemporal.

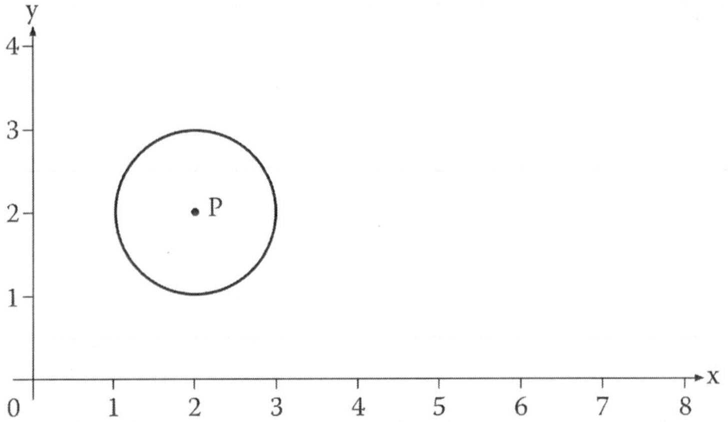

Fig. 4.1 A Cartesian coordinate system

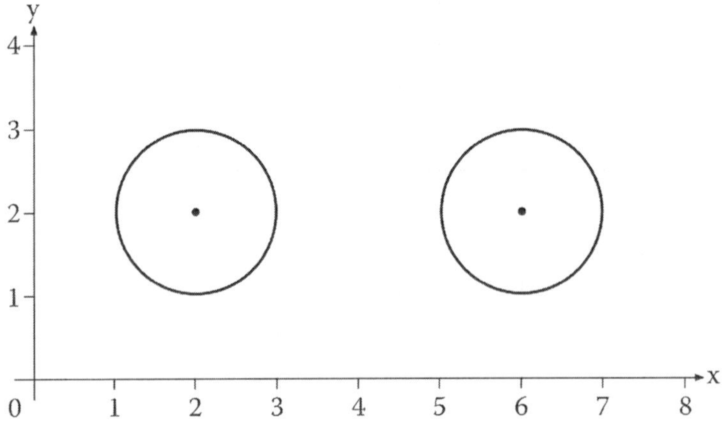

Fig. 4.2 Two circles

points that fall under it, but that are in a different location than any point of coordinate system). Even more problematic becomes such an approach if we introduce a second circle of the same size (see figure 4.2). In this case, we cannot refer to one of the two circles without referring to the Cartesian coordinate system first. For, they are indiscernible apart from their relation to the coordinate system. Hence, we cannot utilize them in order to refer to the coordinate system.

The only way to refer to the coordinate system is by the coordinate system itself as shown above (identifying the X-axis via the Y-axis and vice versa). But this, it seems, has the taint of circularity. However, the problem disappears if we give up on the endeavor of empirically discovering the coordinate system. If we postulate it *a priori*, it makes the entire two-dimensional space accessible. The symmetry is broken and therefore the indiscernibility disappears.

In fact, this is exactly the way first-person reference works in our initial Strawsonian point symmetric universe. We know our location a priori – as it can be expressed in the a priori truth 'I am now here'.[10] Without knowing where I am in terms of places I have visited earlier, I can nevertheless determine the location of any entity in my field of perception by its relation to myself – even if it is the only entity I perceive (like when I am hovering through a black nothingness and encountering there a single solid object). I am not in need of any other entity apart from myself in order to successfully refer to an object within my field of perception. Even in cases of universal symmetry, like in the Strawsonian thought experiment, I locate objects simply by the relation they have to me.

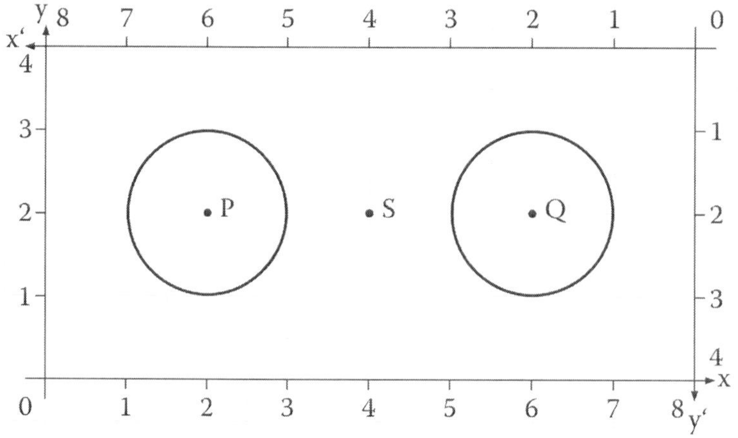

Fig. 4.3 Two point-symmetrical Cartesian coordinate systems

10 Anton Friedrich Koch highlights the a priori nature of this proposition (Koch 1990, p. 37f.). His line of reasoning is inspired by a thought experiment by Elizabeth Anscombe (Anscombe 1975, p. 57), who in contrast tried to argue for the thesis that 'I' does not refer.

A Cartesian coordinate system is similar in this regard. If we introduce complete universal symmetry to the case of our coordinate system by adding a second coordinate system (see figure 4.3), referring to any point is no issue from *within* the framework of one of the two coordinate systems. All that is needed is an a priori postulation of the location of this coordinate system.

Hence, it is our priori self-location that makes it possible to unambiguously refer to all the objects we encounter – even if they have objectively indiscernible counterparts.

But what is the link between personal identity and the fact that we locate ourselves a priori? How does the a priori self-location answer the question *what kind of entity* we are? Without an answer to this question, we still cannot employ the Kantian framework to determine personal identity.

4. What is Located a Priori?

What kind of entity is located by a priori self-location? If we rephrase this question in the analogy of the Cartesian coordinate system, we must ask what entity is a priori postulated by the coordinate system. There are two answers to this question and only one yields implications for the question of personal identity.

The first one claims that a Cartesian coordinate system a priori locates an entity that merely *has* the properties of having or being formed like (but not actually *being*) a coordinate system. According to this approach, a specific spatiotemporal entity is located (like a set of black ink lines on a sheet of paper) that is specifically formed (e.g., like having arrows at some of their ends, letters printed next to them etc.). This a priori located entity *has* necessarily the property that it enables us to provide coordinates.

The second one claims that a Cartesian coordinate system a priori locates *itself as a Cartesian coordinate system*. According to this approach, a means of providing coordinates is located. This a priori located entity *merely has* a

There is, of course, an everyday use of 'I am now here' that is not a priori: For example, we can imagine a situation where someone is waiting for me to arrive with my car at a building where she is. At the moment I arrive, I call her and tell her, 'I am now here'. In this case, 'here' refers to the building and is therefore not a priori. However, we can ignore this everyday use as long as there is also the use that is truely a priori.

certain material realization (like a set of black in lines on a sheet of paper etc.).

Which of the two approaches is the correct one? I believe that only the second approach is viable. As we have seen, in order to refer to an object at the position of the coordinate system (like the black ink lines) we are already dependent on it. What object is in the position of the coordinate system or how it is materially realized is not a priori postulated and therefore it cannot make the access to space possible. Only the coordinate system itself makes reference via coordinates possible.

The same can be said about our spatial consciousness. For demonstrative reference, we need to locate us a priori as expressed in the a priori truth 'I am now here.' We cannot refer demonstratively to an object by the relations it has to an empirically discovered body (e.g., I cannot refer to the chair by the fact that it is next to the table). Because such an empirical discovery is again in need of a relation to an already known location (in this case the location of the table). We need to locate ourselves a priori. But what is it that is located a priori? Is it an entity that merely *has* consciousness of a spatial field of perception that is apt for demonstrative reference (i.e., in short *spatial consciousness*) or *is* it such spatial consciousness itself?

The issue is the same: Reference to an entity that merely *has* spatial consciousness already presupposes spatial consciousness. The expression "the object that makes my spatial consciousness possible" can only refer to a certain position if the spatial consciousness is already located a priori. The location of such an object would not be a priori given itself and therefore it could not make access to space possible. Hence, we *are* spatial consciousness that a priori locates itself, we do not merely *have* it. Like the Cartesian coordinate system that is postulated as a Cartesian coordinate system and not only as an object that has such a system, spatial consciousness is a priori aware of *itself* and not of an entity that merely *has* it. With the indexical 'I', we refer a priori to spatial consciousness.

Thereby, we have found the relevant property for our Kantian framework. The answer to the question what kind of entity we are is *spatial consciousness* (*that locates itself a priori*). What we need to track in space over time to settle the question of transtemporal identity is *spatial consciousness*. But how can we keep track of such an entity? If we want to keep track of a table, we know what properties we need to look for. We can simply use our eyes to keep track of a material object that has a *specific shape* within spacetime. What shape do we look for when keeping track of spatial consciousness?

5. Extension

If spatial consciousness is the crucial concept for determining personal identity, is this not Cartesianism with a spatial twist? In fact, the opposite is the case. To understand the physiological constraints of spatial consciousness, let me go back again to the Cartesian coordinate system.

Thanks to it we can refer to the point P in the center of the circle by the coordinates (2|2). There are certain requirements for providing unambiguous coordinates: The axes need to be different from each other. They cannot be symmetrical. Otherwise, we would not be able to know which axis a coordinate refers to. This asymmetry is achieved by their names X-axis and Y-axis.

In addition, each axis is in need of *extended* subdivisions: the number lines. Without definite extension, it would not be possible to provide coordinates, since an infinite line (like a single point without extension) does not offer any features that can constitute a relation which can be used for successfully providing coordinates. The same is true for the demonstrative reference of spatial consciousness, like when I point my finger to a chair or a table. Without being extended, the reference of the phrase 'this chair' could not be fixed. Without extension, there would be no relation that I could access to refer to an entity. Hence, when I locate myself a priori, I locate myself as an extended entity. Only thanks to my a priori understood extension, I am able to refer demonstratively.

One might raise several objections against my claim that without conceiving myself as extended I could not access a relevant relation to make a demonstrative reference in space.

First, is it not the case that I can refer to an object via other objects, like 'the chair next to this table'? However, referring to a chair by such an expression is in need of fixing the reference of 'this table' first.

A second objection might be the claim that it is possible to refer to an object simply by the limits and properties of my field of perception – like when I use the expression 'the chair in the center of my field of vision'. However, in order to speak of a field of vision it is important that there are objects that you *cannot* see anymore or that you *barely* see at the moment. Hence, the field of vision presupposes already that we are able to refer to certain objects. Only our extension provides us with the means to successfully refer demonstratively to objects. For, if we know of our extension a priori, we can employ the relation between our extension and empirical objects for successful demonstrative reference.

There are two ways to understand this extension requirement. According to the weaker one, self-location simply presupposes extension. According to the stronger one, that what is located in self-location is located *as* extended. What is the difference between those two positions? The first one is only about a (necessary) property. Like each piece of clay (necessarily) has a certain shape, it is no shape – or like each artifact (necessarily) has a maker, but it is not a maker. However, the second understanding goes beyond such a requirement of possession. It claims that we *are* an extended entity and do not only (necessarily) have one. According to the first understanding, it would still be possible that we were similar to Cartesian egos, but necessarily had bodies. In that case, we would not be located in space, but the extension or bodies that we (necessarily) possess would be located in space. The relation to the extended entity that is located in self-location would be a relation of possession, not of identity.

I think that only the second understanding is viable: We are extended entities and do not merely have an extension. In the case of the coordinate system, we need to postulate a priori the extended subdivisions of the number lines. They are not a mere requirement of the coordinate system like for example the color it is drawn in. The number lines *define* the coordinate system.

Hence, I am defined by my extension. In self-location, it is extension that is located a priori. For, otherwise, it would not be possible to refer demonstratively to objects in space. As extension is necessary for demonstrative reference, and as a priori location is necessary for it, that what is located a priori is located as extended. My extension needs to be located a priori and is not merely a requirement like the molecules I am composed of.

With this we arrived at the conclusions outlined in the beginning. As demonstratively referring entities we are (and do not merely have) spatial consciousness that a priori locates itself – and we necessarily locate ourselves as extended in space. Thanks to our extension, we are an entity in spacetime that can be perceived and kept track of.

6. Objections

The line of reasoning presented so far might provoke a series of objections. In the following part, I try to address some of them before I conclude with implications and limits of the position advanced in this article.

a) Extension and the Kantian framework: In the last part, I have argued that we are necessarily extended and claimed that due to our extension we can be kept track of. However, it is also my claim that we are not biological organisms but extended spatial consciousness. We know how to keep track of a biological organism. But how to keep track of extended spatial consciousness?

'Consciousness' is a psychological term. We can know of the psychological states of an entity by its reports – like when a person tells me that she is happy.

But of course, a report is not what we are looking for. We look for a persisting extended entity to keep track of. How can such an entity be a psychological entity?

This objection presupposes that our mental states are solely internal and do not have a spatial side. However, the rich discussion about intersubjectivity teaches us the opposite. Especially, the increasingly prominent approach of direct perception is of relevance for the central thesis of this article (Scheler 1973, Husserl 1963, § 150, 1973a, 1973b, and 1973c, Stein 2008, Wittgenstein 1980, § 170, McDowell pp.379–385, Zahavi 2005, ch. 6 and 2014). This approach claims that we can directly perceive the mental states of other subjects and not only deduce their existence by external indicators. This discussion is beyond the scope of this article, but the upshot is that we do not primarily perceive a specifically shaped object when perceiving a person, but primarily a psychological meaningful entity. Of course, in this regard we are not immune to error. For example, something that seems to be a happy person can turn out to be a doll. But this is also the case for ordinary objects like a table: What seems to be a table can turn out to be a cardboard dummy.

Hence, if the position of direct perception is true, we have all we need to keep track of extended spatial consciousness.[11]

b) Consciousness without spatial perception: The central thesis of this article is that we are extended spatial consciousness (that a priori locates itself). One might think that the spatial requirement can be refuted by a simple modal argument: It is possible that I am (at least momentarily) only conscious of non-spatial issues. In such a case, I do still exist, and I am not spatially conscious. Hence, I am not spatial consciousness.

The question here is whether it is possible to be *only* conscious of non-spatial issues. What reason do we have for such a claim? We might be tempted to accept it because we might imagine a situation where we close our eyes and cannot see anything – and might not even be able to have auditive perception. However, even in such a case there is still spatial perception. We still do have proprioception. There is so much bodily awareness that is spatial, even if we lose the obvious visual and auditive senses.

But even if we granted that all bodily awareness could be lost as well (for which a compelling argument is needed), the objection confuses spatial consciousness with spatial perception. Even with a momentary loss of spatial perception, I can understand myself as located in space. In such a case, I simply would have lost my access to other entities in space, and I would have lost a

11 For my in-depth discussion of the position of direct perception and its applicability to the position advanced in this article cf. Herrmann 2021, §§ 22-25.

definite understanding of my exact extension. Spatial perception would rather be understood as *missing* than as merely *non-existent.*

However, as empirical data of such an extreme fringe case are difficult to obtain, the entire objection does not rest on firm ground to start with.

c) Mislocation: If we locate ourselves a priori, it should not be possible to mislocate ourselves. For, this presupposes that our location is a relation to empirically perceived objects as only such a relation could turn out to be wrong in the end. However, we can dream or hallucinate to be in one place, but in fact we are in another place. Hence, we do not a priori locate ourselves.

This objection does not fully understand what 'a priori self-location' means. The a priori location of spatial consciousness makes it first possible to locate objects to the frame of reference it creates. Hence, it is in fact impossible to locate oneself wrongly a priori. But how can that be? What is the case if I dream to be in Paris when I am in fact in Heidelberg? In this case, I have not mislocated myself, but *I have mislocated Paris*. I locate the Eiffel Tower to be in front of me – which it is not. I do not locate myself in front of the Eiffel Tower. The latter can only happen, when I change my perspective, i.e., if translate my a priori self-location into a second- or third-person perspective. In such a secondary step, I can indeed mislocate myself. But this is a secondary translation of my primary a priori self-location – which as a frame of reference cannot be wrong. It is again similar to the Cartesian coordinate system: If I claim P is at (3|3), but it is in fact in a different place (see image 1). I have not defined the coordinate system to be in the wrong place, but simply provided the wrong coordinates for P.

d) Perception is not demonstrative reference: Throughout this article, I have treated perception like demonstrative reference. One might object that I confused two essentially different phenomena and therefore that my argument might collapse, as soon as it is not possible to infer from questions of perception to issues of reference.

Although demonstrative reference and perception is indeed not one and the same, the differences are not crucial for the aims of this article. All that my line of reasoning is dependent on is that perception is like demonstrative reference insofar as it is *indexical.* If I use a demonstrative reference like 'this' in a sentence, its truth value is context dependent. Is there something similar in perception? Let us consider the case where I see a fox in the woods. In such a perception, the animal occupies a certain percentage of my field of vision – and the same is true of the trees and the relation between the fox and the trees. Now, let us assume that I move closer to the fox. The percentage it occupies in my field of vision and its relations within it have changed. If my perception were not indexical, I would be required to claim that I perceive a change of the size of the fox and that the relation between the fox and the tree has changed. But this is not the case. My representation has changed due to my movement. The fox occupies now different variables in my field of vision. This means that the distinct parts of my field of vision can be filled differently exactly like the expression 'this' in a sentence can be used to refer to different entities depending on the context in which the sentence is uttered.[12]

With these objections out of the way, I want to conclude the article with the implications that the line of reasoning presented here might have (or lack) for other issues in philosophy.

7. Implications (and a Lack Thereof)

a) Consciousness and Self-consciousness: There is a discussion whether all consciousness is self-consciousness or whether the latter is only a special form of consciousness – namely, when consciousness is directed away from everyday objects and directed at ourselves (Zahavi 2005, ch. 1).

The arguments presented above have strong implications for this issue. As we are spatial consciousness *that locates ourselves a priori*, self-consciousness in form of self-location becomes a necessary condition of consciousness. To be more precise, as any spatial reference or perception presupposes the frame of reference that is created by our a priori self-location as an extended entity, each perception of (or a demonstrative reference to) an entity occurs within the frame of reference of a priori self-location. As every time we provide coordinates within the frame of reference of the Cartesian coordinate system requires implicit reference to the coordinate system, the same is true of consciousness and our a priori self-location.

b) Extension, animalism, objects, and processes: The central claim of this article is that we are extended spatial consciousness that a priori locates itself. With that said, it is important to highlight what has *not* been said. This claim is not a mere complicated reformulation of animalism. Claiming that we are no Cartesian Egos, but that we are extended is not tantamount to the claim that we are biological organisms. For, our biological organism can exist without (spatial) consciousness. Hence, we are not a biological organism, we merely have one (and most likely necessarily so). We are not even necessarily bodies (in the sense of material objects). Because there can be spatially extended entities that are not material objects (e.g., also processes, like a storm or when a bar is bended, have a location and are spatially extended). Regarding this question

12 For an in-depth discussion of this issue cf. Herrmann 2021, § 13.

(whether we are material objects or processes), the arguments presented in this article are neutral.[13]

c) *Further essential properties:* The line of reasoning presented here is also neutral regarding our essential properties *beyond* the fact that we are spatial consciousness. By claiming that we are extended spatial consciousness, I do not claim, for example, that we are not essentially agents – as it might turn out that any form of consciousness without agency is impossible. One might also argue that we are rational beings or that we are necessarily temporally conscious and necessarily have memories. In fact, I consider each of these propositions to be true (although I do not consider a specific act, memory, or line of reasoning to be essential). Hence, by claiming that we are spatial consciousness, I do not claim that this is a complete description of what kind of entity a person is. I think that extended spatial consciousness that a priori locates itself comes in a package with a lot of other psychological and physiological traits. But these are beyond the scope of this article.[14]

References

Anscombe, Gertrude Elisabeth Margeret 1975, 'The First Person', in Samuel Guttenplan (ed.) *Mind and Language* (Oxford: Clarendon Press)

Black, Max 1952, 'The Identity of Indiscernibles', in *Mind* 61.242

Baker, Lynne Rudder 1997, 'Why Constitution is not Identity', in *Journal of Philosophy* 44.12

Castañeda, Hector-Neri 2001, '"He": a study in the logic of self-consciousness', in R. Brook and R. DeVidi (eds.) *Self-reference and Self-awareness* (Amsterdam & Philadelphia: John Benjamin Publishing Company)

Geach, Peter Thomas 1973, 'Ontological Relativity and Relative Identity', in Milton K. Munitz (ed.) *Logic and Ontology* (New York: New York University Press:)

Gibbard, Allen 1975, 'Contingent Identity', in *The Journal of Philosophical Logic* 4

Herrmann, Markus 2021, *Das unbestimmte Ich: Selbstbewusstsein, Leiblichkeit und Persistenz* (Paderborn: mentis)

Husserl, Edmund 1963, *Cartesianische Meditationen und Pariser Vorträge*, ed. S. Strasser. 2. ed. (Den Haag: Martinus Nijhoff)

---

13 This issue is given an in-depth discussion in Herrmann 2021, §§ 33–37.

14 Author's Affiliation: Section Translational Medical Ethics, University Hospital Heidelberg, Department of Medical Oncology, National Center for Tumor Diseases (NCT), NCT Heidelberg.

—— 1973a, Zur Phänomenologie der Intersubjektivität, Texte aus dem Nachlass, Erster Teil: 1905–1920, ed. Iso Kern (Den Haag: Martinus Nijhoff)

—— 1973b, Zur Phänomenologie der Intersubjektivität, Texte aus dem Nachlass, Zweiter Teil: 1921–1928, ed. Iso Kern (Den Haag: Martinus Nijhoff)

—— 1973c, Zur Phänomenologie der Intersubjektivität, Texte aus dem Nachlass, Dritter Teil: 1929–1935, ed. Iso Kern (Den Haag: Martinus Nijhoff)

Kant, Immanuel [KrV] 1998, Kritik der reinen Vernunft, ed. Jens Timmermann (Hamburg: Felix Meiner Verlag), trans. Norman Kemp Smith 2003, *Immanuel Kant's critique of pure reason* (London: Palgrave Macmillan)

Koch, Anton 1990, *Subjektivität in Raum und Zeit* (Frankfurt a. Main: Vittorio Klostermann)

—— 2006, *Versuch über Wahrheit und Zeit,* (Paderborn: mentis)

—— 2016, *Hermeneutischer Realismus* (Tübingen: Mohr Siebeck)

Kripke, Saul A. 1980, *Naming and Necessity* (Cambridge: Harvard University Press)

Lewis, David K. 2003, 'Survival and Identity', in Raymond Martin and John Barresi (eds.), *Personal Identity* (Oxford: Blackwell)

Locke, John 1975, *An essay concerning human understanding*, ed. Peter H. Nidditch (Oxford: Clarendon Press)

McDowell, John 1998, *Meaning, Knowledge, and Reality* (Cambridge MA: Harvard University Press)

Olson, Eric T. 1997, *The Human Animal: Personal Identity Without Psychology* (Oxford: Oxford University Press)

Perry, John 2001 'The problem of the essential indexical', in R. Brook and R. DeVidi (eds.) *Self-reference and Self-awareness* (Amsterdam & Philadelphia: John Benjamin Publishing Company)

Scheler, Max 1973, *Wesen und Formen der Sympathie*, ed Manfred S. Frings (Bern and Munich: Francke)

Stein, Edith 2008, *Zum Problem der Einfühlung* (Freiburg: Herder)

Snowdon, Paul 1990, 'Persons, Animals, and Ourselves', in Christopher Gill (ed.), *The Person and the Human Mind: Issues in Ancient and Modern Philosophy* (Oxford: Clarendon Press)

—— 2014, *Persons, Animals, Ourselves* (Oxford: Oxford University Press)

Strawson, Peter Frederick 1959, *Individuals: An Essay in Descriptive Metaphysics* (London: Routledge)

Wittgenstein, Ludwig 1980, *Bemerkungen über die Philosophie der Psychologie / Remarks on the Philsophy of Psychology* (vol. 2), Georg Henrik von Wright and Heikki Nyman (eds.) (Oxford: Basil Blackwell)

Zahavi, Dan 2005, *Subjectivity and Selfhood: Investigating the First-Person Perspective* (Cambridge MA: MIT Press)

—— 2014, *Self and Other* (Oxford: Oxford University Press)

Spatial Cognition and Bodily Objective Presence

Tony Cheng

Abstract

'Bodily presence' refers to the idea that 'one's body is perceived as being one object among others' (de Vignemont 2018, p. 44). This is a kind of bodily self-consciousness. It has two aspects: firstly, one's body is perceived as a *physical* object (bodily physical presence); secondly, one's body is perceived as an object among other objects within an *objective* space (bodily objective presence). On another occasion I have discussed the former (workshop: agency, bodily perception, and the self, Universitat de Barcelona 2022); in this article I shall focus on a version of the latter: Is one *aware of* one's body as an object among other objects within an *objective* space (cf. Cassam 1997)? A Strawsonian thesis has it that certain capacity for spatial cognition requires bodily objective presence, and the major aim here is to provide an argument for this thesis. This argument faces various objections, and here we will deal with three of them, including the missing self problem, the *qua* subject problem, and the problem from Bálint's syndrome. The discussion will then be situated into wider contexts, such as notions of the body in the phenomenological tradition, self-acquaintance in Frege and Russell, the Heidelberg School, and Naturalised Strawsonianism. Towards the end, I will also explain how the ideas here are formulated as transcendental arguments. Crucially, I will borrow the notion of 'Subject-Object' from Merleau-Ponty (1945/2013) and hold that it captures the apt notion of personhood we need in this and various other contexts.

1. State of Play

Spatial cognition is a very important and special capacity in the animal kingdom. Arguably, almost every species of animals can spatially *register* information from the world and their own bodies, otherwise they would not be able to survive. Here we invoke the threefold distinction between registration, perception, and cognition. While perception involves specific kinds of *constancy* that distinguish it from registration (Burge 2010, 2022), cognition involves elements such as *longer-term working memory* that distinguish it from perception (Block 2022). In this article, I will argue that certain capacities for spatial cognition require bodily objective presence. This will be formulated as a

 | DOI:10.30965/9783969752906_006

transcendental argument, and we will provide a partial defence of the viability of transcendental arguments at the end.[1]

Spatial cognition has been a heated topic in developmental psychology. It consists in two sub-capacities:

> Object permanence: When objects are occluded, the subjects perceptually understand or expect that those objects can still persist. (e.g., Piaget 1963)

> Solidity constraint: Two solid objects cannot co-locate at the same time. (e.g., Locke 1690/1998)

From what we know about developmental psychology and animal cognition, we know that human infants below three months and many other animals have two such capacities (e.g., Carey 2010).

The bridges from spatial cognition to bodily presence are varieties of spatial representations. Here we introduce two crucial ones:

> Allocentric spatial representations: They are to be contrasted with *egocentric spatial representations*, which refer to the spatial frames that are specified by locations on one's own body. Allocentric spatial representations are specified by points that do *not* refer to one's own body.

> Primary quality spatial representations: Primary qualities (Locke 1690/1998) include solidity, shapes, and sizes. This kind of representations are about these properties.

Now, we need to introduce two other key notions in the picture. The first is objectivity, understood as *existence unperceived* (Strawson 1959). This is to be contrasted with another notion of objectivity, understood as *the view from nowhere* (Nagel 1986). Although both notions are very important, and might be connected in some ways, what is crucially relevant here is the Strawsonian notion, as bodily objective presence is a feeling of one's body as *being here*, located in an *objective* space (Strawson 1966; Cassam 1997; de Vignemont 2018). The second is physicality, and the notion we need can be traced back to John Locke, specifically his notion of primary qualities.[2] Bodily physical presence

1 For a fuller attempt, see Cheng (in preparation).
2 Christopher Peacocke updates this notion and situates it in the context of intuitive mechanics or physics (1993).

is a feeling of one's body as *being here*, exemplifying varieties of *physical* objecthood.[3]

Now here are some clarifications. Assuming commonsense realism, we know that human bodies *are* objective in the Strawsonian sense, and *exemplify* physical objecthood. The question is: whether a human being in question can *experience* bodily objective presence and bodily physical presence. Moreover, in such bodily experiences, if there is indeed any, whether one can be aware of one's own body, *qua* subject, as an object. In this context, '*qua*' should be understood as 'mode of access' (Longuenesse 2006).

This almost completes the stage setting. Before moving on, I would like to briefly comment on the dialectics, as the above discussions are not very prominent in the contemporary literature, and it might strike some readers as strange and even unnecessary to engage such discussions. First of all, there is the idea that one cannot find oneself in introspection (Hume 1738/2011, B1.4.6). There are also roots from Kant, more specifically Kant's lack of intuition (1787/2007, B135, 155, 408): 'Through the "I", as simple representation, nothing manifold is given [B135]… I am given to myself beyond that which is given in intuition [B155]'. 'This identity of the subject, of which I can become conscious in every representation, does not concern the intuition of it, through which it is given as object [B408]'. Much more recently, there is the idea that one cannot be aware of oneself as an object (Shoemaker 1984). In a different tradition, there is also the idea that awareness of object and that of subject are incompatible (Sartre 1943/2003). These ideas are different from one another, and exactly how to interpret them can be a matter of dispute. However, it seems clear that all of them put pressure on the current line of thought, so they serve as nice backgrounds or foils for what we are going to consider in the following sections.

2. Object Permanence and Objectivity

The major argument we will consider in this article is called 'the Permanence Argument', naming after the phenomenon of object permanence. However, it is embedded in the larger context of 'the Object Cognition Argument', so we will briefly consider it first. It has two premisses and one conclusion:

3 The objectivity and physicality in the relevant sense are key themes in *Spatial Representations* (Eilan, McCarthy, and Brewer 1993).

P1. The possibility of spatial cognition requires bodily presence, i.e., being aware of one's own body as oneself *qua* subject as an object in an objective space.
P2. Some non-linguistic subjects are capable of spatial cognition.

C. These non-linguistic subjects enjoy bodily presence, i.e., being aware of one's own body as oneself *qua* subject as an object in an objective space.

This argument is very hard to defend (Cheng 2021), and it is not today's business of defending it. As promised, we will focus on objectivity, leaving aside physicality for the moment. Now in order to proceed, we need to look into a bit more details of animal cognition and infant cognition, as unlike Cassam (1997), our target of analysis is non-linguistic creatures.

Some animals, such as bats, dolphins, and beluga whales, due to the fact that they rely heavily on echolocation, understand 'occlusion' in a way that is different from animals like us. Therefore, they might have less good understanding of object permanence: for them, information about many objects is available from sounds, which travels differently compared to lights (Mitchell and Hoban 2010). Also, self-awareness in our sense is different from one version that is prominent in cognitive sciences, i.e., recognising oneself in a mirror; the so-called 'mirror test' (Gallup 1970). Many animals have been said to pass the test, including a certain species of ants (Cammaerts and Cammaerts 2015). Human infants in their second year seem to be able to recognise themselves in mirrors (Anderson 1983/1996), though things remain to be controversial.

About infant cognition, Piaget (1954) thought that human infants develop full object permanence only during 18–24 months-old. He pointed out that younger infants, when seeing something they are interested in being hidden, often do not actively try to find them, even with the ability to crawl. He also speculated that object permanence presupposes crossmodal correspondence, which might be in place only after one-year-old. Later empirical studies – including those involve eye trackers (e.g., Diamond 1991) – have shown that Piaget underestimated infants' abilities in this regard. Nowadays the consensus is that below one-year-old they already have good understanding of object permanence. Whether it is innate, several-week-old, or several-month-old, is a matter of dispute (Carey 2010).

Now we are in a position to introduce and consider the Permanence Argument:

SAP1. The possibility of object permanence understanding requires the practical capacity for allocentric spatial representations.

SAP2. The practical capacity for allocentric spatial representations requires awareness of one's own body, *qua* subject, as an object, in an objective world.

SAC. The possibility of object permanence understanding requires awareness of one's own body, *qua* subject, as an object, in an objective world.

'SAP' stands for 'sub-argument premiss,' while 'SAC' stands for 'sub-argument conclusion'. Now why should we accept the two premisses? It is polemically useful to consider why they might be rejected, and how we can go about rescuing them. For SAP1, the possibility of object permanence understanding does require *egocentric* spatial representations, as one needs to represent the spatial relations between the target, the occluder, and one's own body; but why does it also require *allocentric* spatial representations? In response to this, consider the idealist or subjective space thought experiment: imagine a confused creature who somehow misunderstands that the entire space, though huge, is dependent on its mind. Within this idealist or subjective space, object permanence can still happen, but there will not be any idea of *objectivity* available. In order for objectivity to be in place, allocentric spatial representations have to be in place too.

About SAP2, one might think that the capacity for allocentric spatial representations seems to be very abstract; why does it require anything about bodily presence, or more specifically, awareness of one's own body, *qua* subject, as an object, in an objective world? In response to this, consider the contrast between studying maps theoretically and navigating *via* maps practically. For the former, it is true that no awareness of oneself in the relevant sense is involved. But for the latter, since practically navigating in space requires knowing where one is and the spatial relations between other objects and oneself, the kind of bodily presence is needed.

This completes my minimal defence of bodily *objective* presence. In defence of bodily *physical* presence, an argument called 'the Solidity Argument' needs to be introduced, but again for the present purposes, we will focus on the objectivity side of the story. Now we will consider several objections, including the missing self problem, the *qua* subject problem, and the problem from Bálint's syndrome.

3. Objections Considered: The Missing Self, *Qua* Subject, and Bálint's Syndrome

Let's begin with the missing self. There seems to be a gap between the body and the self: even if the above argumentation is roughly correct, it does not show anything about *self*-awareness. At best, it shows something about bodily presence without self-awareness. In response, note that 'body' and 'self' are abstract concepts in our thinking; for those who fall under the scope of the Object Cognition Argument, i.e., non-linguistic animals, there is no such gap in their minds. Note also that this does not concern the mind-body problem: no matter which *metaphysics* we take, the question is about our *epistemological* relations to ourselves.

For the *qua* subject problem, seeing oneself in a mirror can provide a certain kind of bodily presence, but that is a kind of awareness of oneself as an object, which involves *tracking*. How can such awareness be awareness of oneself *qua* subject, which does *not* involve tracking? In response, it is true that for awareness of objects, it *usually* involves tracking, which is in tension with awareness *qua* subject. However, one's own body is such a special object that in normal cases, there is *no* tracking needed. We simply bring our bodies with ourselves. Note that sometimes we do 'track' our bodies in the sense that when we learn new skills, we need to pay attention to specific parts of our bodies, but that is a different meaning of tracking.[4]

Now, what about Bálint's Syndrome? It is a condition consisting in simultanagnosia (the inability to enjoy the visual field as a whole), oculomotor apraxia (the difficulty in fixating one's eyes), and optic ataxia (the inability to reach specific objects with the help from vision). Typically, patients suffered from strokes and have their posterior parietal cortex seriously damaged. As a result, they are unable to localise perceived objects by sights (Robertson 2004). Now why is this a threat to the Permanence Argument? This is because patients with Bálint's Syndrome seem to retain capacities for object permanence, but lost visual allocentric spatial representations. If this is the case, then it seems to threaten SAP1.

This is indeed a difficult problem. One response is to question whether those patients *do* retain capacities for object permanence in the relevant sense. After all, they can only see one simple object at one time. Perhaps they only retain abstract understanding of object permanence.[5]

At this point, it will be helpful to situate the discussions into wider contexts, so that we have better perspectives on what have been gone through.

4 Both in my dissertation *Sense, Space, and Self* (2018) and Cassam's *Self and World* (1997), there are more discussions of these two objections and replies. Here I provide minimal summaries only to focus on the mainline.

5 For more on this, see Cheng (2018).

4. Wider Contexts: The Phenomenologists, the Logicists, the Heidelberg School, and Naturalised Strawsonianism

Continental phenomenologists tend to think hard about issues about the body and self-consciousness. For example, Husserl argues that the *Body* (Leib) is the 'animated flesh of an animal or human being', i.e., a bodily self, while a *mere body* (Körper) is simply 'inanimate physical matter' (1913/1998, p. xiv). The Body presents itself as 'a bearer of sensations' (ibid., p. 168). For Merleau-Ponty, '[t]he body is not one more among external objects' (1945/2013, p. 92); his distinction between phenomenal/lived body and the objective body is close enough for Husserl's distinction for our purposes. Sartre argues that one's body is either 'a thing among other things, or it is that by which things are revealed to me. But it cannot be both at the same time' (1943/2003). And there are more. It is difficult to take issues with them in details, as they are all very systematic philosophers. But I will say something minimal in response for gesturing at general directions for future research.

To begin with, we can readily admit that there is a key distinction between Leib and Körper, or between the phenomenal/lived and the objective body. What is crucial is to insist that the objective body is being aware of *via* the phenomenal or the lived body. And as we just saw, Sartre mentions *time* as a crucial element. It is unclear, though, whether that specific temporal element is at issue. Merleau-Ponty's notion of 'subject-object' (1945/2013) is congenial to the current picture, and it seems to capture the apt notion of personhood we need in this and various other contexts.

The Logicists in the early analytic tradition, notably Frege (1918–9) and Russell (1912/2001), invoke certain notion of 'self-acquaintance' to capture self-awareness. The major motivation for this move is that the kind of self-awareness in question seems *primitive* and non-conceptual. It is unclear, though, whether the present picture needs to involve self-acquaintance in its formulation. The main concern is that acquaintance might imply *incorrigibility*, and this might be too strong for our purposes.

What about the Heidelberg School? The first use of the term 'Heidelberg School' is found in Tugendhat, Ernst, *Selbstbewubtsein und Selbstbestimmung* (Frankfurt am Main: Suhrkamp 1979), 10, 53. Cf. Frank, Manfred, *Die Unhintergehbarkeit von Individualität* (Frankfurt am Main: Suhrkamp 1986), 35. The name reflects the crucial influence of Dieter Henrich's seminar in Heidelberg (Zahavi 2007). The Heidelberg School explicitly denies that the self-consciousness that is present the moment I consciously experience something is to be understood in terms of some kind of *reflection*, or introspection, or higher-order monitoring. Would this be in tension with the current picture?

The picture Zahavi prefers, and the one he attributes to the Heidelberg school, is that the sophisticated kind of self-awareness 'always presupposes a prior unthematic and pre-reflective self-awareness as its condition of possibility' (Zahavi 2007, p. 276). This is actually compatible with the current picture, because it only says that spatial cognition requires a certain rather sophisticated kind of self-awareness; it does not say that such intellectualist self-awareness does *not* presuppose pre-reflective self-awareness.

Now, it is interesting to observe that the inference from exteroceptive, objective experiences to spatial representations and then to self-awareness is a Strawsonian framework (1959, 1966). The naturalised version introduced in this chapter is more similar to his followers, such as Evans (1980, 1982) and Bermúdez (1995). This should then be called 'Naturalised Strawsonianism'. It is also important to note that some concepts from J. J. Gibson's ecological optics also connect exteroceptive experiences and self-specifying information (1979). However, it is often pointed out that self-specifying information is weaker than self-awareness *qua* subject, and that is why we need to onerously consider various arguments and objections above.

5. Transcendental Arguments?

At the beginning of this article, I mentioned the relevance of transcendental arguments. Although here is not the appropriate occasion to dive into all the details concerning such arguments, it seems apt to say something about them before closing.[6]

To begin with, 'transcendental' in Kant roughly means 'prior to experiences and make (objective) experiences possible'. In *Critique of Pure Reason*, Kant's transcendental deductions, transcendental expositions, and transcendental proofs are akin to present-day transcendental arguments. The basic form according to the contemporary literature goes like this:

> *X* is a necessary condition for the possibility of *Y* – where then, given that *Y* is the case, it logically follows that *X* must be the case too (Stern 2011/2019)

One key question arises here is: how many modalities are here? There is the possibility of *Y*, there is a necessary condition, and there is a logical consequence. This will not be resolved on this occasion. In Kant's original context,

6 For more about transcendental arguments and their places in transcendental epistemology, see Cheng (in preparation).

perhaps this transcendental conditional should be understood as synthetic *a priori*. Let's not repeat those familiar dialectics here. The next question is: can we invoke the present-day modal metaphysics to understand the condition? For example, we can perhaps say that one of P's conditions of possibility is Q. This means that in *no* metaphysically possible world, P obtains while Q does *not* obtain. This amounts to the idea that it is *not* metaphysically possible that P obtains while Q does *not* obtain. With several simple transitions, we can say that necessarily, if P then Q. This can be our preliminary understanding of transcendental arguments with the help of contemporary machineries.

With the assumption that transcendental conditionals are metaphysically necessary, we can have some corresponding linguistic and epistemic considerations. For example, are the conditionals analytic or synthetic? Are they *a priori* or *a posteriori*? Putnam (1981) regards transcendental conditionals as synthetic *a priori*. Bermúdez (1995), when discussing O'Shaughnessy (1980, 1989, 1995) on the will and the body, holds that this kind of conditionals should be analytic *a priori*. The consensus seems to be that transcendental conditionals have to be *a priori* (also see e.g., Schwenkler 2012). On another occasion, I will explore the possibility that some transcendental conditionals point to *de re* necessity; they are synthetic necessary *a posteriori* propositions (Cheng, in preparation), but this is hard to defend, and is only a premature working hypothesis.

However, even if the above considerations are roughly correct, can we really invoke 'necessarily, if P then Q' to understand transcendental conditionals? I think the correct verdict is that even if it is not wrong, it cannot be the whole story. To see this, consider: 'Necessarily, if *x* is a dog, then *x* is a mammal'. This is true, but there is nothing transcendental about it! My diagnosis is that for conditionals of this form to be transcendental, formal considerations are insufficient.

So what are the relevant informal considerations? In the literature, philosophers often emphasis that there are specific *purposes* of transcendental arguments. The first purpose is to answer *how possible questions*. In this case, the emphasis is placed on *the antecedent*: how is the antecedent possible? The consequent as a specific kind of necessary condition to make the antecedent possible; Transcendental Deduction is the paradigm example.[7] The second purpose is to respond to *scepticism*. In this case, the emphasis should be placed on *the consequent*: it is supposed to be the target of scepticism, so we need to deduce it from something that is much less controversial; Refutation of Idealism is the paradigm example. The two purposes do not need to be construed as incompatible; e.g., Kant's refutation of idealism (purpose 2) can also be understood

7 For an objection to this understanding, see Cassam (2007), especially ch.2.

as answering the question of how temporal experiences are possible (purpose 1). There is a potential problem for purpose 2, though: if the point is to establish the consequent, then it is unclear why we need "necessarily" to begin with. Perhaps in this case we need to consider things such as essence or constitution. We leave this open on this occasion. In addition to modal metaphysics, modal epistemology such as considerations about conceivability is relevant too (Mizrahi 2017), but we also leave this open for now.

To conclude, in this article I have attempted to argue that the possibility of spatial cognition requires bodily objective presence. This thesis itself is formulated as a transcendental conditional, and both the Object Cognition Argument and the Permanence Argument are formulated as transcendental arguments, so we discussed the nature of such argument. Along the way, key notions such as object permanence, allocentric spatial representations, primary qualities, etc., were introduced. We then considered several objections, such as the missing self problem, the *qua* subject problem, and the problem from Bálint's syndrome. After that, the entire discussion was situated into wider contexts, including considerations from the phenomenologists, the Logicists, the Heidelberg School, and Naturalised Strawsonianism. It is not reasonable to try to settle all the difficult issues concerning these convoluted discussions, but it is the hope that the article has provided a roadmap for further research in this area. Much more relevant materials are contained in my dissertation *Sense, Space, and Self*, but many of them are far from mature, and need to be reworked completely.

References

Anderson, John 1983/1996, *The Architecture of Cognition* (New Jersey: Lawrence Erlbaum Associates)

Bermúdez, José Luis 1995, 'Transcendental Arguments and Psychology: The Example of O'Shaughnessy on Intentional Action', in *Metaphilosophy* 26(4), 379–401

Block, Ned 2022, *The Border between Seeing and Thinking* (Oxford: Oxford University Press)

Burge, Tyler 2010, *Origins of Objectivity* (New York: Oxford University Press)

—— 2022, *Perception: First Form of Mind* (Oxford: Oxford University Press)

Cammaerts, Marie-Claire, & Cammaerts, Roger 2015, 'Are ants (hymenoptera, formicidae) capable of self recognition?' *Journal of Science* 5(7), 521–532

Carey, Susan 2011, *The Origin of Concepts* (Oxford: Oxford University Press)

Cassam, Quassim 1997, *Self and World* (Oxford: Oxford University Press)

Cheng, Tony 2018, *Sense, Space, and Self* (UCL Dissertation)

Cheng, Tony 2021, 'Sensing the Self in World', *Analytic Philosophy* 62(1), 57–60

Cheng, Tony in preparation, *Transcendental Epistemology* (Cambridge: Cambridge University Press)

Diamond, Adele 1991, 'Neuropsychological Insights into the Meaning of Object Concept Development', In S. Carey & R. Gelman (eds.), *The Epigenesis of Mind: Essays on Biology and Cognition* (Hillsdale, NJ: Erlbaum)

de Vignemont, Frédérique 2018, *Mind the Body: An Exploration of Bodily Self-Awareness* (Oxford: Oxford University Press)

Eilan, Naomi, McCarthy, Rosaleen, & Brewer, Bill 1993 eds., *Spatial Representation: Problems in Philosophy and Psychology* (new edition) (New York: Oxford University Press)

Evans, Gareth 1980, 'Things without the Mind', In Z. V. Straaten (ed.), *Philosophical Subjects* (Oxford: Oxford University Press)

—— 1982, *The Varieties of Reference* (New York: Oxford University Press)

Frank, Manfred 1986, *Die Unhintergehbarkeit von Individualität* (Frankfurt am Main: Suhrkamp)

Frege, Gottlob 1918–1919, Der Gedanke. In *Beitrage zur Philosophie des deutschen Idealismus* I, 58–77. Trans. as Thought by Peter Geach and Robert Stoothoff, in Beaney 1997, 325–345.

Gallup, Gordon Jr. 1970, 'Chimpanzees: Self Recognition', *Science* 167(3914), 86–87

Gibson, James Jerome 1979, *The Ecological Approach of Visual Perception* (New Jersey: Lawrence Erlbaum Associates)

Hume, David 1738/2011, *A Treatise of Human Nature: Volume 1: Text* (USA: Oxford University Press) (Original work published 1738).

Husserl, Edmund 1913/1998, *Ideas Pertaining to a Pure Phenomenology and to a Phenomenological Philosophy – First Book: General Introduction to a Pure Phenomenology*, trans. Fred Kersten (Dordrecht: Kluwer Academic Publishers)

Kant, Immanuel 1787/2007, *Critique of Pure Reason*, trans. N. K. Smith, 2nd edition (Basingstoke: Palgrave Macmillan) (Original work published 1781/1787).

Locke, John 1690/1998, *An Essay Concerning Human Understanding* (New York: Oxford University Press) (Original work published 1690).

Longuenesse, Béatrice 2006, 'Self-Consciousness and Consciousness of One's Own Body: Variations on a Kantian Theme', *Philosophical Topics* 34(1/2), 283–309

Merleau-Ponty, Maurice 1945/2013, *Phenomenology of Perception*, trans. Donald Landes (London: Routledge) (Original work published 1945).

Mitchell, Robert. & Hoban, Esmé 2010, 'Does Echolocation Make Understanding Object Permanence Unnecessary? Failure to Find Object Permanence in Dolphins and Beluga Whales. In F. L. Dolins & R. W. Mitchell (eds.), *Spatial Cognition, Spatial Perception: Mapping the Self and Space* (Cambridge: Cambridge University Press)

Mizrahi, Moti 2017, 'Transcendental Arguments, Conceivability, and Global vs. Local Skepticism', *Philosophia* 45(2), 735–749

Nagel, Thomas 1986, *The View from Nowhere* (New York: Oxford University Press)

O'Shaughnessy, Brian 1980, *The Will, Vol. 1* (Cambridge: Cambridge University Press)

—— 1989, 'The sense of touch', *Australasian Journal of Philosophy* 67(1), 37–58

—— 1995, 'Proprioception and the Body Image', in J L. Bermúdez, A. J. Marcel, & N. Eilan (eds.), *The Body and the Self* (Cambridge, MA: MIT Press)

Peacocke, Christopher 1993, Intuitive Mechanics, Psychological Reality and the Idea of a Material Object. In N. Eilan, R. McCarthy, and B. Brewer (eds.), *Spatial Representation: Problems in Philosophy and Psychology* (Oxford: Basil Blackwell)

Piaget, Jean 1954, *The Construction of Reality in the Child* (London: Routledge)

—— (1963). *The Origins of Intelligence* (New York: W. W. Norton & Company, Inc.)

Putnam, Hilary 1981, 'Brains in a Vat', in his *Reason, Truth and History* (Cambridge, UK: Cambridge University Press)

Robertson, Lynn 2004, *Space, Objects, Minds and Brains* (New York: Psychology Press)

Russell, Bertrand 1912/2001, *Problems of Philosophy* (Oxford: Oxford University Press)

Sartre, Jean-Paul 1943/2003, *Being and Nothingness: An Essay on Phenomenological Ontology*, trans. H. E. Barnes (Oxford: Routledge) (Original work published 1943)

Schwenkler, John 2012, 'Does Visual Spatial Awareness Require the Visual Awareness of Space?' *Mind and Language* 27(3), 308–329

Shoemaker, Sydney 1984, 'Personal Identity: A Materialist's Account', in S. Shoemaker and R. Swinburne (eds.), *Personal Identity* (Oxford: Basil Blackwell)

Stern, Robert 2011/2020, 'Transcendental Argument', in E. N. Zalta (ed)., *The Stanford Encyclopedia of Philosophy* < https://plato.stanford.edu/entries/transcendental-arguments/ >

Strawson, Peter 1959, *Individuals: An Essay in Descriptive Metaphysics* (London: Routledge)

—— 1966, *Bounds of Sense: Essay on Kant's Critique of Pure Reason* (London: Methuen & Co Ltd)

Tugendhat, Ernst 1979, *Selbstbewußtsein und Selbstbestimmung* (Frankfurt am Main: Suhrkamp)

Zahavi, Dan 2007, 'The Heidelberg School and the Limits of Reflection', in S. Heinamaa, V. Lahteenmaki, & P. Remes (eds.), *Consciousness: From Perception to Reflection in the History of Philosophy* (Dordrecht, Netherlands: Springer)

The Metaphysics of the Continuity of Consciousness

Amit Anurag

Abstract

In this chapter I propose that consciousness is an enduring process. This claim is revisionist for it challenges the classical notion that consciousness is stream-like; I suggest that rather than stream, consciousness is like a whirlwind or a tornado.

I make a distinction between two problems of continuity of consciousness- the phenomenality of continuity and the metaphysics of continuity. The problem of the phenomenality of continuity of consciousness is how do we experience continuity of consciousness, or how does continuity appear in our experience? The problem of metaphysics of continuity is about how consciousness itself as an entity continues. My chapter is about the latter problem.

So, how does consciousness continue in time? This chapter takes an ontological path to answer this question. If abstract and concrete are the two broadest ontological categories, then consciousness would fall into the category of concrete entities, for it is causally efficacious, and undergoes change. I try to understand how concrete entities continue in time. The paradigmatic example of concrete entities is physical things. I explore two classical theories of persistence – eternalist perdurantism and presentist endurantism. I argue against eternalist perdurantism and the allied ideas of temporal parts and space-time analogy. I show that the argument for temporal parts and that of space-time analogy is circular, therefore, the doctrine of temporal parts should be rejected. I conclude that presentist endurantism is the most appropriate theory of persistence, which is that the present is the only real time, and things persist by being wholly present throughout its persistence. Then I analyse the ontological categories of events, processes, and states, and concluded that events and states are not concrete, for they are causally inefficacious. Processes, on the other hand, are causally efficacious, they undergo change, and they can be interrupted. Therefore, processes belong to the category of concrete. Now we have two ontological categories, which include concrete entities- things and processes. So, consciousness must fall into either of them. I introduce a thought experiment which I call experience in frozen time. If time is frozen, all processes cease to occur; we cannot conceive of any occurrence taking place. But we can conceive of things, albeit immutable. I then suggest that consciousness too is not conceivable in frozen time. If consciousness were a thing, we could have conceived it. But our inability to conceive implies that it is a process. Following my argument, we

 | DOI:10.30965/9783969752906_007

can say that consciousness continues in time as a process by being wholly present at each moment of its occurrence. This can be captured into a slogan that 'consciousness is an enduring process'.

Consciousness is a purely temporal entity; therefore, the if consciousness is stream-like, it must be a purely temporal stream. But a temporal stream has an allusion to spatialized time. As the stream flows, it is not 'wholly present' at any spatial location. I have argued that time is not space-like; therefore, consciousness cannot be stream-like. So, we need to look for a different metaphor that can fit into the temporal ontology. I suggest that the most suitable metaphor is that of a tornado or a whirlwind. A whirlwind is a process, it moves from one place to another, but wherever it goes, it is 'wholly present'. Although the metaphor of whirlwind too is not totally free from spatial connotation, but it is a phenomenon that comes closest to the argument followed in this chapter.

1. Introduction

This chapter investigates the problem of continuity of consciousness. But what is the problem? I draw a distinction between two problems of continuity of consciousness- the phenomenality of continuity, and the metaphysics of continuity. The problem of the phenomenality of continuity of consciousness concerns how we experience continuity of consciousness. From the time you wake up until you sleep, you undergo different experiences, and they all appear in an experiential continuum. William James famously uses the metaphor of stream to describe this experiential continuum:

> Consciousness, then, does not appear to itself chopped up in bits. Such words as 'chain' or 'train' do not describe it fitly as it presents itself in the first instance. It is nothing jointed; it flows. A 'river' or a 'stream' are the metaphors by which it is most naturally described. *In talking of it hereafter, let us call it the stream of thought, of consciousness, or of subjective life.* (James 1983, p. 233)

Phenomenal continuity should not be confused with phenomenal sameness. Once you lock your house and step into the street, there is a change in atmosphere, the silence of the house is replaced by the cacophony of the traffic, there may be a sudden explosion, a change in weather, a flash of light, a happy thought may be replaced by a sad one. However, according to James, these discrete occurrences do not affect the stream of consciousness. Therefore, a change in the content of consciousness does not amount to the discreteness of experience. The stream of subjective life continues uninterrupted.

The metaphysical problem of continuity of consciousness is about how consciousness itself continues in time. Consciousness is a naturally occurring phenomenon (by natural, I do not mean physical, I simply mean that it is part of nature). Therefore, it has a place in nature. So, consciousness, as a naturally occurring phenomenon, also continues in time. The phenomenal continuity (or consciousness of continuity) is not the same as the metaphysical continuity (or continuity of consciousness). This distinction has been captured in the slogan that 'a succession of feelings, in and of itself, is not a feeling of succession' (James 1983, p. 591). Therefore, a separate study in the metaphysics of continuity is required. When we look at the *stream* metaphor, it is not clear whether James uses it exclusively in a phenomenal sense or if the metaphysical continuity is also stream-like.

This chapter primarily deals with the metaphysical problem, that is, 'how does consciousness continue in time?' This question may resemble a question such as 'how birds fly'. If I were to study how birds fly, I would study the mechanism involved with birds' flying, including their anatomy and physiology. The emerging work would be explanatory rather than argumentative. But a similar methodology will not work here, for it is not a matter of observation of the movement of consciousness in time. Therefore, we need a different method to study metaphysical continuity.

This chapter hinges on the ontological categories. First, I argue that the broadest ontological category into which consciousness falls is that of a concrete entity. A concrete entity is something that exists in space and time (or space or time). I argue that concrete entities endure by being wholly present. I analyze the ontological categories of things, events, processes, and states, and I argue that only objects/things and processes are concrete, therefore, if consciousness is concrete, it must be one of the two. I conclude that consciousness is an enduring process, best captured through the metaphor of a whirlwind or a tornado, and not that of a stream, as typically described.

2. Consciousness is Concrete

Everything that is there can be categorised into two broad ontological categories- abstract or concrete. Two of the commonly accepted distinctions between abstract and concrete entities are:

i. Abstract entities have no spatio-temporal location, whereas concrete entities are located in space and time (or either in space or in time).

ii. Abstract entities are absent from the causal order of the world (they are causally inefficacious). Concrete entities play an active role in the causal order of the world (Cowling 2017).

Accepting these distinctions, we must see whether consciousness is concrete or abstract. One of the hallmarks of consciousness is that it is causally efficacious. The change in the world affects my experience and vice-versa. The concreteness of consciousness is largely uncontroversial, as Galen Strawson observes that 'the only sense in which the existence of experience and subjects of experience is mysterious is the sense in which the existence of any concrete reality at all is mysterious' (Strawson 2017, p. 5).

3. Two Ways of Persistence

Since consciousness is concrete, it should continue in time like any other concrete entity. Before we discuss persistence, it would be relevant to talk about time, for every theory of persistence is grounded in its temporal ontology. There are two major theories of time- presentism and eternalism. According to presentism, the present time is ontologically privileged, for it the only real time, and only the present things exist. Eternalism, by contrast, proposes that all times are equally real, and the present is not ontologically privileged. Therefore, both present and non-present things exist. So, if the presentist makes a list of all things that exist, it will include Barack Obama and Donald Trump, but it will not include Abraham Lincoln and Mahatma Gandhi. However, if an eternalist makes such a list, it will include Lincoln and Gandhi as well. It does not mean that all of them exist now, but they do exist at some temporal location.

David Lewis proposes that there are two ways of persistence- endurance and perdurance:

> something *persists* iff, somehow or other, it exists at various times ... Something *perdures* iff it persists by having different temporal parts, or stages, at different times, though no one part of it is wholly present at more than one time; whereas it endures iff it persists by being wholly present at more than one time. (Lewis 1986, p. 202)

Perdurantism argues that concrete things persist by being extended in time- they have temporal parts, just like spatial entities have spatial parts. You can compare a perduring entity with that of a road- a road continues in space by having a spatial extension, and at one spatial location, only a spatial part of the road is present. Likewise, for a perduring entity, at a temporal location, only a temporal part of it is present. Endurantism, on the other hand, argues that concrete things do not continue in time as spatial things continue in space. At a time, it is not an atemporal part of the thing that is present, but a thing is 'wholly present' at each moment of its persistence. You can compare endurantism with a ball being rolled on; as it moves from one point to another, it is wholly present. A perduring entity is never wholly present.

4. Perdurance and the Doctrine of Temporal Parts

The doctrine of temporal part is a radical but problematic idea. I will discuss two problems with the doctrine – (a) it rules out change, and (b) it presupposes spatio-temporal analogy.

4.1 *Change and Temporal Parts*

In this section, I argue that the doctrine of temporal parts excludes the possibility of change in the properties. Any theory of change and persistence faces the challenge of explaining the differences occurring within the object as well as the sameness despite the difference. Any attempt by a theory to explain away either of them leads to the failure of the theory, for it will not capture our intuitive idea of change. A theory of persistence is often attacked on the ground that either it does not explain the change or it does not explain the sameness. We should all agree that 'Although not every change requires the survival of the subject of the change, every change entails a change in something which itself survives the change. Hence every substantial change entails a non-substantial change' (Oderberg 2004, p. 686). If I paint a white cup with red color, the cup survives the change, but if I break the cup and turn it into powder, the cup does not survive the change, but the ceramic which made the cup does survive. Therefore, sameness or identity is inextricably linked with change. Suppose John is happy on Sunday and sad on Monday, there is a change in the mood of John. But if John is happy on Sunday, and Smith is sad on Monday, we cannot say that there is a change in anybody's mood because John and Smith are two entirely distinct entities. We cannot find something which has survived the change.

Change by replacement is not a real change. The idea of change involves the presence of incompatible properties in one and the same object. Hence one may say of the object O that it is P and that it is not P; however, the transience of time saves the proposition from being a contradiction. But, if O is P and S is not P, there is no real change. When a banana changes its color from green to yellow, that is a real change in the banana. But if a magician makes a green banana disappear and, in its place, produces a yellow banana, there is no change, this is the case of replacement.

According to its proponents, a temporal part is neither a conceptual nor an abstract entity; rather it is as much a concrete entity as a spatial part. A spatial part is composed of yet further spatial parts; likewise, a temporal part is made up of yet smaller temporal parts. The idea of change that temporal part theorists suggest is the idea of change by replacement; in other words, they simply explain away change.

4.2 *Spatio-Temporal Analogy*

Ted Sider (2001) presents the most detailed defense of the doctrine of temporal parts. He claims that one of the reasons to accept the doctrine of temporal parts is that time is space-like.

> A common argument in favor of temporal parts is based on the analogy between space and time. We observe an analogy between these dimensions in many respects. All physical objects are represented in our experience as located in both space and time ... The more this analogy holds, the more entitled we are to expect it to hold in new areas. We thereby should expect the part–whole relation to behave with respect to time as it does with respect to space. (Sider 2001, p. 87)

It is not hard to see why the temporal part view needs an analogy between space and time. The temporal part implies temporal extension. An object can have different temporal parts only if it is extended in time. For something to be extended in time, time has to be space-like. But why should one believe that time is space-like?

4.2.1 Taylor's Argument for the Analogy

Temporal part theorists draw the support for the analogy between space and time from Taylor's (1955, 1959) seminal papers in which he argues that space and time are analogous. I argue that using Taylor's argument in support of temporal parts theory is circular.

Taylor says that certain words like place, location, part, distance, length, and presence can be used for both space and time. We refer to spatial place when we use expressions such as 'at home', 'in Mumbai'. We refer to a temporal place in dated expressions, like 25 December 2021. Similarly, distance can be designated spatially, e.g., the distance between Paris and London, and temporally, e.g., the temporal distance between George Washington and Donald Trump. Also, things are present both spatially and temporally. 'The allied notion of being present, incidentally, is in fact commonly used in both senses, as meaning "here" or "now" or both' (Taylor 1955, p. 599).

Taylor considers several objections against the analogy and defends the analogy against them. The most significant objection is that 'An object cannot be in two places at once, though it can occupy two or more times at only one place (Taylor 1955, p. 601). Let us split the conjunction first, for it will be easier to analyze each of the conjuncts separately.

Conjunct 1: 'An object cannot be in two places at once.'

Conjunct 2: 'An object can occupy two or more times at any one place.'

The first possible reply to the objection (although not Taylor's) could be that an object too cannot occupy more than one time at one place. A thoroughgoing presentist will be happy with this reply because for him, there is only one time, the present time, which an object can occupy. But from this similarity, the presentist will not conclude temporal extension or temporal parts. Now coming back to Taylor's reply. He does not deny the second conjunct, he denies the first. The objection presupposes that an object is wholly (spatially) present at a spatial location, and Taylor counters that presupposition. At a place, only a part of the object is present. A bed kept at the middle of the doorway is present in the bedroom as well as in the living room.

So far, so good, but then how does it suggest that space and time are analogous? The underlying assumption with both the conjuncts is that things are wholly (spatially) and wholly (temporally) present. Now the falsity of Conjunct 1 depends upon the falsity of the proposition that things are wholly (spatially) present. But the bed is not wholly (spatially) present in the bedroom. So, the correct way to put Conjunct 1 is as follows (Slowik 2002):

Conjunct 1a: An object cannot wholly (spatially) be in two places at once. Or,

Conjunct 1b: An object can be partly (spatially) be in two places at once.

Now, if you say:

Conjunct 2': An object can (wholly) occupy two or more times at any one place, then space and time cannot be analogous. Therefore, to maintain the analogy, you will have to write:

Conjunct 2a: An object cannot wholly (temporally) occupy two or more times at any one place. Or

Conjunct 2b: An object can partly (temporally) occupy two or more times at one place.

So, all the spatial parts of an object (say a car) exist at one temporal location, but all the temporal parts of an object may not exist at one spatial location (for a car may move from one place to another).

Now let us understand why Taylor's construal of the analogous statements (1b and 2b) is problematic. We should keep in mind that he is not arguing for temporal parts; he is arguing for spatio-temporal analogy. The proposition that there are temporal parts is the premise of his argument that space and time are analogous. The plausibility of temporal parts is questionable, and hence the premise is questionable. But Sider (although he acknowledges this problem) and other advocates of temporal parts use spatio-temporal analogy to support the doctrine of temporal parts. Therefore, the entire temporal parts and the analogy argument is outright circular. The doctrine of temporal parts presupposes that space and time are analogous, and the space-time analogy presupposes the doctrine of temporal parts.

5. Persistence by Enduring

Presentism does not allow temporal extension, for the only real time is the transient present time. Therefore, the only temporal parts can exist is that which exist in presentist time. It is analogous to saying that the only spatial part of the road that exists is the one which exists here. If only a part of the road exists, then the road is not continuous. For a road to be continuous, all its parts need to exist. Likewise, for temporal continuity, all the temporal parts need to exist (or needs to be real). But presentism will not allow all the temporal parts to be real. Therefore, an object cannot perdure in presentist time.

Presentism and endurantism are consistent metaphysics. Trenton Merricks defines endurantism thus: 'For any presently existing object O, O *endures* if and only if O persists and *all* of O's parts *simpliciter* exist at the present time' (Merricks 1999, p. 424).

When we take tense into account, we must grant that the present is distinct from the past and the future. In other words, time is not homogeneous. The very idea of tense implies that there is no temporal parity, and the present is ontologically privileged. Thus, we have the theory of presentism, according to which only present things exist, whereas 'past and future things become nearly-bare particulars, unreal echoes of their ones or future selves' (Zimmerman 2006, p. 400). It is possible to combine presentism with endurantism. If we do so, then we get a coherent theory of persistence. Presentism holds that time is not space-like, and endurantism says things are not extended in time like they are extended in space. Thus, both reject the spatial analogy- presentism about time, endurantism about continuity. Therefore, the presentist endurantism would go like this: only the present things exist, and they are wholly present. But then, it faces a problem- how to account for change. Change requires possession of incompatible properties- being green, being yellow. But an object cannot possess incompatible properties at the same time, as it would be a contradiction. Hence, the incompatible properties must be possessed at different times. But the only time that is there is the present time. Therefore, the first step is to say that the object, say O, exists in the present. And then add that either O did exist, or O will exist.

Following Baron, let us formulate it as follows:

> An object O endures from the past to the present iff O is wholly located in the present and either O was wholly located at some time in the past when that time existed or O will be located at some time in the future when that time comes into existence. (Baron 2018, p. 663)

The only property that O has, is that it has presently. Thus, the banana is green, the banana is yellow, but the banana is not both green and yellow presently. The banana is yellow, and the banana was green. Since, 'is' and 'was', that is, 'present' and 'past' are not ontologically at par, therefore the fact represented by 'the banana is yellow' and 'the banana was green' are also ontologically not at par. Therefore, there is no contradiction. Being green is a way the banana was, not a way the banana is. And the way the banana is, is the way it presently is- that is yellow.

6. Events, Processes, States, and Objects

In sections 6, 7, and 8 I will analyze the ontological categories of events, processes, states, and objects. I will argue that both events and states are changeless and causally inefficacious; therefore, they cannot be concrete. Objects and processes are concrete, but with a distinction.

Donald Davidson has argued that there are events, and they form an independent ontological category. According to Davidson, what makes events ontologically distinct is that they are unrepeatable, concrete, and dated particulars. The reason to consider events to be particular lies in our natural language. He states that

> Our language encourages us in the thought that there are, by supplying not only appropriate singular terms, but the full apparatus of definite and indefinite articles, sortal predicates, counting, quantification, and identity-statements; all the machinery, it seems, of reference. If we take this grammar literally, if we accept these expressions and sentences as having the logical form they appear to have, then we are committed to an ontology of events as unrepeatable particulars ("concrete individuals"). (Davidson 1970, p. 25)

Events behave as particulars. Think of an event such as a *battle*. We can ascribe predicate to it (a *fierce* battle), it can be counted (*three* battles), events can also be quantified over (*all* battles are bloody, *some* battles are justified), and so on. Davidson uses the following example to show the particularity of events:

> the conditions under which (1) 'Sebastian strolled through the streets of Bologna at 2 A.M.' is said to be true must make clear why it entails (2) 'Sebastian strolled through the streets of Bologna.'If we analyze (1) as 'There exists an x such that Sebastian strolled x, x took place in the streets of Bologna, and x was going on at 2 A.M.' then the entailment is explained as logically parallel with (many cases of) adjectival modification; but this requires events as particulars. (Davidson 1970, p. 30)

In the above example, when Sebastian strolled through the streets of Bologna, an event occurred. This event is different from the event where Michael strolled through the streets of Bologna or Sebastian strolled through the streets of Paris. So, an event can be individuated like other particulars. These events are different because they occurred at different places and times and involved different people.

Although Davidson uses the term 'events' for all kind of occurrences, occurrences can be classified into events and processes; the basis of the classification, however, can differ. Philosophers, especially till the first half of the 20th century, did not explicitly distinguish between events and processes, and these terms had often been used interchangeably. But in the last fifty years, a section of philosophers has started to consider them as separate ontological categories.

In his example, Davidson uses *x* for both 'x took place' and 'x was going on' as though they are interchangeable, but linguistically, they differ in aspect. Aspects 'are different ways of viewing the internal temporal constituency' (Comrie 1998, p. 3) of an occurrence. The perfective aspect is about what has happened/will happen, that is, a completed occurrence. It looks at the occurrence from outside and in its totality. The progressive aspect is about what is/was/will be happening, that is, an ongoing occurrence. It looks at the occurrence from within, and since what is going on is not yet complete, it cannot be seen in its totality. Aspects are different from tenses for tenses (linguistically) describe the objects and occurrences with respect to the present. Aspects can be past, present, or future.

In Davidson's example, 'Sebastian strolled through the streets of Bologna' is a perfective occurrence whereas 'Sebastian strolling through the streets of Bologna' is a progressive occurrence.

'X took place' has perfective aspect, whereas 'x was going on' has progressive aspect.

Although aspect is a linguistic notion, aspectual difference has significant metaphysical implications. Therefore, the *x* in 'x took place' and that in 'x was going on' would be metaphysically different. Rowland Stout (1997, 2016) makes it the basis for distinction between events and processes.

7. The Metaphysics of Events and Processes

Changes take place in time. Some properties are atemporal and they do not change with time- such as a triangle having three sides. Do occurrents also change? Rowland Stout argues that process is the class of occurrents that change, and in this sense, they resemble concrete things. Events, on the other hand, do not change, and they have properties atemporally.

Think of an ongoing football game. Twenty minutes into the game, and no goal is scored. The commentator, describing the game, says- 'the game is slow and dull'. A few minutes later, both the teams score a goal each and now the commentator says- 'the game has become fast and exciting'. Something has changed from 'slow and dull' to 'fast and exciting', what is it? It is an ongoing football game. We can also say that it is something that is *happening*. Whatever is happening here can become 'dull', 'exciting', 'nasty', or 'bloody'. So, anything that is happening can undergo change. Once the game is over, the commentator says, 'the game was sensational'. But this time, he is not referring to the ongoing game; it is not something that is *happening*, but something that has *happened*. The game referred to earlier was an ongoing occurrence, and the game referred to later is a completed occurrence. Can what has happened change its property? It should be uncontroversial to say that what has happened cannot change its property. If the completed occurrence was 'sensational', it will always be so, whereas if the ongoing occurrence is/was dull, it may not always remain so. Of course, it is possible that the entire game may not be sensational, we can talk about 'stages' of the game. If the game was dull in the beginning, it will always be so; the property that the game was dull in the beginning will never change. Thus, that 'stage' of the game has the property of dullness timelessly. So, we can say that some occurrences change, and some do not.

Stout uses the above distinction between occurrences for his formulation of the difference between events and processes. He proposes that a process is an ongoing occurrence; an event is a completed occurrence:

'When something is/was/will be/etc. happening, let me call what is/was/will be happening a *process*. When something happened/will happen/etc, let me call what happened/will happen an event'. (Stout 1997, p.19)

As we can see, processes are occurrences with progressive aspect and events have perfective aspect. But perfective occurrences are not identical or identifiable with their progressive correlates. Therefore, what is happening is not identical to what has happened. Why should we distinguish what is happening from what has happened? Because they are two different things and have different incompatible properties. Their stark dissimilarities make them ontologically different.

Another difference, according to Stout, between events and processes is that what is happening (a process) can be interrupted, but what has happened (an event) cannot be interrupted. Suppose a banana has been decaying, but not for a very long time; maybe it has just begun to decay. I put the banana in the refrigerator such that it is no longer decaying. Thus, the process of decaying has been halted. The banana has not decayed. This act is not going to affect the identity of the process before it was interfered with. But the event depends upon or is affected by, whether the banana is kept in the refrigerator. So, the process and the event cannot be literally identical.

We can talk of events in terms of parts or stages. These parts or stages are completed occurrences. Since the part which constitutes events are occurrences that are completed and no longer happening, they cannot change. Events are changeless entities. Thus, if an event part of a protest is peaceful, it will always remain so. Therefore, events have their properties atemporally. An ongoing football match has different possible outcomes, so can an ongoing protest. This makes processes 'modally robust' (Steward 2013).

Processes are real and concrete, for we can see them (at least some of them), interact and engage with them, and they affect us. Only the things that are going on can affect us; things that have happened cannot affect us. A finished brutal war does not cause damage to the world the way an ongoing war does. Also, you can stop an ongoing war, but you cannot stop a finished war. You can stop a war that is happening, but you cannot stop the war that has happened. Also, the outcome of an ongoing war can change, but the outcome of a finished war cannot change.

There cannot be an identity relation between events and processes. The protest that has happened is not the same as the protest that is happening and vice-versa. This may not be intuitively appealing as we tend to believe that what is happening is the same as what has happened. But events and processes are two distinct ontological categories. An ongoing protest can become violent from being peaceful until the police come and manage the violence, and the protest becomes peaceful again.

When asked 'What is there on the table?' you can answer 'There is a cup on the table'; likewise, when it is asked 'What is happening on the street?', you can reply 'A protest is happening on the street'. You can refer to a process, in the same manner you can refer to an object. We have seen in the earlier section that concrete objects do not have a temporal extension or temporal parts, they are 'wholly present' throughout their existence, and they persist by enduring rather than perduring. Events are not affected by interruptions. Events have their properties atemporally. Therefore, events are not causally efficacious. Nothing can affect events, and nothing can be affected by events. Stout says:

> Events and structures of stages have temporal parts- they are *extended* in time. But being extended in time precludes something from *persisting* in time. Processes persist in time. Therefore, processes are not identical with events or structures of stages. (Stout 1997 p. 23, emphasis added)

Since events have all their properties atemporally, they cannot be temporal. Therefore, events are not concrete entities. When we say events have temporal parts, they are not concrete and real as spatial parts. We mean that we can conceptualize being spread out in time with different temporal parts bearing different properties. But such a conceptual entity does not have a corresponding entity in the real temporal world. Stout says events are atemporal because they are temporally extended.

> Things that have their properties atemporally may have their presence in time in just the same way they have presence in space- namely by being extended or located in a region ... But things that have their properties at a time ... do not have a presence in time in the same way they have a presence in space. (Stout 2016, p. 48).

Stout's argument can be formulated as follows:
(1) If something is temporal, then it is not extended in time.
(2) Events are extended in time.
(3) Therefore, events are not temporal.
The validity of this *modus tollens* presupposes the truth of (2). But if we grant temporal extension to events in reality, then it is difficult to understand how it be devoid of temporal properties. Therefore, temporal extension of events cannot be real. Then what else is it? I suggest the temporal extension is merely linguistic. It is just a linguistic manner to refer to an occurrence. But if the temporal extension of events is linguistic, then the atemporality of events will be linguistic too. My suggestion is that we should understand the atemporality of events not in the sense we understand the atemporality of universals or numbers for we can still make temporal references to events which we cannot about universals. Remember Davidson's notion that events are dated particulars. We can ask 'When was the wedding?' but we cannot ask 'When was red?' Events are not concrete entities, they are atemporal, but not eternal in the sense numbers or universals are. Events are not modally necessary; for example, the occurrence of the Second World War is contingent, it may not have happened. I think events can be compared with fictional entities. Fictional entities are abstract too, but they are not like universals. That is why many philosophers

refer to them as 'abstract artefacts' (van Inwagen, 1977; Thomasson, 1999). We can make dated references to fictional entities (e.g., Sherlock Holmes met Watson on Thursday morning), but these entities exist nowhere in space and time. However, I am not claiming that events are fictional entities. Events are not artefacts, but they are contingent abstract particulars.

7.1 *Objects and Processes*

Ordinary physical objects are paradigmatically concrete. Therefore, it is unnecessary to argue for its concreteness. However, there is a key difference between them and processes. Objects are static whereas processes are necessarily dynamic. Hence, processes are more intimately related with time than objects. Objects are located in space, instantiate certain properties- both intrinsic and relational, and have distinct criteria of identity. However, none of them necessarily require time. But that does not affect the concreteness of objects. The key difference between objects and processes are that the former is essentially spatial whereas the latter is temporal.

8. The Metaphysics of States

The metaphysical sense of 'state' is not very clear despite the widespread use of the term. Ordinarily, 'state' means the way something is. *Oxford English Dictionary* defines it as 'the condition of someone or something'. When philosophers use 'state', they assume that the readers already know what it means. van Inwagen has expressed his frustration with the ontological status of 'states'.

> Philosophers of mind like to talk about "states" – mental states, physical states, what-have-you states. And when you ask a philosopher of mind what a "state" is, the reply is generally either a blank stare or something along the lines of, "Well, *you* know – *states*. Please, none of your metaphysician's ontological quibbling. We philosophers of mind know what we mean when we talk about mental states and physical states, and if you don't, that's *your* problem." I insist on ontological quibbling, however. I insist on asking whether a state is an *attribute* (or a *property, quality, characteristic,* or *feature*). These are abstract objects, things that exist in all possible worlds and which are without causal powers. And the answer to this question I insist on asking (when any answer is given) is usually something like, "Well of course that's not what states are. A person's mental states exist only when he or she is *in* them, and they're constantly causing and being caused by other states." And then I have to ask, "But what is there for a state to *be* but a property? Aunt Milly's mental and physical states aren't *substances*, are they? – that is, things that belong to the same ontological category as Aunt Milly herself?" It is rare for the conversation to get as far as this, but if it does, I'm told (I paraphrase), "Well, they're neither substances nor attributes, they're

> *states*. Don't expect the things we talk about in the philosophy of mind to fit into the neat a priori categories you metaphysicians dream up." And my rejoinder is, "I don't see any reason to believe that there are any things with the combination of properties you assign to 'states'. It looks to me as if the very idea of a thing that has those properties makes no sense. All the stuff you say about or in terms of 'states' looks to me as if it's *not even wrong*. (van Inwagen 2014, p. 21–22)

State, in its ordinary sense, is 'a stylistic variant on ordinary predication' (Robinson 1990 p. 33), and since a predicate or a property cannot be concrete, a state cannot be concrete. In this section, I will argue that states cannot be concrete for they are changeless, they are not causally efficacious, and they do not have criteria of identity.

8.1 *States Do Not Change*

Change, as we understand it, involves continuity of identity; something survives the change. When we say the banana has changed from green to yellow (or the banana has changed from the green state to the yellow state), there has been a change in the exemplification of state, not in the state itself. There is no numerical continuity of a token state. But what if we say that 'The yellowness of the banana has changed from light to dark', has not the state endured the change? Actually not. Here we are not talking about *yellowness* but the *yellowness of banana*. *Yellowness* is a state; *yellowness of banana* is a trope. Tropes are particularised properties. The existence of tropes is metaphysically controversial, and I am not arguing either in their favour or against as it will steer our discussion into a different direction. But tropes are not states. Two objects can share the same state, but they cannot share the same trope.

8.2 *States Are Causally Inefficacious*

In this section, I will follow the argument advanced by Skow (2018) to show that states are neither causes nor effects. Skow makes a distinction between causation and background condition. The distinction can be understood with the following example (originally discussed in Mackie 1980). You light a matchstick in a room by striking it. So, it is the striking that caused the matchstick to light. But there is the presence of oxygen in the room, and we know that oxygen is required for something to light. So, did the presence of oxygen in the room also cause the matchstick to light? Striking of matchstick is an occurrence, whereas the presence of oxygen in the room is a state. If the latter caused the matchstick to light, then we cannot say that states are causally inefficacious. Skow says that the presence of oxygen is a background condition. A background condition is a state which is neither a cause nor an effect for the following reason:

> The relation that a cause bears to one of its effects is different from the relation a background condition bears to that effect. *Cause* is binary, but *background condition* is ternary: a background condition is not a background condition to an effect alone, it is a background condition to *a cause's causing that effect.* The presence of oxygen is a background condition to the striking's causing the lighting, not to the lighting in isolation. (Skow 2018, p. 25–26)

A background condition cannot be equated with causation since causation is transitive and binary. If B is a background condition to E1 and also a cause to E1, and E1 further causes E2, then by the rule of transitivity, B is also a background condition to E2. But background conditions are not transitive. If I light a matchstick by striking and the lighting of the matchstick terrifies a child, then we cannot say that the presence of oxygen is the background condition for the child to become terrified.

8.3 *States Do Not Have Criteria of Identity*

I have maintained in this chapter that consciousness is a concrete entity. Therefore, if consciousness is a state, as it is widely held, then states in themselves must be concrete entities. But what is an entity? Quine answers that an entity must have an identity criterion:

'We have an acceptable notion of class, or physical object, or attribute, or any other sort of object, only insofar as we have an acceptable principle of individuation for that sort of object. *There is no entity without identity.*' (Quine 1981, p. 102, emphasis added)

The slogan 'no entity without identity' is ontologically liberal in one sense for it does not rely on concrete existence and restrictive in another sense for it eliminates the possibility of entities with indeterminate identity conditions. At the same time, this dictum is compelling, for it is necessary for unity and multiplicity of things. You can count something as one or many only when you have criteria of identity; as Lowe notes, 'There can only be many if each of the many is a one that is identical only with itself and distinct from each of the rest' (Lowe 2006, p. 198). Barack Obama and Donald Trump are entities for they have definite identities, and they can be individuated. Likewise, Harry Potter and Robinson Crusoe are entities. On Quine's formulation of entities, it does not matter whether they are actually located in space or time or not; what matters is a determinate (or determinable) identity criteria or principle.

An event is an entity. If Sebastian has walked on the streets of Bologna seven times a week, there are seven token instances of an event. Processes too are entities as they too have determinable identity criteria. For an ongoing protest, you can ask, 'is it the same protest that was going on yesterday?' For an object too it is perfectly legitimate to ask, 'is it the same table in the room that was there yesterday?' But the state does not have a determinable principle of identity for we cannot ask if x is the same state as y. It does not make sense to ask, 'is it the same redness as yesterday?' This is so because 'redness' provides no criteria of identity.

Peter Geach (Geach 1962/1980), referring to Frege, says that the problem with counting 'red things' is not that there are innumerable red things but that it is not possible to know whether you have already counted one 'because "the same red thing" supplies no criteria of identity' (Geach 1962/1980, p. 63)

Geach says that countability is the sufficient condition for the identity, for you cannot count something if you do not know whether you have counted it before. However, this does not preclude stuff that is mass quantified such as gold or water from having identity. We do not ask 'how many water?' but we can certainly ask 'is the water in the glass the same water as that in the bottle?' Therefore, countability is a sufficient condition for identity but not necessary.

> The trouble about counting the red things in a room is not that you cannot make an end of counting them, but that you cannot make a beginning; you never know whether you have counted one already, because "the same red thing" supplies no criteria of identity. (Geach, 1962/1980, p.63)

Geach makes a distinction between substantival and adjectival terms. A substantival term has a determinate criterion of identity, whereas the adjectival term does not. A substantival term can be both count quantified and mass quantified. Thus, countability is not necessary for identity. Dummett (1973), elaborating on Geach's distinction between substantival and adjectival terms, states that the former has criteria of identity whereas the latter has criteria of application. So, we can apply 'redness' to certain objects but we cannot use 'the same red' locution. Redness is *exemplified* by the objects (say, balls), whereas objects themselves are *instantiated* (Lowe 1999, p. 78–79). A token ball is an instantiation of the type ball, and there can be multiple instantiations of the type ball (although a token itself has no instantiation). We can count how many token instantiations of type ball are in the room. Thus, every token instantiation has a determinate identity criterion. But redness has no token instantiation because 'states are universals that have no principles of identity' (Marcus 2009, p. 223).

9. Consciousness as a Process

When a philosopher singles out a sensation or thought for an analysis of mind, it does not reveal the complete picture of the mind. As Charles Travis notes, although in a slightly different context, that experience is a 'far from innocent count noun' (2004, p. 57). We would agree that whatever happens in the mental domain is much more complex than a single sensation or a single thought. The sight of cake evokes certain childhood memories, generates a desire to eat it, also an occurrence of a belief that it is not healthy for me. All this (and many other sensations and thoughts- like the smell of cake/bakery, the background noise, the dietary advice of my physician, etc.) happen almost simultaneously and non-discretely. How it happens is a different question, and it constitutes the problem of the unity of consciousness, but what is important here is that consciousness is a complex occurrence. Thus, we can say that 'perceptions, thoughts, emotions, images, etc. They are all members of the one tribe. And they continue in an unbroken 'stream' as long as consciousness endures ...'(O'Shaughnessy 2000, p. 36). Therefore, consciousness should be looked at in its entirety for any big picture study.

In this section, I am going to present three thought experiments to show that consciousness is necessarily a process. Processes are more intimately temporal than any other ontological category. Not only processes cannot be atemporal, but they cannot occur in a temporally frozen world. Processes necessarily presuppose time (or flow of time) to happen or go on. If time freezes, no processes can occur, but a thing can exist. This thought experiment is an attempt to show that if consciousness were a thing or a state, we could conceive it in a temporally frozen world. The reason we cannot conceive such is because consciousness is necessarily a concrete occurrence, a process.

In the first scenario, suppose God decides to freeze the time; thus, all temporal properties like movement, qualitative change etc. are ceased. Flying birds are hung in the sky, rivers cease to flow, a green banana does not turn yellow, and so on. You can conceive such a frozen world populated with (changeless) things, such as birds and trees. You can also conceive obtaining of certain states, such as the presence of oxygen in the room and rock being solid. What you cannot conceive in such a world is the occurrence of processes. If consciousness is a substance or thing or a state, we should be able to conceive existence or obtaining of experience in such a world. Suppose Sam is bald, being bald is a state, and we can conceive Sam to be bald in the temporally frozen world. But we cannot conceive his heart to be beating and blood running through his veins. Now, can we conceive Sam to be experiencing pain or making calculations (thingly or stately) in such a world? Most certainly not. Now one can argue that the reason why we cannot conceive experience or thought in a temporally frozen world is because such a world ceases all neuronal activities, like all cardiovascular ones. But here, the issue is metaphysical rather than nomological. Think of the possibility of consciousness to be a purely immaterial, non-relational thing, which does not supervene on any neuronal activity (or any kind of activity whatsoever). Such a thing-consciousness should be conceivable in a frozen world, but again we cannot conceive a happiness-thing or pain-thing in such a world.

Lastly, one can say that consciousness is not a thing, rather a modification of a mental thing. A crumpled sheet of paper is a modification of the sheet of paper. We can, again, conceive the crumpled sheet of paper in the frozen time, manifesting the modification. If the feeling of happiness is the modification of the mental thing, it too should be conceivable. It can be argued that the examples I am presenting are not that of dynamic modifications or dynamic states. A heart that beats is in the dynamic state- or beating state. Likewise, a thinking thing is in a dynamic (or active or occurrent) state, as and when consciousness occurs. But can a state be dynamic? Soteriou (2013) has proposed a hybrid category of occurrent states. But occurrent state is a category mistake. Occurrents occur whereas states obtain. They have different modes of being. And as we have seen earlier, occurrents (processes) are concrete and states are not, so there cannot be a hybrid category of abstract and concrete. The beating of the heart is an occurrence of a process, and the process continues as long as there is beating of the heart. Likewise, the so-called dynamic modification of the thinking thing will be nothing but an instance of a process.

In the second scenario, let us suppose that God decides to freeze the time but makes an exception for consciousness. So, for consciousness, the 'inner clock' ticks as usual. Once again, nothing changes, moves, or happens in the external world. But since consciousness has been kept out of the frozen world, can we conceive there being experience? Yes, we can. Although the external world is frozen, consciousness continues to occur. However, the content of the experience will not be a dynamic representation of the external world. One can still feel anxiety, happiness, can recollect a past experience, and so on.

The third scenario is the reverse of the second. Time is frozen, but only for mental life. The birds fly in the sky as usual; leaves fall from the tree. But we cannot conceive a subject undergoing any experience. A state (e.g., presence of oxygen in the room) can obtain even in a temporally frozen world. If consciousness is a state, Sam is in a state of happiness, the state will obtain in freezing. Once again, I want to emphasize that I am not arguing that consciousness is processive because neuronal activity is processive (or processive consciousness is identical to some neuronal process). Even in a possible world where consciousness does not have a neuronal basis, this thought experiment will hold.

9.1 *O'Shaughnessy on Processive Consciousness*

O'Shaughnessy argues that consciousness is necessarily processive and never a state, and our experience is always in flux. He states that within the realm of experience, 'whatever endures necessarily does so processively (O'Shaughnessy 2000, p. 44). If experience is in continuous flux, what is changing? O'Shaughnessy answers

> even when experience is not changing in type or content, it still changes in another respect: it is constantly *renewed*, a new sector of itself is there and then *taking place* ... each momentary new element of any given experience is a further happening or *occurrence*. (O'Shaughnessy 2000, p. 42)

First, the flux he is talking about is not phenomenal (or phenomenal content) but metaphysical. If the process is metaphysical, how can we know it? We cannot have an experience of such a process, rather any knowledge of it can be only a priori.

All experiences are necessarily processive, but all processive mental occurrences are not necessarily experiential. Mental phenomena such as forgetting are non-experiential and yet processive. Therefore, certain mental processes may go on even when there is no experience, for example, a mental process of deep, dreamless sleep or being comatose.

10. Conclusion

Coming back to our question: 'how does consciousness continue in time?' How can we answer it? Following my argument in this chapter, we can say that consciousness continues in time as a process by being wholly present at each moment of its occurrence. This answer can be captured into a slogan that 'consciousness is an enduring process'.

Finally, I return to the James' metaphor of stream of consciousness. Consciousness is a purely temporal entity; therefore, the stream of consciousness must be a purely temporal stream. But a temporal stream alludes to spatialized time. As the stream flows, it is not 'wholly present' at any spatial location. As I have argued that time is not space-like; therefore, consciousness cannot be stream-like. So, we need to look for a different metaphor that can fit into the temporal ontology followed in this chapter. I suggest that the most suitable metaphor for the continuity of consciousness is that of a tornado or a whirlwind. A whirlwind is a process, it moves from one place to another, but wherever it goes, it is 'wholly present'. Although the metaphor of whirlwind too is not completely free from spatial connotation, but it is a phenomenon that comes closest to the argument followed in this chapter.

Acknowledgements

I would like to thank Elena Popa for her extensive comments on an earlier draft of this chapter. I would also like to thank C. A.Tomy and Rognvaldur Ingthorsson for their comments on my Ph.D. thesis, from which this chapter is drawn.

References

Baron, Sam 2019, 'How to endure presentism', *Inquiry* 62:6.

Comrie, Bernard 1998, *Aspect: An introduction to the study of verbal aspect and related problems* (Cambridge University Press).

Cowling, Sam., 2017, *Abstract entities* (Routledge, Taylor & Francis Group).

Davidson, Donald 1970, 'Events and particulars', *Noûs* 4:1.

Geach, Peter 1980, *Reference and generality: An examination of some medieval and modern theories* (Cornell University Press).

James, William 1983, *The principles of psychology* (Harvard University Press).

Lewis, David 1986, *On the plurality of worlds* (Blackwell Publishers).

Lowe, E. Jonathan 2006, *The four-category ontology: A metaphysical foundation for natural science* (Oxford University Press).

Mackie, J. L. 1980, *The cement of the universe: A study of causation* (Clarendon Press).

Merricks, Trenton 1999, 'Persistence, parts, and presentism', *Noûs* 33(3).

Oderberg, David 2004, 'Temporal parts and the possibility of change', *Philosophy and Phenomenological Research* 69:3.

O'Shaughnessy, Brian 2000, *Consciousness and the world* (Oxford University Press).

Quine, Willard. 1981, *Theories and things* (Harvard University Press).

Robinson, William 1990, 'States and beliefs' *Mind* 99:393.

Sider, Theodore 2001, *Four-dimensionalism: An ontology of persistence and time* (Oxford University Press).

Skow, Bradford 2018, *Causation, explanation, and the metaphysics of aspect* (Oxford University Press).

Slowik, Edward 2002, 'Spatiotemporal analogies: Are space and time similar?', *Southern Journal of Philosophy* 40:1

Soteriou, Matthew 2013, *The mind's construction: The ontology of mind and mental action*, (Oxford University Press).

Stout, Rowland 1997, 'Processes' *Philosophy* 72:279.

Stout, Rowland 2016, 'The category of occurrent continuants', *Mind* 125:497.

Strawson, Galen 2017, *The subject of experience* (Oxford University Press).

Taylor, Richard 1955, 'Spatial and temporal analogies and the concept of identity', *Journal of Philosophy* 52:22.

Taylor, Richard 1959, 'Moving about in time', *The Philosophical Quarterly* 9:37.

Thomasson, Amie 1999, *Fiction and metaphysics* (Cambridge University Press).

Travis, Charles 2004, 'The silence of the senses', *Mind* 113:449.

van Inwagen, Peter 1977, 'Creatures of fiction', *American Philosophical Quarterly* 14:4.

van Inwagen, Peter 2014, *Existence: Essays in ontology* (Cambridge University Press).

Zimmerman, Dean. 2006, 'Temporary intrinsics and presentism' in Haslanger S., Kurtz R. (Eds.), *Persistence: Contemporary readings*, 393–424 (Bradford Books/MIT Press).

III

Personal Identity and Normativity

A Narrative Pattern-Theory of the Self

Muriel Leuenberger

Abstract

Building on the account of a pattern-theory of self introduced by Shaun Gallagher, this article investigates the unique role of the narrative dimension of the self within the self-pattern. According to a pattern-theory, the self is constituted by a cluster of dimensions that interact with each other. A particular variation of this pattern constitutes a self. This article advances the argument that for selves who narrate, the narrative dimension of the self takes a special role that cuts across the other dimensions. First, the pattern-theory of self is introduced and a conceptual and ethical argument for employing a pattern-theory is developed. Second, the distinct role of the narrative dimension of the self is analysed. Through the narrative dimension of the self, we engage in self-definition, integrate and connect the other dimensions of the self, make them intelligible, and ascribe personal meaning to them. And third, the narrator type of self is characterized. Organizing one's experiences through a self-narrative changes the self. Narrators constitute a unified self, they can actively plan and lead a life and engage in forensic practices, and they integrate the subjective and objective nature of the self.

1. Introduction

Philosophy offers a broad range of suggestions on how best to explain and define the self – from the self as a moral agent, to a self as an experiential subject, a physical individual, a mental entity, or a social construct. One of the more recent additions to the debate is the pattern-theory of self (PTS). Inspired by pattern-theories of emotions (Izard and Ackerman 2002; Izard 2013; Mendonça 2012; Newen, Welpinghus and Juckel 2015), Shaun Gallagher (Gallagher 2013; Gallagher and Daly 2018) introduces the pattern-theory of self[1] as an interdisciplinary approach that accounts for the neural as well as the embodied and enactive nature of the self. According to a PTS, the self emerges

1 Gallagher avoids the expression 'the self' to emphasize that the different aspects of self do not simply modify something that has its own independent existence (Gallagher 2013).

 | DOI:10.30965/9783969752906_008

from a cluster of dimensions that interact with each other dynamically. Instead of reducing the self to one aspect, PTS understands the different theories of the self as compatible. The patterned self encompasses embodied, minimal experiential, affective, behavioral, intersubjective, cognitive, reflective, narrative, extended/situated, and normative elements (Gallagher and Daly 2018). None of those dimensions is by itself necessary or essential to a particular self but PTS remains open to the possibility that a subgroup of aspects of the self may be jointly sufficient or necessary to constitute a self.

In the following, I argue that for individuals who narrate, the narrative dimension takes a special role within the patterned self as an organizing and self-defining principle. It is not but one element among others but cuts across the other dimensions of the self. Through the narrative dimension of the self, we engage in self-definition, integrate and connect the other dimensions of the self, make them intelligible, and ascribe personal meaning to them. Gallagher and others have already pointed to the unique role of the narrative dimension in retrieving, disclosing, mapping, and connecting the other aspects (Daly and Gallagher 2019; Dings and de Bruin 2022; Gallagher and Daly 2018). They have argued that through the narrative, we can track the dynamical relations among the different dimensions of the self which can be particularly useful in the medical context to diagnose and treat patients with mental disorders. This article expands on this work by giving a more comprehensive argument for and analysis of the role of the narrative in PTS, as well as by characterizing the narrating self.

In this article, I proceed in three steps. First, I provide a more detailed introduction of the PTS and argue for a PTS on the basis of conceptual and ethical considerations. Second, I introduce the narrative dimension of the self and argue that it takes a special role within PTS because it allows for self-definition, integration, intelligibility, and ascription of meaning. Third, I characterize the narrator type of self as a unified self who can lead their life and engage in forensic practices and who integrates the subjective and objective nature of the self in the self-narrative.

2. Pattern-Theory of Self

According to a pattern-theory, what we call a 'self' is a cluster concept (Gallagher 2013). The self is constituted by a cluster of dimensions that interact with each other. Those variables can take a different value and weight in the dynamic constitution of selves. Changes to one dimension may cause modulations in others. A particular variation of this pattern constitutes a self, which may also change over time for an individual. A self is a complex system that emerges from the dynamic interactions of those constituents. It is not reducible to any one of these aspects. However, a sufficient number of self-dimensions is necessary to constitute a self. In a more recent paper than the one introducing PTS, Gallagher and Daly (Gallagher and Daly 2018) suggest a revised list of dimensions of the self:

1) Embodied elements: Core biological, ecological, and interoceptive factors, allowing the system to distinguish between itself and what is not itself.
2) Minimal experiential elements: First-person, pre-reflective, conscious experience, reflecting the self/non-self distinction, including a sense of ownership ('mineness') and a sense of agency for one's actions.
3) Affective aspects: Affect/emotion/temperament, ranging from bodily affects to what may be a typical affective or emotion pattern.
4) Behavioral aspects: Behaviors and actions make us who we are – behavioral habits reflect, and perhaps actually constitute, our character.
5) Intersubjective interactions and capacities: Humans are born with a capacity for attuning to intersubjective existence, which develops into a social self-consciousness.
6) Psychological/cognitive elements: May range from explicit self-consciousness to a conceptual understanding of self as self, personality traits, psychological continuity, and memory.
7) Reflective capacities: The ability to reflect on one's experiences and actions – closely related to the notions of autonomy and moral personhood.
8) Narrative capacities: Our self-interpretations have a narrative structure.
9) Extended/situated elements: Not only may we identify with our material belongings, the technologies we use, our professions, and the institutions we work in, but we are dynamically related to the action possibilities they afford.
10) Normative factors: Ranging across possibilities presented by the kind of family structure and situation in which we grew up to cultural and normative practices, involving physical and mental health, gender, race, and economic status, that define our way of living.

Those ten elements are presented as a tentative list of dimensions that may contribute to constituting a self.[2] It depicts a schema of possible pattern theories of self. On the basis of this list, we may identify some dimensions as necessary or sufficient to constitute a specific type of self or analyze which elements contribute to the self of a single individual and how they interact with each

2 I remain neutral on whether this list is accurate or complete.

other. In case someone no longer exhibits a dimension of the self (for instance, if they lose narrative capacities), they do not experience a complete loss of the self but rather a modulation. Their self-identity may continue to be supported by other dimensions of the self, such as minimal bodily and experiential aspects, as well as intersubjective relations or extended aspects in one's surroundings. An individual may lack some of the characteristic features of the self and still constitute a self.

An advantage of PTS is that it understands various accounts of the self, such as the self as a moral agent, an experiential subject, a physical individual, or a mental entity, as compatible instead of in opposition (Gallagher 2013). Its modular, flexible structure allows us to analyze a broad range of elements of the self and the relationships and interactions between them. The narrative self theory, for instance, has been accused of neglecting the importance of minimal experiential elements for the self (Zahavi 2007). A PTS can do justice to the different dimensions of the self without having to reduce the self to any one of them.

A further conceptual advantage of PTS is that it allows for a more sensible and nuanced application to marginal cases such as toddlers, individuals with a mental disability, or some non-human animals. Marginal cases can make it difficult to determine when to apply concepts like 'self' or 'person'. As DeGrazia argues for personhood (DeGrazia 1997), picking one of the typical characteristics, such as moral agency, autonomy, subject of experience, or self-awareness, as crucial seems arbitrary. Moreover, those characteristics do not seem to be all-or-nothing properties but are themselves multidimensional and gradational. There are, for instance, different kinds of self-awareness and they come in degrees (DeGrazia 1997). Both person and self are vague concepts that do not let us decide non arbitrarily in every case whether they apply to an individual. Defining the self in terms of a pattern theory does justice to this vagueness. It also allows us to understand in what sense an individual is a self or which typical characteristics of selves are lacking.

Ethical considerations also speak in favor of a broad conception of the self. The self as well as personhood which is a closely related concept and sometimes even used interchangeably are what we may consider 'thick concepts' (DeGrazia 1997; Gunnarsson 2008; Williams 2006). This means they are both descriptive *and* normative. To be a self or a person one must fulfill certain descriptive conditions, such as exhibiting a sufficient number of characteristic self-dimensions. But being a self or a person also comes with an exclusive or superior moral status. We treat selves and persons differently than beings we do not consider as constituting selfhood or personhood. The descriptive and normative dimensions of the concept are interrelated – the moral status is granted because the descriptive features apply. Even though some authors defending more restrictive definitions of self or person assure that the lives of non-persons or non-selves are not inferior (see, for instance, Schechtman 1996), we should nonetheless be aware of the normative power that comes with denying that someone is a person or a self. Think concepts do not shed their normative dimension that easily. Overly narrow conceptions of selves and persons can lead to undesirable ethical implications (e.g., that people with mental disabilities or toddlers have inferior moral status). Especially in light of the vagueness of the concept, it seems risky to create narrow conceptual boundaries with potentially severe ethical implications on seemingly arbitrary grounds. A PTS allows us to establish different types of selves constituted by specific types of self-patterns. The distinction between different types of selves can be used as a conceptual tool in a more fine-grained moral landscape of how different types of selves should be treated and what rights they have based on the descriptive features that apply to them (for instance, I will argue that a subset of narrator type selves can enter into binding commitments and contracts).

3. A Narrative Pattern-Theory of the Self

Having considered the definition and advantages of a PTS, I turn to the role of the narrative dimension of selves. In philosophy, narrativism has been developed as a neo-Lockean response to the persistence question (i.e., what does it take for a person to exist at two different times). Narrative identity theorists argue that the self is narrative in form. Versions of the narrative self view have been developed by Marya Schechtman, Charles Taylor, Alasdair MacIntyre, Paul Ricoeur, David Velleman, Jerome Bruner, and Daniel Dennett, among others (Bruner 1990; Dennett 1992; MacIntyre 1984; Ricoeur 1991; Schechtman 1996; Taylor 1989; Velleman 2006). Furthermore, there is abundant literature on narrativism in psychology (Fivush, Habermas, Waters and Zaman 2011; McAdams 1992; McAdams 2011; McLean, Pasupathi and Pals 2007; Singer 2004). In contrast to the narrative self view, according to a PTS, narratives are not necessary and sufficient for constituting a self. Some selves do not narrate. But, as will be argued in the following, the narrative dimension takes a special role that cuts across the other dimensions of the self.

The general idea of narrativism is that narrators integrate their experiences into an evolving, internalized life story and project themselves into narratives of the future. This self-narrative is a story telling one's life-events from a personal perspective, reflecting character traits, goals, and values. The self-narrative defines the self on an individual, characterizing level, answering the question 'what makes me *me*?'. It is more than just a chronology of life events, or a neutral list of all the experiences of one's life. A self-narrative is selective and reflects personal evaluations. The stories of our lives are colored by our views on what occurred. Since your view on your past and future can change, we should understand the narrative dimension of selves as an ongoing process of self-interpretation and self-definition. A person may have thought that he was very confident and tough or that being from Scotland is an important part of his identity, but later in life came to understand that he acted out of insecurity or considers his Scottish origins as accidental and not self-defining.

The self-narrative is both explicit and implicit. We explicitly give an account of who we are or what we do to others and ourselves in terms of a narrative. In doing so, we summarize, abridge, highlight, find repeating patterns, or combine a span of weeks or years into a distinctive period (Glover 1988). Through such accounts, we make sense of ourselves and our actions and communicate it to others. When making the self-narrative explicit to others or to ourselves, we do not just express the implicit self-narrative we already had but we reflect on and make decisions about who we take ourselves to be and the intentions and responsibilities of our actions. At the same time, the self-narrative is implicit in the sense that our awareness of where we come from and expect to go shapes the experience of the present moment even if we are not explicitly or consciously considering the self-narrative. Parts we have made explicit before but are not consciously present at the moment as well as inchoate, vague notions of our life trajectory that have never been made explicit shape our experience implicitly and provide the framework through which we interpret, evaluate, and filter our experiences. Thereby, the self-narrative provides an individual, phenomenological point of view. For example, a person winning a marathon is experiencing this moment not in isolation but connected to the hours she put in the training and her ambitions for the future. Even if she does not reflect on the hours of training or her future goals at this moment, the implicit awareness of her life trajectory forms this experience.

For individuals who narrate, the narrative dimension is not just one among the other aspects of the patterned self. It cuts across the other dimensions and serves as an organizing and self-defining principle. How and to what degree the individual dimensions contribute to defining the self is shaped by the self-narrative. As argued in the following, the self-narrative takes this role because through it we engage in self-definition, integrate different features of the self, make them intelligible, and ascribe meaning. For non-narrators, the remaining aspects of the self can support their self-identity and the narratives others construe about them can partially fulfill the functions of self-definition, integration, intelligibility, and meaning for them. The narrative dimension of the self depends itself on other aspects of the self. It certainly requires minimal experiential and cognitive elements, but likely also embodied, situated, reflective, and interpersonal aspects. This article does not investigate how the other dimensions of the patterned self contribute to making the construction of a self-narrative possible. Instead, it is focused on the mechanisms of how the self-narrative organizes and shapes the self across all dimensions as well as how having a narrative shapes the self to identify what characterizes narrating selves.

3.1 *Self-Definition*

Not all your actions, characteristics, and life-events are equally defining you. Some elements are considered merely accidental, as in the above example of the Scottish origin, whereas others are central to one's identity. For some, being a philosopher is a central part of who they take themselves to be, for others it's just a way to pay the bills. What is part of the self is to some degree a matter of interpretation. The hard facts about yourself, such as where you were born, the things you did in your life, or how you look like, do not define your identity in its entirety (Leuenberger 2020). They leave ample room for different interpretations, emphasis, and choices about relevance. A child, friend, spouse, or mother of someone likely construes a very different but potentially equally true narrative of this person. They would all emphasize different elements and interpret some actions or emotions differently while remaining true to the hard facts. The narrative of the individual itself is the one that matters for self-definition because it guides her actions (Velleman 2006) and shapes her first-personal perspective (Schechtman 1996).[3] His mother might see him as a talented artist but as long as he does not see himself as an artist, he will not pursue a career in arts or look at galleries as a potential space to exhibit his work.

In construing a self-narrative, you take an active role in defining yourself. Through narrative accounts of yourself and your actions, you make choices about what defines you. For example, someone might be explaining to her friend that her aggressive outbursts weren't really her because they were caused by a tumor. In this narrative account of what caused her actions, she defines herself across multiple dimensions of the self. She rejects the tumor as part of her embodied self and she decides that certain behavior and emotions

3 This leaves a lot open concerning self-definition for cases of delusional self-narratives which commit errors of facts or errors of interpretation. I do not have the space to cover this topic here. Schechtman's work on the reality constraint is discussing those issues extensively (Schechtman 1996).

are not a real part of herself. Self-definition through narratives cuts across the other dimensions of the self and determines which elements belong to them or to what degree they are part of those dimensions. By giving accounts of who we are and what we do, we define ourselves, decide what is important and what is irrelevant about ourselves, and create, embrace, or reject interpretations of ourselves.

3.2 *Integration*

As argued by Dings and de Bruin (Dings and de Bruin 2022), narrativity constitutes the highest level of integration for an agent or cognitive system. Narratives provide temporal integration, by connecting past, present, and future. Through the self-narrative, we represent ourselves as diachronic, as being at a certain point in an ongoing life. Temporally separated episodes of our lives are held together through a narrative that connects them and they are extended into the future through narrative projections of how we expect our lives to develop. Having a self-narrative means experiencing present moments as tensed moments that expand into the personal past and future. Not everyone is experiencing this temporal integration to the same degree (e.g., Strawson's episodics (Strawson 2008)), and not every situation lends itself equally to experiencing its temporal extension. Nonetheless, through the self-narrative we are implicitly and explicitly situating ourselves along a life trajectory and integrate the episodes of our lives into it.

Narratives can furthermore provide integration by identifying patterns and structures. An individual can identify a pattern of helpful behavior and continue to interpret and account for their actions through their identified trait of helpfulness. Other patterns and structures identified in self-narratives would be life periods (angsty teenage years, punk-rock phase, or a period of depression), social roles, or cultural influences (e.g., 'I keep falling into patriarchal patterns of thought'). In identifying and defining those patterns and structures, we connect features of ourselves across the dimensions of the PTS. The punk-rock phase integrates elements of behavior (listening to this music genre, going to concerts), embodiment (e.g., a fashion style or physical reaction to the music), intersubjectivity (a circle of like-minded friends), values, beliefs, and more into a coherent element of one's identity.

Similarly, self-narratives can integrate elements with different degrees of abstraction and specificity. They can connect single actions to overarching goals, a single behavior to a repeating character disposition, or an isolated feeling of affection to a relationship of love and care. Narratives allow us to zoom in on specific actions, thoughts, or emotions and consider their details as well as to zoom out to more abstract features of the self. In the self-narrative, those levels are integrated and connected such that the specific aspects can be understood as exemplifying the abstract ones.

3.3 *Intelligibility*

Through the self-narrative, actions are made intelligible (Butler 2001; MacIntyre 1984; Velleman 2003). To modify an example by MacIntyre (MacIntyre 1984), if I ask you why you are reading this article, you may reply that you are an academic researching the topic, that you just stumbled upon it and do not have anything better to do, or that you read it to count all the spelling errors. To understand what you are doing, we have to know the causal and temporal order of short- and long-term intentions and beliefs (do you want to write a paper on the topic or just fill the time until dinner) as well as the cultural and social framework structuring the action (e.g., what is academia) (MacIntyre 1984). This means we are telling a story. We have to embed actions in narratives to understand them.

Making an action intelligible also entails understanding how the different dimensions of the self impact our actions. By integrating the different dimensions of the self into the self-narrative, we come to understand how they influence what we do. In construing narratives such as how his constant back pain makes him grumpy and lash out at his friends, how he hopes to impress his colleagues by talking about a prize he won, or how he avoids mowing the lawn on Sundays because it is frowned upon in his cultural context, he connects embodied, intersubjective, cultural, and other dimensions of himself to his actions such that actions and what influences them are rendered intelligible. This allows us to understand the impact of different dimensions of the self on our lives, to reflect on them and to try to change or abandon some aspects of those dimensions. Only if we understand our actions and what causes them are we in a position to manage them. This means the self-narrative provides crucial conditions that allow us to manage the different features of the patterned self and thereby ourselves.

3.4 *Meaning*

The final reason the narrative aspect of the self takes a special role for narrators is that we ascribe personal meaning to events, beliefs, values, traits, embodiment, and other aspects of ourselves through narratives (Bruner 1990; Leuenberger 2021). Personal meaning refers to the subjective value or relevance something has for the individual. The events and aspects of our lives gain their personal meaning through their position in the self-narrative. By integrating events into a self-narrative, they receive the necessary context of intentions, beliefs, personal history, and institutional settings to be meaningful. What it means for someone to win a marathon depends on whether she trained for this her whole life, whether she just participated on a whim, or whether this is her last run before retiring as a professional athlete. This moment becomes personally meaningful only in light of the narrative of her life.

Besides providing context, narratives provide intentionality. Through narratives, we account for events in intentional terms, i.e., in terms of intentions, beliefs, emotions, and cultural settings. In contrast, a purely naturalistic, reductionistic description of an event cannot depict its meaning. For instance, the personal meaning of a person's belief in God cannot be grasped through the underlying physical and biochemical processes, such as the neural activation pattern. To make sense of the personal meaning of this belief, we need to know how it connects to their values and other beliefs, what they have given up or gained through it, or what its cultural significance is. The intentional, contextual, and diachronic perspective of a narrative is needed to ascribe subjective value (i.e., meaning). Taking this narrative perspective on one's life impacts the self on a phenomenological level. The moment of winning the marathon in the above example is meaningful because it is not experienced in isolation but as a point in an ongoing life. To ascribe personal meaning and to experience moments as meaningful, this perspective that connects past, present, and future in intentional and contextual terms is necessary.

In the context of the PTS, the self-narrative ascribes meaning and relevance to the different dimensions of the self. What your body, gender, moods, friendships, character traits, or behavior mean for you in an individual, characterizing sense is determined by the narrative in which they are embedded. Again, the narrative dimension of the self is not just one among the others but determines the personal relevance for all of them.

4. The Narrator Type of Self

So far, I have argued that the narrative dimension of the self serves as an overarching organizing principle by allowing for self-definition, integration, intelligibility, and meaning. Having a self-narrative that takes over all those roles changes the self. This section analyzes how having a narrative shapes you. It provides a characterization of the narrator type of self to pinpoint what distinguishes selves that are constituted by a self-pattern that includes narrative elements – selves who take a narrative perspective and organize their experiences through a story of their lives. I argue that we can identify three characteristics of the narrator type of self: the self is unified through the narrative, narrators can lead their lives and engage in forensic practices and the subjective and objective nature of the self are brought together in the narrative.

4.1 *Unified Self*

Through a self-narrative, the self is unified in two ways. It construes unity as persistence, meaning unity across time, and unity as oneness, meaning unity across the different dimensions of the self (Schramme 2014). The self-narrative construes unity as persistence by integrating different moments and periods of one's life into a bigger whole. It provides a perspective of oneself as being at a certain point in an ongoing life. Thereby, the stages of this life are understood as parts of a unified self that spans from birth to death (and some construe narrative projections beyond death). This temporal unification through the narrative perspective might only be a construction and not a metaphysical truth (I leave this question open). But it has far-reaching practical consequences for how we can and do lead our lives, as I will discuss in the next section (see also Schechtman 2008).

Furthermore, through narration, the self is unified in the sense that different aspects of the self are brought together to make sense in light of each other as part of one. The single dimensions of the self are part of a bigger whole emerging from the self-narrative through which they become intelligible. The raised heart rate when holding a presentation in front of colleges only makes sense if it is part of a self that integrates, for instance, intersubjective dimensions of work relationships, normative and cultural dimensions connected to institutions of employment, and the psychological dimension of being shy or insecure. Self-narratives create a bigger whole by providing structures of interpretation – a network of meaning and intelligibility – that make you into a unified self that is persisting and one. Of course, we also have a certain physical unity. You are one organism throughout your lifetime who is distinct from others. But through the self-narrative, we construe coherence and unity in a broader sense, that integrates those purely bodily aspects with the intentional level of goals, values, aspirations, and characteristics. In the case of multiple personality disorder, for instance, an individual is unified as an embodied self but not in the sense of the individual characterizing self that defines what makes me *me*.

4.2 *Leading a Life and Forensic Practices*

The self-narrative allows for a particular kind of self-understanding and engagement with the world: as an agent that actively plans and leads their life. Through the phenomenological perspective of the self-narrative, the present moment is experienced in relation to the past and the anticipated future. We experience this diachronicity to different degrees, depending on idiosyncratic characteristics as well as the nature of the experience. The experience of absentmindedly scratching your head is not colored by your self-narrative in the same way as when you win a marathon you spent years training for. In the marathon case, the self-narrative gives depth and meaning to the experience it would lack without the narrative background. In a comparatively meaningless moment of your life, when you just sit and scratch your head, the narrative perspective lets you know how you got to be where you are and sets expectations of what happens in the future. Sometimes we may lose this narrative connection when we walk into a room and forget why and some mental disorders can lead to a more severe lack of narrative, diachronic organization (Mackenzie and Poltera 2010).

Narrators come to see themselves as temporally extended subjects whose histories impact the present and whose choices and current circumstances will influence the future. In the self-narrative, we represent ourselves as diachronic, as aging. Only if I think of myself as a diachronic entity, it makes sense to actively plan and lead my life, take responsibility for past actions, or hold special concern for my own future (Schechtman 1996). The perception of oneself as an agent shapes the self as a subject (Schechtman 2011). Because we represent ourselves as ageing, we have to somehow manage this ongoing life as we age, using these coordinating self-representations (Taylor 2011). You want to know who you are and construe self-defining narratives not just out of curiosity but because your life is given to you as something you undertake. This is why it is important to know whether you really are a philosopher or not, whether this reflects your norms, goals, and desires because you have to make choices based on who you take yourself to be. Moreover, by projecting ourselves into the future through a narrative, the self-narrative is action-guiding. We try to enact the imagined futures suggested by the self-narrative (McConnell 2016; Velleman 2006). Taking this integrative, diachronic, and meaning-generating narrative perspective generates a qualitatively different experience that allows us to understand ourselves as ongoing agents engaged in meaningful activities and thereby constituting the self.

If the individual furthermore adheres to the reality and articulation constraints, as introduced by Schechtman (Schechtman 1996), they 'unlock' another set of (inter)actions: social, forensic practices concerned with responsibility and accountability. To adhere to the reality constraint, the self-narrative should fundamentally cohere with a shared understanding of reality. Holding each other accountable or entering into binding commitments or contracts requires common ground. With individuals who do not have a solid grasp of reality and with whom we do not share some very basic assumptions of how the world works, we do not enter into a contract, hold them accountable, or see them as deserving blame or praise for their actions (at least not in the same way). A highly delusional self-narrative prevents the individual from engaging in certain social practices. Someone who believes, for example, that he is Napoleon may have construed a unifying, though delusional, narrative self through which he can ascribe meaning to life-events, actions, and emotions and which he uses to try to make himself intelligible. But he cannot successfully navigate his life and we would not assign responsibility to him or bind him to his promises (Schechtman 1996). The articulation constraint requires that at least parts of the self-narrative can be made explicit, meaning the individual can explain why she is performing this action, feeling this feeling, or holding this belief. To be held accountable we have to be able to give an account of ourselves. Of course, whether one meets the reality and articulation constraints is gradual and may be temporary. Insofar as narrators construe their self-narratives within these constraints they can engage in such forensic practices.

The reality and articulation constraints are not required for the self-narrative to allow for self-definition, integration, intelligibility, meaning, unity, and the integration of the subjective and objective nature of the self. To fulfill those functions, the self-narrative needs to provide a phenomenological point of view that positions the self as being at a certain point in an ongoing life and comes with structures of interpretation. This only requires a minimal coherence with reality (most importantly, the self-narrative needs to be the story of a life and it has to feature the individual's perspective). The details of this minimal requirement are too complex to work out at this point, but it would be weaker than the reality and articulation constraints. The narrative dimension of the self as I have discussed it in this article does not necessarily describe your 'true' or 'real' self in a deep metaphysical sense. It constitutes the dimension of the self (together with and across the other aspects of the self) through which we experience, organize, and engage with the world. Insofar as this self-dimension has far-reaching, real-life consequences there is a reality to it, but I do not engage with the metaphysical question of how this relates to one's 'true self'.

4.3 *Subjective and Objective*

Lastly, I want to argue that the narrator type of self can make sense of the subjective and objective duality of the self. Nagel famously argued that by giving an objective account of the self, its subjective nature is lost. We cannot account for the subjective point of view through an objective viewpoint. 'Any attempt to conceive persons completely as a kind of thing in the world persisting through time will come up against this obstacle. The self that appears to the subject seems to disappear under external analysis.' (Nagel 2012) The narrator self is fundamentally subjective due to the phenomenological point of view constituted by the narrative perspective. The narrative self constitutes the subjective framework through which we experience and engage with the world (Postan 2016; Schechtman 1996). At the same time, we regularly give third-personal, objective accounts of ourselves in the self-narrative. We often describe our bodies, actions, emotions, behavior, and character traits from an objective stance.

Narrators take the role of the protagonist, the author (or more realistically, co-author), and the critic of the self-narrative at the same time (Schechtman 2011). In the role of the protagonist and the author, you take the subjective position of experiencing life through the point of view shaped by the self-narrative and of making decisions and acting them out from the subjective perspective. But you are also a critic who reflects on his or her life, tries to make sense of it, and ascribes meaning to it. In this role as a critic, you take an objective perspective on yourself. Narrators combine the subjective and objective nature of the self through the different perspectives ingrained in the narrative.

5. Conclusion

To conclude, let me briefly summarize the argument of the article. Conceptual and ethical considerations speak in favor of understanding the self as constituted by a dynamic pattern of variables. For selves who narrate, the narrative dimension serves as an organizing principle. It can take this role because 1) through the self-narrative you define yourself across other dimensions of the self, 2) the self-narrative integrates the self temporally, by identifying patterns and structures, and across degrees of abstraction, 3) it allows us to understand and manage the different dimension of the self, and 4) through the self-narrative we ascribe personal meaning to other elements of the self. Thereby, the narrative dimension of the self is revealed to be crucial for the constitution of the dimension of self through which we experience, organize, and engage with the world. The narrator type of self is characterized as constituting a unified self (as persistence and as oneness) who actively plans and leads their life and may engage in forensic practices, and who accounts for the subjective and objective nature of the self.

The narrative pattern-theory of the self laid out in this article raises important ethical questions about how others may support or disrupt the functions and roles of self-narratives for the self. In this article, I have not touched upon the topic of how others influence the self-narrative but of course, we do not create narratives in isolation. The social context is required to develop capacities for self-narration (Fivush, Habermas, Waters and Zaman 2011; McAdams 2011; McAdams 2013), we make ourselves intelligible and give an account of ourselves to others in narrative terms (Brison 2002; Butler 2001; Schechtman 1996; Velleman 2006), we define ourselves through our relations with others and by being part of social and cultural groups (Baylis 2012; Lindemann 2001; MacIntyre 1984; Taylor 1989), others shape what can be considered as meaningful characteristics of a person (Taylor 2003), and others provide inputs and constraints for our self-narratives (Baylis 2012; Fivush, Habermas, Waters and Zaman 2011; Lindemann 2001; Lindemann 2016; McConnell 2016; Mihailov, Zorila and Iftode 2021; Schechtman 1996; Schechtman 2014). In view of what the narrative dimension of the self allows us to do and how it shapes the self, it is important to consider how others may impact our abilities for self-definition, integration, personal intelligibility, and ascription of meaning. Moreover, further empirical and conceptual research is necessary to work out in more detail how the other elements of the patterned self interact with and are impacted by the narrative dimension, notably which aspects are necessary to construe a narrative, as well as how this theory of the self can be used in the applied context, particularly in the medical field to improve how we define, diagnose, and provide treatment for individuals suffering from disorders of the self. This analysis of the role of the narrative dimension of the self and the narrator type of self can serve as a starting point for this research.[4]

References

Baylis, Françoise 2012: 'The Self in Situ: A Relational Account of Personal Identity'. In *Being Relational: Reflections on Relational Theory and Health Law*. Downie, Jocelyn and Llewellyn, Jennifer J. (eds) Vancouver: UBC Press, pp. 109–31

Brison, Susan J. 2002: *Aftermath: Violence and the Remaking of a Self*. Princeton: Princeton University Press

Bruner, Jerome S. 1990: *Acts of Meaning*. Cambridge, MA: Harvard University Press

Butler, Judith 2001: 'Giving an Account of Oneself'. *Diacritics*, 31, pp. 22–40

Daly, Anya and Gallagher, Shaun 2019: 'Towards a phenomenology of self-patterns in psychopathological diagnosis and therapy'. *Psychopathology*, 52, pp. 33–49

4 I would like to thank the participants of the Heidelberg Workshop on Personhood, Self-Consciousness, and the First-Person Perspective for valuable feedback on this article.

DeGrazia, David 1997: 'Great apes, dolphins, and the concept of personhood'. *The Southern journal of philosophy*, 35, pp. 301–20

Dennett, Daniel 1992: 'The Self as a Center of Narrative Gravity'. In *Self and Consciousness: Multiple Perspectives*. Kessel, Frank S., Cole, Pamela M. and Johnson, Dale L. (eds) Hillsdale, NJ: Erlbaum Associates, pp. 103–15

Dings, Roy and de Bruin, Leon C. 2022: 'What's Special About 'Not Feeling Like Oneself'? A Deflationary Account of Self(-illness) Ambiguity'. *Philosophical Explorations*, pp. 1–21

Fivush, Robyn; Habermas, Tilmann; Waters, Theodore E. A. and Zaman, Widaad 2011: 'The Making of Autobiographical Memory: Intersections of Culture, Narratives and Identity'. *International Journal of Psychology*, 46, pp. 321–45

Gallagher, Shaun 2013: 'A Pattern Theory of Self'. *Frontiers in Human Neuroscience*, 7, pp. 443–43

Gallagher, Shaun and Daly, Anya 2018: 'Dynamical relations in the self-pattern'. *Frontiers in Psychology*, p. 664

Glover, Jonathan 1988: *I: The Philosophy and Psychology of Personal Identity*. London etc.: Penguin Books

Gunnarsson, Logi 2008: 'The Great Apes and the Severely Disabled: Moral Status and Thick Evaluative Concepts'. *Ethical Theory and Moral Practice*, 11, pp. 305–26

Izard, Carroll E and Ackerman, Brian P 2002: 'Self-Organization of Discrete Emotions, Emotion Patterns, and Emotion-Cognition'. In *Emotion, development, and self-organization: Dynamic systems approaches to emotional development*. Lewis, S. E. and Granic, I. (eds) New York: Cambridge University Press, p. 15

Izard, Carrolle E 2013: *Patterns of emotions: A new analysis of anxiety and depression*. New York: Academic Press

Leuenberger, Muriel 2020: 'In Defense of Narrative Authenticity'. *Cambridge Quarterly of Healthcare Ethics*, 29, pp. 656–67

—— 2021: 'Losing Meaning: Philosophical Reflections on Neural Interventions and their Influence on Narrative Identity'. *Neuroethics*, 14, pp. 491–505

Lindemann, Hilde 2001: *Damaged Identities, Narrative Repair*. Ithaca: Cornell University Press

—— 2016: *Holding and letting go: The social practice of personal identities*. Oxford: Oxford University Press

MacIntyre, Alasdair C. 1984: *After Virtue*. Notre Dame, IN: University of Notre Dame Press

Mackenzie, Catriona and Poltera, Jacqui 2010: 'Narrative Integration, Fragmented Selves, and Autonomy'. *Hypatia*, 25, pp. 31–54

McAdams, Dan P. 1992: 'Unity and purpose in human lives: The emergence of identity as a life story'. In *Personality structure in the life course*. Zucker, R. A., Rabin, A. I., Aronoff, J. and Frank, S. J. (eds) New York: Springer, pp. 131–48

—— 2011: 'Narrative identity'. In *Handbook of identity theory and research*. New York: Springer, pp. 99–115

—— 2013: 'The psychological self as actor, agent, and author'. *Perspectives on Psychological Science*, 8, pp. 272–95

McConnell, Doug 2016: 'Narrative Self-Constitution and Recovery from Addiction'. *American Philosophical Quarterly*, 53, pp. 307–22

—— 2016: 'Narrative Self-constitution and Vulnerability to Co-authoring'. *Theoretical Medicine and Bioethics*, 37, pp. 29–43

McLean, Kate C; Pasupathi, Monisha and Pals, Jennifer L 2007: 'Selves creating stories creating selves: A process model of self-development'. *Personality and social psychology review*, 11, pp. 262–78

Mendonça, Dina 2012: 'Pattern of sentiment: following a Deweyan suggestion'. *Transactions of the Charles S. Peirce Society: A Quarterly Journal in American Philosophy*, 48, pp. 209–27

Mihailov, Emilian; Zorila, Alexandra and Iftode, Cristian 2021: 'Taking Relational Authenticity Seriously: Neurotechnologies, Narrative Identity, and Co-Authorship of the Self'. *AJOB Neuroscience*, 12, pp. 35–37

Nagel, Thomas 2012: *Mortal Questions*. Cambridge: Cambridge University Press

Newen, Albert; Welpinghus, Anna and Juckel, Georg 2015: 'Emotion recognition as pattern recognition: the relevance of perception'. *Mind & Language*, 30, pp. 187–208

Postan, Emily 2016: 'Defining Ourselves: Personal Bioinformation as a Tool of Narrative Self-Conception'. *Journal of Bioethical Inquiry*, 13, pp. 133–51

Ricoeur, Paul 1991: 'Life in quest of narrative'. In *On Paul Ricoeur: Narrative and Interpretation*. Wood, David (ed) New York: Routledge, pp. 20–33

Schechtman, Marya 1996: *The Constitution of Selves*. Ithaca NY, London: Cornell University Press

—— 2008: 'Diversity in unity: practical unity and personal boundaries'. *Synthese*, 162, pp. 405–23

—— 2011: 'The Narrative Self'. In *The Oxford Handbook of the Self*. Gallagher, Shaun (ed) Oxford: Oxford University Press, pp. 394–416

—— 2014: *Staying alive: Personal identity, practical concerns, and the unity of a life*. Oxford: Oxford University Press

Schramme, Thomas 2014: 'On being wholeheartedly ambivalent: indecisive will, unity of the self, and integration by narration'. *Ethical Theory and Moral Practice*, 17, pp. 27–40

Singer, Jefferson A. 2004: 'Narrative identity and meaning making across the adult lifespan: An introduction'. *Journal of personality*, 72, pp. 437–60

Strawson, Galen 2008: 'Against Narrativity'. In *Real Materialism and Other Essays*. Oxford: Oxford University Press, pp. 189–207

Taylor, Charles 1989: *Sources of the Self: The Making of the Modern Identity*. Cambridge etc.: Cambridge University Press

—— 2003: *The Ethics of Authenticity*. Cambridge, MA: Harvard University Press

Taylor, Kenneth 2011: 'The Narrative Construction of the Self'. In The Human Experience [Video file]. University, Stanford (ed) https://www.youtube.com/watch?v=kDSH9Xb_oAg 05.12.2011

Velleman, J. David 2003: 'Narrative explanation'. *Philosophical Review*, 112, pp. 1–25

—— 2006: *Self to Self: Selected Essays*. Cambridge: Cambridge University Press

Williams, Bernard 2006: *Ethics and the Limits of Philosophy*. Cambridge: Harvard University Press

Zahavi, Dan 2007: 'Self and Other: The Limits of Narrative Understanding'. *Royal Institute of Philosophy Supplement*, 60, pp. 179–202

Humans and Persons: A Compatibilist Account

Jörg Noller

Abstract

What is the relationship between a person's living body and her identity? In this article, will argue for compatibilist account of personal identity, according to which persons are life forms. For this reason, I will sharply distinguish between species and life form. Morphologically speaking, the relation of species and life form can be determined in such a way that the latter is a configuration of the individual life under the species form. Seen in this way, the relationship between species and life form does not imply a dualism of two forms or substances, but an integrative combination of forms. While the species form composes living organisms such as humans, the personal life form integrates a supra-individual structure in them, thereby configuring their living capacities reflexively and intersubjectively. This allows to understand a person's identity not only in logical or ontological, but also in normative terms.

1. What are We?

From a philosophical point of view, there are many ways to determine 'the kind of beings that we fundamentally are' (Baker 2008, p. 10). Among the most important philosophical attempts to determine our very identity conditions count (i) (Neo)Lockeanism, (ii) animalism, and (iii) constitutionalism. In this article, I shall argue that these three attempts fall short. They fall short because they merely focus on relations of *identity* but not on the relations of the *form* of our existence. I shall argue that we need to distinguish between species and life form. According to my view, we are fundamentally personal life forms, and our personal life form is compatible with our human species form.[1] My article is structured as follows. First, I will present the main arguments of (Neo) Lockeanism, thereby focusing on the relationship between human and personal identity, which I interpret in terms of human species and personal life form. Second, I will discuss the main arguments of animalism, thereby referring to Eric T. Olson's account and the 'too many thinkers problem' (Parfit 2012, p. 7), which I shall interpret as a problem to unify species and life form. Third,

1 For an extensive discussion of this thesis, see Noller 2022. For the distinction between life form and species form, see Buchheim and Noller 2016, and Toepfer 2020.

© BRILL MENTIS, 2023 | DOI:10.30965/9783969752906_009

I shall discuss the arguments of constitutionalism proposed by Lynne R. Baker and its attempt to avoid both reductionism and the 'too many thinkers problem'. I shall argue that constitutionalism cannot escape Olson's objections, and argue for a compatibilist account of personal identity based on the distinction between human species and personal life form. Drawing on Marya Schechtman's 'Person Life View', I will explain the personal life form from a morphological point of view, thereby combining the human and the person life as a kind of morphological compatibilism. According morphological compatibilism, we are personal life forms that are compatible with the human species form. This allows me to avoid the animalist problem of reductionism as well as the 'too many thinkers problem' of Lockeanism and constitutionalism.

2. Lockeanism

According to Locke, the concept of a person is 'a forensic term appropriating Actions and their Merit; and so be-longs only to intelligent Agents *capable* of a Law, and Happiness and Misery' (Locke 1975, p. 346; emphasis added). Persons are thus constituted in terms of their identity in such a way that they are *normatively responsive*: 'In this *personal Identity* is founded all the Right and Justice of Reward and Punishment; Happiness and Misery, being that, for which every one is concerned for *himself*' (Locke 1975, pp. 341–2). According to Locke, personal identity grounds normative facts. The (self-)attribution of personal identity is not only a theoretical, but also a practical-axiological matter. Locke's theory thus closely connects questions about the numerical identity of a person, its persistence, and its moral imputability. Harold Noonan has therefore rightly argued, following A. N. Whitehead's well-known dictum, that the more recent theories of personal identity are only 'footnotes to Locke'[2]. However, in doing so, Noonan has referred primarily to those recent theories that are in the Lockean tradition of our identity with regard to the identity of self-consciousness. However, less attention has been paid to Locke's theory of the *identity of life* and its relation to his theory of the person, since Locke does not elaborate on the precise ontological relation between person- and life-identity. In what follows, I will place Locke's theory of personal identity in closer relation to his theory of the identity of life than is usually done.

Locke categorically distinguishes three *forms* of identity and their principles:

---

2 See Noonan 2003, p. 34: 'On this topic [of personal identity, J.N.], at least, it can be truly said that all subsequent writing has consisted merely of footnotes to Locke.'

> 'It being one thing to be
> [1] the same *Substance*, another
> [2] the same *Man*, and a third
> [3] the same *Person*;
> *Person, Man*, and *Substance*, are three Names standing for three different *Ideas*.'
> (Locke 1975, p. 332)

Locke analyzes these three forms of identity as follows:

[1]: The identity of a material and inanimate body is founded by the ontological principle of 'cohesion'. Locke speaks of a 'Cohesion of Particles of Matter any how united' (Locke 1975, p. 330).[3] He explains the specific 'identity' of such mass bodies as follows: '[I]f one of these Atoms be taken away, or one new one added, it is no longer the same Mass, or the same Body' (Locke 1975, p. 332). In this respect, inanimate bodies, as Locke conceives them, are characterized by a *weak* or *unstable* identity principle, which is sensitive to (even minimal) mass exchange. The identity principle of inanimate material substances is therefore the weakest of the three discussed, since it is maximally numerically *mass-sensitive*.

[2]: Identity of the living bodily organism, especially the *human* one. In contrast to the arbitrary unity of matter particles of inanimate masses, the identity of living bodies is more flexible and robust, since it is *immune* to mass exchange: '[T]he Identity of the same *Man* consists [...] in nothing but a participation of the same continued Life, by constantly fleeting Particles of Matter, in succession vitally united to the same organized Body.' (Locke 1975, pp. 331–2) Locke speaks of a 'disposition' and 'organization' of the animate matter, which thereby 'constitutes' the parts of the animate substance (Locke 1975, pp. 330–1) The principle of identity here is no longer weak cohesion, but the dynamic *organization* of life. In the animated and organized body, the identity of life is 'communicated' (Locke 1975, p. 331) to the individual particles of matter. Organized and communicated matter differs in this from merely mereologically aggregated matter, because in mere mass bodies and aggregates the particles are not uniformly organized, but only constantly loosely connected. Locke speaks here of a 'coherent body' instead of the merely material 'cohesion of particles' (Locke 1975, p. 331).

[3]: Identity of the person, especially identity of self-consciousness. Compared to the identity of inanimate bodies as well as organisms, persons are characterized by an even more stable identity principle. Persons obey other identity conditions and principles than humans do. In contrast to human or general living identity, personal identity is not exclusively bound to one and

3 For a discussion of the ontology of cohesion, see Hübner 2007, p. 66.

the same substance. In comparison to aggregates, personal identity is not only immune to mass exchange, but also, in comparison to living beings, to the change of the living *substance*. It is not decisive according to Locke

> whether the same *self be* continued in the same, or divers Substances. For since consciousness always accompanies thinking, and 'tis that, that makes every one to be, what he calls *self;* and thereby distinguishes himself from all other thinking things, in this alone consists *personal Identity, i.e.* the sameness of a rational Being: And as far as this consciousness can be extended backwards to any past Action or Thought, so far reaches the Identity of that *Person;* it is the same *self* now it was then; and 'tis by the same *self* with this present one that now reflects on it, that that Action was done. (Locke 1975, p. 335)

For Locke, the only thing in question is 'what makes the same Person, and not whether it be the same Identical Substance, which always thinks in the same Person, which in this case matters not at all.' (Locke 1975, p. 336) Thus, the only relevant question is whether self-consciousness can bind itself to an individual substance or maintain itself in the succession of different substances (see Locke 1975, p. 336).

Crucial to Locke's theory of personal identity is a formal analogy between the identity of life and the identity of the person:

> Different Substances, by the same consciousness (where they do partake in it) being united into one Person; *as well as* different Bodies, by the same Life are united into one Animal, whose *Identity* is preserved, in that change of Substances, by the unity of one continued Life [emphasis added]. (Locke 1975, p. 336)

Let us dwell for a moment on this distinction. It is striking that Locke conceives the relationship between (3): identity of the person and (2): identity of the (human) organism analogously to the relationship between (2): identity of the organism and (1): identity of the mass.[4] While the identity of the organism is unaffected by the change of matter, the same is true of the person qua self-consciousness in the case of a changing bodily organism or substance. Locke thus conceives of the form of self-consciousness in terms of a 'second-order organism'. However, he does not explain this higher-order structure further concerning the relationship with the bodily organism. Locke's morphology suggests to understand the form of the organism and the form of the person in terms of of species form and life form.

---

4 Noonan 2003, p. 52 argues that this analogy is 'at the heart of Locke's position'.

According to Locke, what transforms the human organism into a person is self-consciousness. Personhood is thus not something substantial, but something *formal*: 'For the same consciousness being preserv'd, whether in the same or different substances, the personal Identity is preserv'd.' (Locke 1975, p. 338) Self-consciousness is not something which is ontologically added to the bodily organism, but rather *structures* the underlying living bodily substance. Therefore, two persons organized according to the species form can exchange their personal identity, as Locke illustrates with his famous example of the prince and the cobbler:

> [S]hould the Soul of a Prince, carrying with it the consciousness of the Prince's past Life, enter and *inform* the Body of a Cobler as soon as deserted by his own Soul, every one sees, he would be the same Person with the Prince, accountable only for the Prince's Actions [emphasis added] (Locke 1975, p. 340).

Due to the (onto)logical independence of organism and self-consciousness, it is therefore possible for the same human organism to represent different persons at different times (see Locke 1975, p. 344), just as it is possible for the same person to be embodied by different humans or substances at different times. Thus, Locke dynamizes the identity of the person through her independence from substance. By epistemically as well as practically *forming* the living body, self-consciousness allows to identify, individuate, and morally judge persons.

Even though Locke conceives of the identity of living beings and the identity of persons in terms of an analogy, he at the same time conceives of them as ontologically independent of each other. This becomes clear by Locke's famous finger example:

> [E]very one finds, that whilst comprehended under that consciousness, the little Finger is as much a part of it *self*, as what is most so. Upon separation of this little Finger, should this consciousness go along with the little Finger, and leave the rest of the Body, 'tis evident the little Finger would be the *Person*, the *same Person*; and *self* then would have nothing to do with the rest of the Body. (Locke 1975, p. 341)

The severed little finger of which Locke speaks here is not a living organism, but only a part of the body without which the organism continues to live, and to that extent inanimate matter. It follows that Locke dissociates personal identity and biological life again in the end, despite his analogy. Personal identity does not presuppose organic life, but is formally analogous to it. Locke thereby determines the identity of the person as a function of consciousness: 'That with which the *consciousness* of this present thinking thing can join it self, makes the same *Person,* and is one *self* with it.' (Locke 1975, p. 341) However, here the question arises of whether consciousness can in fact also be united with inanimate matter. I will argue below that this is not the case, because self-consciousness is a *personal* form of life. In this respect, I suggest to interpret Locke's analogy between the identity of life and the identity of the person in a stronger sense: The identity of the person is grounded by the identity of life, and it can be analyzed by a specific relationship between species form and life form.

3. Animalism

An alternative way of defining the relationship between human and personal identity is to abandon Locke's criterion of self-consciousness altogether and to ground personal identity in human life. This position is called 'animalism', of which Eric T. Olson may be regarded as the main representative.[5] Olson speaks of the 'Biological Approach' (Olson 1995, p. 160), which he conceives as the only consistent theory of our personal identity as living beings. Olson speaks less of persons than of 'people' or even only of 'us' (see Olson 1997a). He avoids using the term 'person', because he argues that our identity conditions are those of animals. Psychological properties such as self-consciousness are therefore not decisive for our numerical identity. Nevertheless, (human) animals or organisms can possess properties that are not of a genuinely biological nature. Olson gives the example that biological organisms like us can very well be philosophers and Europeans (see Olson 1997a, p. 17). Nor does Olson deny that there can be major differences between human animals and other species with respect to mental and even moral properties. However, these properties are not so ontologically crucial as to determine our conditions of identity (see Olson 2003a, p. 321).

In order to plausibilize his thesis of animalism, Olson carries out a thought experiment (see Olson 1997b, p. 94). Let us assume that we fall into a permanent vegetative state due to an injury of our brain (Olson speaks here of a 'human vegetable') and thus no longer possess (self-)consciousness. According to (neo-)Lockean positions, our existence, which is always personal, would hereby be extinguished. According to Olson, however, it is not our existence that is extinguished, insofar as the human animal survives us, but rather we

5 Other current proponents of animalism include Reuter 2019, Snowdon 1990, 2014, 2020, and van Inwagen 1997. Blatti 2020 provides a comprehensive overview of the various differentiations of this position.

survive the human person. Our identity conditions are those of a human animal. Olson emphasizes that his theory of animalism, although biologically informed, is by no means trivial in philosophical terms: '[A]nimalism is a substantive metaphysical thesis with important consequences. There is nothing harmless about it [...]. Our being animals has important and highly contentious metaphysical implications.' (Olson 2003a, pp. 325–6)

What are these metaphysical implications of animalism? Olson's argument against the 'standard view' of the self-consciousness theory of personal identity considers the two temporal edges of human existence – birth as well as death. Concerning the temporal beginning of our existence, Olson develops the following argument, which he also calls the 'fetus problem' (see Olson 1997b, p. 98):

(1) We (as persons) were once fetuses.
(2) We have no consciousness of ourselves as fetuses.
(3) Hence, our identity cannot consist in the continuity of consciousness.

In a very similar way, this argument can be used in favor of animalism if we reflect upon the end of our existence – as a 'human vegetable' (Olson 1997b, p. 96) without consciousness and only maintaining the most vital functions. We can describe Olson's argument against Lockeanism as follows (see Olson 1997a, p. 94):

(1) We (as persons) can once enter a purely vegetative state.
(2) In the vegetative state no continuity of self-consciousness exists anymore.
(3) Our human animal cannot outlive us.
(4) Accordingly, our identity cannot consist in the continuity of self-consciousness.

Olson's 'Animalism Argument' (hereafter 'AA') reads as follows:

(1) There is a human animal sitting in your chair.
(2) The human animal sitting in your chair is thinking.
(3) You are the thinking being sitting in your chair. [...]
(4) Hence, you are that animal. (Olson 2003a, p. 325)

In order to better understand Olson's animalism, we have to take a closer look at his concept of life. Olson explicitly refers to Locke's concept of life:[6]

6 See Olson 1997a, p. 136: 'This is reminiscent of Locke's account of the identity of organisms.'

> By a life I mean more or less what Locke meant [...]: a self-organizing biological event that maintains the organism's complex internal structure. The materials that organisms are made up of are intrinsically unstable and must therefore be constantly re-paired and renewed, or else the organism dies and its remains decay. An organism must constantly take in new particles, reconfigure and assimilate them into its living fabric, and expel those that are no longer useful to it. An organism's life enables it to persist and retain its characteristic structure despite constant material turnover. (Olson 2007, p. 28)

Olson defines life as 'a special kind of event, roughly the sum of the metabolic activities the organism's parts are caught up in.' (Olson 1997, p. 136) Metaphorically speaking, life is 'a sort of storm of particles in constant motion.' (Olson 1997, p. 136) In contrast to storms, however, lives – Olson speaks here in the plural – are 'self-directing' and 'self-organizing' by internal principles. Thus, lives maintain their form for a very long time, while storms are only 'short-lived' and unstable. However, this is only a quantitative difference to phenomena like storms. A qualitative difference between lives and storms is that the lives are uniquely determined with respect to their outer boundary, which gives them a particularly strong (numerical) identity: 'Lives are *well-individuated* events: there is usually a definite answer to the question whether a given particle is or is not caught up in a particular life.' (Olson 1997, p. 136)

Olson argues that life has a 'characteristic organization', i.e. that it provides a form for its changing particles. However, he emphasizes that not every self-directed and homeodynamic biological event represents a life. Rather, a life must always contrast with its environment in a specific way (Olson 1997, p. 138). Olson conceives this contrasting performance as a moment of the concept of life itself. This shows that life is not only significant through its internal organic relations, but also through *external* relations. However, Olson's term 'substance concept' suggests that he represents a reductionist concept of life that conceives of the relations of life only in terms of self-sustaining self-referentiality, but not in terms of external referentiality. As I shall argue below, the concept of the personal life form represents the *unity* or *compatibility* of self-reference and other-reference.

To summarize: Olson's approach to the problem of personal identity is essentially reductionist. Within Locke's categories, the reduction is not to (3): self-consciousness, but to (2): organic life: According to Olson's theory of animalism, the human person is nothing but a living being of the species 'human'.[7]

7 See Olson 2003a, p. 318: 'When I say that we are animals, I mean that each of us is numerically identical with an animal. There is a certain human organism, and that organism is you. You and it are one and the same.'

Thus, Olson does not distinguish between species form and life form: we, as persons, are animals, essentially, in a non-derivative way.

4. Constitutionalism

Lynne R. Baker has attempted to open an intermediate path between (Neo) Lockeanism and animalism, and to avoid the 'too many thinkers problem' and reductionism. Baker conceives of constitutionalism as 'a genuine third alternative beyond the recognized alternatives of either identity or separate existence.' (Baker 2000, p. 57) She argues against animalism, according to which our identity conditions are essentially identical to those of other, even lower organisms: '[A]ccording to animalism [...], there is no ontological distinction between us and earthworms. By contrast, I think that metaphysics should tell us about what is fundamental to our being the kind of thing that we are (as opposed to earthworms), and about what is significant about us.' (Baker 2016, p. 58). In contrast to Olson's animalism, Baker emphasizes the metaphysical relevance of the practical dimension to the identity of the person. By means of her conception of constitutionalism, she attempts to unify the identity of self-consciousness and the identity of life and thus further analyze the relationship between the person and the bodily organism, since Locke had famously left this question open. While according to animalism we are essentially animals and only contingently persons, according to constitutionalism the exact opposite is true: 'I am a person essentially, and an animal contingently' (Baker 2008, p. 9).

Baker's concept of a person is situated within a 'metaphysics of everyday life' that allows to explain the identity of quite different entities by the relation of constitution:

> Constitution is a very general relation, ubiquitous in the world. It is a relation that may hold between granite slabs and war memorials, between pieces of metal and traffic signs, between DNA molecules and genes, between pieces of paper and dollar bills – things of basically different kinds that are spatially coincident. The fundamental idea of constitution is this: when a thing of one primary kind is in certain circumstances, a thing of another primary kind – a new thing, with new causal powers – comes to exist. (Baker 2002a, p. 32)

Against Olson's animalism, according to which practical and moral qualities are merely accidental to the organism, Baker emphasizes the genuinely practical dimension of personal identity, which she determines within the framework of her metaphysics of everyday life:

> Should metaphysics be sealed off from all practical and moral concerns? If so, why? I take metaphysics to be the study of fundamental reality. And I take fundamental reality to include all the objects and properties whose omission from ontology would render an account of reality incomplete. [...] What we consider to be real should not be independent of what we consider to be important. Else, why bother with metaphysics? (Baker 2008, p. 10)

Baker methodologically distinguishes two concepts of metaphysics, which she calls 'big-tent metaphysics' and 'pup-tent metaphysics'. The metaphor of the tent is to be understood in such a way that Baker wants to grasp and conceptually clarify as many aspects of reality as possible in her metaphysics. Thus, Baker argues for a unified concept with respect to the identity of the person, which takes into account both theoretical and practical dimensions: 'Big-Tent Metaphysics does not relegate what is unique about us to some second-rate realm of the merely practical, but rather welcomes it into the domain of basic reality.' (Baker 2008, p. 12) Baker counts Olson as 'Pup-Tent-Metaphysics', since she accuses him of not being able to do justice to the theoretical-practical unity of the person within the framework of animalism: 'Olson wants to keep what is distinctive about us and what is most significant about us out of metaphysics. He does not discuss what is distinctive about us at all, and he consigns what is significant about us to a sphere of practical concerns outside the purview of metaphysics altogether.' (Baker 2008, p. 10).

Baker argues that our conditions of identity are not those of animals but of persons. But this difference is not meant to establish an ontological *dualism*. According to Baker, although we are basically persons, we are equally 'fully animals' (Baker 2008, p. 9), i.e. we stand in an evolutionary relation to the animal kingdom. Hence, Baker argues for a compatibilism between animal and personal identity. We are animals insofar as we are *constituted* by human animals, i.e. the living organism (see Baker 1999b, p. 157). However, Baker, in contrast to Olson, denies that our conditions of identity as persons thereby arise equally from our biological nature. Thus, although we are animals, we are not identical with them.[8] Rather, she argues that we could exist as persons without our biological nature.

Baker develops thought experiments concerning our personal survival in order to substantiate her theory (see Baker 2008, p. 9, and especially Baker 2016, pp. 58–61) According to Baker, it is logically consistently conceivable, and moreover scientifically not impossible, that lower brain functions, such as those concerning our metabolism, could be taken over by an artificial prosthetic

8 See Baker 2001: '[T]he Constitution View holds that we are not identical to the animals that constitute us.'

device. Thus it is possible that different parts and organs of our body would be gradually replaced by inorganic parts, and thus in the end we would no longer consist of carbon, as all terrestrial animals do. Opposed to Olson's argument, Baker argues that it is possible for a person to survive the human animal that constitutes her, insofar as the latter is successively replaced by artificial organs. Even if the human animal died in the process, we – understood as identical with a person – would nevertheless continue to exist. Baker ties in here with Locke's theory of the (onto)logical independence of person and substance, even if she explains the relationship between personal identity and organic identity more precisely through her theory of constitution.[9] However, here the question arises in what framework and compound these artificial parts can continue to keep the person alive. A mere additive or substitutive relationship of artificial parts to a biological organism cannot explain the question of the specific *unity* of the parts constituting the person. This demands that Baker define the concept of life more precisely.

Baker criticizes Olson's animalism for using a concept of life that cannot adequately grasp what characterizes us as persons. His concept of life is both too broad and too narrow to understand human life (see Baker 2008, p. 11). According to Baker, Olson's concept of life is *too broad* because it is not able to grasp what specifically characterizes human life – its personhood – but rather includes all organic activities. It is *too narrow* because it uses only a biological concept of life, which is not able to grasp specifically personal life. However, Baker does not use a general concept of life that can be applied unambiguously and equally to different phenomena, but argues for a concept that is only concretized in different respects: 'The word 'life' by itself is incomplete until we know what kind of thing that we are talking about.' (Baker 2008, p. 11) Baker argues for the existence of a specifically *personal* life, which must be distinguished from biological life, but which is at the same time related to it:

> A person's life is a personal life, and the personal life of a human being has biological aspects. A purely biological life, however, is the career of an organism. If the organism constitutes a person, then what would have been a biological life on its own becomes subsumed by, or incorporated into, a personal life. (Baker 2008, p. 11 f.)

This means that Baker formally conceives of the concept of life in a broader way so that it is not identical with the biological concept of life. The biological concept of life is only a case or a specific form of the more general form

9 See Baker 2016, p. 59: 'On Constitutionalism, the person is necessarily embodied, but does not necessarily have the body that she has at a particular time.'

of life.[10] According to Baker, it is possible for non-human persons to live a life which is in no way biological (see Baker 2008, p. 12 n.). However, with regard to humans, Baker does not oppose personal life to biological life, which would imply a dualism of lives. Rather, she relates both lives within the framework of her constitutionalism:

> [A] person-constituted-by-an-organism does not have two lives, but one integrated personal life that has biological as well as nonbiological aspects. The connection between an injury to one's organs and one's resulting dread of a long recovery is a causal connection *within* a personal life. Biological life is what is continuous throughout the animal kingdom. But if I am right, biological life is only one aspect of personal life. In a strict and philosophical sense, your life is a personal life that includes your successes and failures, and loves and losses, as well as your high cholesterol. To equate human life, in a strict and philosophical sense, with biological life severely truncates what we intend to talk about strictly and philosophically. A wholly biological conception of your life is simply not adequate. (Baker 2008, p. 12)

What remains unclear in Baker's definition of life, however, is how she can conceive of biological life as an 'aspect' of personal life, and thereby avoiding ontological dualism. Baker assumes that organisms, i.e. biological lives, constitute personal lives. Based on the relation of constitution, she concludes that persons are higher life forms, which is why personal life cannot be an aspect of biological life, as Olson argues (see Baker 2008, p. 12 n.).

5. A Person's Life

One of the currently most promising approaches to integrate the ontological and practical identity of a person into a unified concept is Marya Schechtman's 'Person Life View' (PLV) (Schechtman 2014). The Person Life View can be understood as an extension and critical modification of Schechtman's narrative self-constitution theory.[11] Schechtman's PLV is both distinguished from Locke's theory of personal identity as well as from animalism. The former, by its focus on the actualization of rational capacities, is *too demanding*, the latter, by its focus on mere biological life, *too indifferent* when it comes to the practical concerns of personal identity (see Schechtman 2010, p. 283 and

10 For a formal definition of the concept of life, albeit in a different argumentative direction, see Buchheim 2019.

11 See Schechtman 2007 and 2014, p. 103, where she defines her goal as follows: 'Expanding the narrative self-constitution view – narratives and lives'.

Schechtman 2019, pp. 133–4). In particular, the problem of 'marginal agents' (Jaworska 2007 and Svirsky 2020), such as infants and dementia patients, is one reason for extending her narrative self-constitution towards a more specific concept of life, which Schechtman understands as a biographical life narrative (Schechtman 2014, p. 104): '[A] plausible account of *literal* identity will need to allow for the personhood of infants and the cognitively impaired, and so to explain how a Lockean person can be the same person as her earlier infant self and later demented self.' (Schechtman 2014, p. 103) Literal identity, according to Schechtman, does not concern the actualization of a mental capacity, but what grounds it. Schechtman calls her conception of biographical identity the 'expanded view', according to which even marginal agents such as 'infants or those with severe dementia or cognitive impairments' (Schechtman 2014, p. 7) can be considered persons. In doing so, Schechtman refers to a *personal* conception of life:

> What I propose is that we think of identity-constituting narratives not just as the narratives we create for ourselves, but the narratives of our lives that are created in conjunction with other people. Infants and the demented cannot self-narrate, but other people can and do form narrative conceptions of them. [...] [T]he claim is not about the way in which others can form narrative conceptions of what infants and the demented are *like* [...] but rather about the way in which they can begin or continue an *individual* life narrative that anticipates or recalls the unfolding of that *individual* life, bringing past and future into the present, as it were, on behalf of the person who cannot do it herself. (Schechtman 2014, p. 104)

Such a co-narrative is not to be understood as a narrative *about* another person, but rather as a continuation of that person's life.

Schechtman understands persons as 'complicated biological-psychological-social loci more fundamental than the animalist's "organisms," which are viewed as abstractions.' (Schechtman 2014, p. 198) Persons as life forms are 'complicated kinds of animals', which usually realize higher cognitive capacities, but – and Schechtman points this out against Locke – can also lose them again without ceasing to be persons:

> [T]here is more to the practical significance of human life than the capacity for moral agency, reflective self-consciousness, and reason, and this is why, when they are lost, we are confused not just about metaphysical identity questions but also (as bioethical dilemmas clearly reveal) about how someone should be treated. (Schechtman 2010, p. 277)[12]

12 See Schechtman 2010, p. 28: 'Because of the way different kinds of concerns are integrated in our lives, a 'residue' of the implications of the Lockean capacities remains even when those capacities are lost.'

Schechtman conceives of the practical dimension of persons not as something contrary to their animal nature, but as a 'core feature of animal life'. In contrast to other animals, however, personal human lives take a different form. Therefore, Schechtman further distinguishes the concept of animal: "'Animality' is not monolithic […]. [I]t is more helpful to think of the uniqueness of human persons not in terms of an opposition to our animality, but in terms of the unique *kind* of animal that persons are, where this includes attention to both the ways in which they *are* and the ways in which they are not like other animals." (Schechtman 2010, pp. 277–8) Thus, Schechtman attempts to unify the human person with the human organism: 'Our personhood, in the sense of our unique endowments, *informs* the whole of our lives and does not represent a tidy package of concerns and activities that can be removed from our animal nature [emphasis added].' (Schechtman 2010, p. 278) In what follows, I shall draw on Schechtman's conception of what I call *personal information* and relate it to the distinction between human species and personal life form. I will develop what I call a compatibilist account of human species and personal life form.

Schechtman defines a person more precisely as 'the being who lives a person-life' (Schechtman 2010, p. 278). But what is meant by a person life? Schechtman describes it as a 'kind of life typically lived by an enculturated human', whereby human beings can be considered 'paradigmatic cases of personhood,' although she explicitly accepts non-human beings as possible candidates for persons as well. Because of the various forms of life that humans pursue, Schechtman first questions whether there can be such a thing as a single person life, or whether each person can exemplify a multiplicity of forms of life. Schechtman argues for the latter option: 'The view does not imply that there is some single, highly specific, way in which persons live but only that there is a cluster of general, structural features in terms of which we can provide a broad characterization of such lives.' (Schechtman 2010, pp. 278–9)

Schechtman bases her Person Life View on a 'developmental trajectory' model of the human person and her life. According to this model, personal development does not consist in a mere addition of personal capacities to a mere animal organism, but in the sense of multiform differentiation. This differentiation manifests itself in such a way that not only higher personal capacities are realized, but that everyday practices are transformed by cultural personal practices (see Schechtman 2010, p. 279). Schechtman argues that personal life does not take place individually, but only intersubjectively, and introduces the concept of a person space:

> One is not a person in isolation. To be a person is to be engaged in certain kinds of characteristic interactions with other persons-to take up a place in what I will call person-space. [...] To be a person thus requires one to occupy a place in the space of interpersonal interactions, and a person's identity is determined by her path through person-space in the living of a single person-life. (Schechtman 2010, pp. 279–80)

Schechtman anticipates the objection that her conception of person space is arbitrary, because any living being could be made a person by merely including it in the person space, even non-human animals such as dogs. However, her answer to this objection remains vague and circular, because she refers to the normal case of personhood: '[S]ince most humans do develop in this way, and there are cultures, person-space is culturally constituted in a way that accords personhood to other humans.' (Schechtman 2010, p. 280). Schechtman's PLV cannot explain the relationship between the human species form and the personal life form as expressed in the concept of a person space.

6. Configuration and Infiguration

In order to avoid the 'too many thinkers problem', I shall apply the difference between human species form and personal life form to Peter van Inwagen's and Eric Olson's theory of composition (see van Inwagen 1990 and Olson 2007, p. 231). My argument can be formulated as follows: Lives are not only composed – in the sense of the species form – by the activity of material particles, but also – when it comes to particularly complex compositions such as persons by a composition in two stages. This means that the personal life form must be *infigured* in the individual life under the species form. Olson's '*new composition question*' '[u]nder what circumstances do particles compose something other than a mass?' (Olson 2007, p. 231), shall thus be extended to persons.

It is striking that in the current debate about the concept of life form it is usually referred to the human species form, i.e. that no distinction is made between species form and life form (see Toepfer 2020, p. 3). With regard to the concept of a person, this leads to the problem of speciesism, insofar as the human species form is interpreted normatively (see Toepfer 2020, p. 9). In what follows, I shall clarify the relationship between species and life form by distinguishing between human species form and personal life form.[13] I shall

13 For a similar distinction, see Buchheim and Noller 2016 as well as Buchheim 2019.

argue for a compatibilism of human species form and personal life form in order to avoid the fact that different principles of identity must be applied here. This compatibilism is in a certain respect analogous to the compatibilism of the causality of nature and the causality of freedom. The personal life form must be fitted into the species form of the individual human being in such a way that the 'too many thinkers problem', by which (Neo)Lockenanism and Baker's constitutionalism are affected, does not arise. Species form and life form represent two dimensions of life that do not exist independently of each other, but are as it were *orthogonal* to each other. Different species forms can belong to the same life form, like lions and owls are predators, although they are biologically, as species, quite different.[14] I shall understand the life form as a dimension of life that can be inscribed in the individual life under the species form while preserving identity. *Biologically*, the human being can thus be assigned to a species, but *biomorphically* it exists personally.

In contrast to the relation of constitution, the relation of composition between material particles and human person consists in strict numerical identity, so that the 'too many thinkers problem' does not arise here. Therefore, the composition relation can be understood in the sense of an identity relation, although it operates with ontologically quite different relations.[15] However, as I shall argue below, the relation of composition does not suffice for a compatibilism between species and life form.

In contrast to Baker's constitutionalism, which considers the ontological and practical status of the person independently of the concept of life but only by reference to self-consciousness, I will develop a concept of life that allows the person to be understood as a particular form of life. According to my view, human person and human organism are identical, but without having to share the practical indifference of animalism and the neglect of personal acts and capacities. The position of animalism, by its sole concentration on the individual organism, will prove to be an underdetermined form of life, which does not consider the difference between species and life form.

According to morphological compatibilism, life is not to be understood materially, as animalism and constitutionalism do, but formally.[16] Viewed closely, van Inwagen's 'composition question', which admits composition only

14 For this distinction, see Buchheim and Noller 2016.

15 See Lewis 1991, p. 82: 'I say that composition – the relation of part to whole, or, better, the many-one relation of many parts to their fusion – is like identity. The 'are' of composition is, so to speak, the plural form of the 'is' of identity. Call this the Thesis of *Composition as Identity*.' I build my argument on Hübner 2007, pp. 202–3.

16 For a similar approach, albeit disregarding the infigurative dimension of the individual living person, see Buchheim 2019, pp. 49–53.

in the case of life[17], turns out to be undifferentiated. Van Inwagen understands persons as material objects ('living human organisms') (van Inwagen 2007, p. 206). However, it is possible to further distinguish the relation of composition with respect to life in such a way as to take into account the species form and life form of the person. For this purpose, let us consider again the 'Master Argument for Animalism' (Zimmermann 2008, p. 26):

> (P1) Presently sitting in your chair is a human animal.
> (P2) The human animal sitting in your chair is thinking.
> (P3) You are the thinking being sitting in your chair.
> (C) Therefore, the human animal sitting in your chair is you. (Blatti 2020)

According to the relation of composition, I as a person am identical with the living being sitting in the chair and am not constituted by it in such a way that I am different from it in my personal identity conditions. But here the term 'human animal' is morphologically underdetermined. We can integrate the personal life form into its species form without having to change its identity conditions. The relation of composition must therefore be extended by a second-order morphology so that it is clearly determined under which form the respective composition of matter takes place.

The personal life form relates reflexively to the individual human life under the species form insofar as it configures *all* its capacities – and not only its rational capacities – in a personal way – namely (i) reflexively and (ii) intersubjectively. This ensures that the personal life form is formally independent of the species form: The personal life form is not exclusively dependent on a certain species, such as humans, but is applicable *across* species just as lions and owls share the life form as predators (see Buchheim and Noller 2016). In the combination of reflexivity and intersubjectivity, but while preserving the identity with the individual life, a supra-species form is established, which structurally corresponds to what Kant calls 'humanity in its person' (Kant, CpR, 5:87) with regard to the human being.

It is crucial that in the configuration of the person the two forms – human species form and personal life form – are integrated into each other in such a way that the same material particles, in spite of both forms, do not compose two different objects – a human being and a person – which would lead to the 'too many thinkers problem' as in the case of the constitution relation and of Lockeanism. Rather, the personal life form further determines the species form. The species form composes an individual (for example a human organism), while the life form does not contribute to the *individuation* of life, but

17 See van Inwagen 1990, p. 82: '(∃*y* the *x*s compose *y*) if and only if the activity of the *x*s constitutes a life (or there is only one of the *x*s)'.

confers a supra-individual structure to it, which can be axiologically interpreted as person space by a personal configuration of an organism's living capacities. According to morphological compatibilism, the personal life form is not to be understood as separate form *besides* the species form, but rather as a determination and orientation of it. The personal life form represents a kind of internal framework that relates the capacities under the species form in a personal way, which corresponds to what Marya Schechtman has called a 'person-space'.

7. Conclusion

I have argued that it is essential to distinguish between species and life form in order to determine what we essentially or most fundamentally are. According to my compatibilist account, we are neither self-conscious beings (against Lockeanism and constitutionalism) nor mere animals (against animalism), but personal life forms. As such, we are nothing *beyond* our animality or our lives (not a thinking substance), but rather something that *informs* our life. Our being alive and being a person are not mutually exclusive. Rather, they are compatible insofar we understand ourselves as personal life forms: living beings, whose capacities are formed in a reflexive and intersubjective way.

References

Baker, Lynne R. 1999a, 'Unity without Identity: A New Look at Material Constitution', in *Midwest Studies in Philosophy* 23 (1): 144–165

Baker, Lynne R. 1999b, 'What Am I?', in *Philosophy and Phenomenological Research* 59 (1): 151–159

Baker, Lynne R. 2000, *Persons and Bodies. A Constitution View* (Cambridge: Cambridge University Press)

Baker, Lynne R. 2001, 'Précis of *Persons and Bodies: A Constitution View*', in *Symposium on Persons and Bodies. A Field Guide to Philosophy of Mind* (Spring 2001) <http://www.uniroma3.it/kant/field/bakersymp_precis.htm>

Baker, Lynne R. 2002a, 'On Making Things Up: Constitution and Its Critics', in *Philosophical Topics* 30 (1): 31–51

Baker, Lynne R. 2002b, 'The Ontological Status of Persons', in *Philosophy and Phenomenological Research* 65 (2): 370–388

Baker, Lynne R. 2007, 'Persons and the Natural Order', in P. van Inwagen and D. Zimmermann (eds.), *Persons. Human and Divine* (Oxford: Oxford University Press)

Baker, Lynne R. 2008, 'Big Tent Metaphysics', in *Abstracta*, Special Issue I: 8–15

Baker, Lynne R. 2016, 'Animalism vs. Constitutionalism', in S. Blatti and P. F. Snowdon (eds.), *Animalism: New Essays on Persons, Animals, and Identity* (Oxford: Oxford University Press): 50–63

Blatti, Stephan 2020, 'Animalism', in: E. N. Zalta (ed.), *The Stanford Encyclopedia of Philosophy* (Fall 2020 Edition) <https://plato.stanford.edu/archives/fall2020/entries/animalism/>

Buchheim, Thomas/Noller, Jörg 2016, 'Sind wirklich und, wenn ja, warum sind alle Menschen Personen? Zu Robert Spaemanns philosophischer Bestimmung der Person', in J. Kreiml and M. Stickelbroeck (eds.), *Die Person – ihr Selbstsein und ihr Handeln. Zur Philosophie Robert Spaemanns* (Regensburg: Friedrich Pustet): 145–179

Buchheim, Thomas 2019, 'What Are Persons? Reflections on a Relational Theory of Personhood', in J. Noller (ed.), *Was sind und wie existieren Personen? Probleme und Perspektiven der gegenwärtigen Forschung* (Leiden and Boston: Brill): 31–55

Hübner, Johannes 2007, *Komplexe Substanzen* (Berlin and New York: De Gruyter)

Jaworska, Agnieszka 2007, 'Caring and Internality', in *Philosophy and Phenomenological Research* 74 (3): 529–568

Kant, Immanuel 1900 ff., *Critique of Practical Reason* (CpR), in Preußische Akademie der Wissenschaften (ed.), *Akademie-Ausgabe* (Berlin: De Gruyter)

Lewis, David 1991, *Parts of Classes* (Oxford: Oxford University Press)

Locke, John 1975, [1]1690, *An Essay Concerning Human Understanding*, ed. P. H. Nidditch (Oxford: Oxford University Press)

Noller, Jörg 2022, *Personale Lebensformen. Identität – Einheit – Würde* (Leiden: Brill)

Noonan, Harold W. 2003, *Personal Identity* (London: Routledge)

Olson, Eric 1995, 'Human People or Human Animals?', in *Journal for Philosophy in the Analytic Tradition* 80 (2): 159–181

Olson, Eric T. 1997a, 'Relativism and Persistence', in *Philosophical Studies: An International Journal for Philosophy in the Analytic Tradition* 88 (2): 141–162

Olson, Eric T. 1997b, *The Human Animal. Personal Identity without Psychology* (Oxford: Oxford University Press)

Olson, Eric T. 1999, 'Reply to Lynne Rudder Baker', in *Philosophy and Phenomenological Research* 59 (1): 161–166

Olson, Eric T. 2003, 'An Argument for Animalism', in R. Martin and J. Barresi (eds.), *Personal Identity* (Malden, MA: Blackwell): 318–334

Olson, Eric T. 2007, *What are We. A Study in Personal Ontology* (Oxford: Oxford University Press)

Parfit, Derek 2012, 'We Are not Human Beings', in *Philosophy* 87 (1): 5–28.

Reuter, Gerson 2019, *Was wir grundlegend sind: Menschen unter anderen biologischen Einzeldingen. Überlegungen zu unserer Natur und unseren transtemporalen Identitätsbedingungen* (Frankfurt/M.: Klostermann)

Schechtman, Marya 2007, 'Stories, Lives, and Basic Survival: A Refinement and Defense of the Narrative View', in: *Royal Institute of Philosophy Supplement* 60: 155–178

Schechtman, Marya 2010, 'Personhood and the practical', in *Theoretical Medicine and Bioethics* 31: 271–283

Schechtman, Marya 2014, *Staying Alive. Personal Identity, Practical Concerns, and the Unity of a Life* (Oxford: Oxford University Press)

Schechtman, Marya 2019, 'Practice and Identity: An Anthropological View of Persons', in: J. Noller (ed.), *Was sind und wie existieren Personen? Probleme und Perspektiven der gegenwärtigen Forschung* (Leiden and Boston: Brill): 133–146

Snowdon, Paul F. 1990, 'Persons, Animals, and Ourselves', in: Christopher Gill (ed.): *The Person and the Human Mind: Issues in Ancient and Modern Philosophy* (Oxford: Oxford University Press): 83–107

Snowdon, Paul F. 2014, *Persons, Animals, Ourselves* (Oxford: Oxford University Press)

Snowdon, Paul F. 2020, 'The nature of persons and the nature of animals', in A. S. Meincke and J. Dupré (eds.), *Biological Identity. Perspectives from Metaphysics and the Philosophy of Biology* (London and New York: Routledge): 233–250

Svirsky, Larisa 2020, 'Responsibility and the Problem of So-Called Marginal Agents', in *Journal of the American Philosophical Association* 6 (2): 246–263

Toepfer, Georg 2020, 'Der Begriff der Lebensform als typologisches, nicht-normatives Konzept der Biologie', in: M. Hähnel and J. Noller (eds.), *Die Natur der Lebensform. Perspektiven in Biologie, Ontologie und praktischer Philosophie* (Leiden: Brill): 3–16

van Inwagen, Peter 1990, *Material Beings* (Ithaka/NY: Cornell University Press)

van Inwagen, Peter 1997, 'Materialism and the psychological-continuity account of personal identity', in *Philosophical Perspectives* 11: 305–319

van Inwagen, Peter 2007, 'A Materialist Ontology of the Human Person', in P. van Inwagen and D. Zimmermann (eds.), *Persons. Human and Divine* (Oxford: Oxford University Press): 199–215

Zimmermann, Dean 2008, 'Problems for Animalism', in *Abstracta*, Special Issue I: 23–31

List of Contributors

Amit Anurag
is assistant professor of philosophy at FLAME University in Pune, India. He received his Ph.D. from the Indian Institute of Technology, Delhi. His main areas of research include metaphysics, philosophy of mind, and process philosophy. He is currently working on the metaphysics of processes and events. E-Mail: amit.anurag@flame.edu.in

Irene Breuer
holds degrees in Architecture and in Philosophy from the Universidad de Buenos Aires (UBA), Argentina, and a PhD in Philosophy from Bergische Universität Wuppertal (BUW), Germany. She was a lecturer for Architectural Design and Theory at the UBA and later a lecturer for Theoretical Philosophy and Phenomenology at the BUW. As part of a DAAD scholarship, she has conducted research on the reception of German Philosophical Anthropology in Argentina. She currently continues this research with the support of the BUW. E-Mail: ibreuer@hotmail.com

Tony Cheng
is a full-time philosopher and part-time psychophysicist. He is the director of the NCCU Centre for Phenomenology, and is affiliated with the Research Centre for Mind, Brain, and Learning. In addition to philosophy, he holds a degree in psychiatry. His research centres the senses and consciousness as they mediate varieties of minds and the world. More abstractly, his research attempts to understand how transcendental, phenomenological, and empirical psychologies can mesh with one another.

Heidi Haanila
currently works as a postdoctoral researcher in Theoretical Philosophy with the University of Helsinki. She defended her PhD in philosophy at the University of Turku. Her doctoral thesis is concerned with neurophilosophy of self-consciousness, and her research has focused on a multidimensional account of self and the dynamics of self-consciousness. More generally, Haanila is interested in a multidisciplinary approach to the philosophy of mind. E-Mail: heidi.haanila@helsinki.fi.

Markus Herrmann
is a lecturer at the Department of Philosophy at the University of Heidelberg, where he received his PhD and completed his habilitation. He has also taught and conducted research at the University of Tübingen and at the Duquesne University in Pittsburgh as part of a DAAD short-term lectureship. His research project 'The indeterminate I' was funded by the German Research Foundation (DFG). E-Mail: markus.herrmann@ps.uni-heidelberg.de

Muriel Leuenberger
is a hosted research fellow at the Oxford Uehiro Centre for Practical Ethics. Her research is focused on identity and authenticity in medical ethics (neuroethics in particular) and ethics of technology/AI. In her current project (funded by the Swiss National Science Foundation) she analyses how personal information provided by novel and emerging technologies (specifically bioinformation and algorithmic profiling) impact identity. E-Mail: muriel.leuenberger@philosophy.ox.ac.uk

Maik Niemeck
is a postdoctoral researcher at the University of Marburg, where he also received his Ph.D. He worked as a research assistant at University College Freiburg, earned his M.A. from the University of Göttingen and his B.A. from the University of Halle. During this time, he also spent visiting periods at King's College London and the University of Notre Dame. His main research interests are philosophy of mind and language, particularly theories of consciousness and self-awareness. E-Mail: maik.niemeck@uni-marburg.de

Jörg Noller
is currently private lecturer (Privatdozent) at the University of Munich. He specializes in the philosophy of personhood, Classical German Philosophy, and the philosophy of digitalization. E-Mail: joerg.noller@lrz.uni-muenchen.de